Business Sponsorship

Business Sponsorship

Caroline Gillies

Butterworth-Heinemann Ltd
Halley Court, Jordan Hill, Oxford OX2 8EJ

 PART OF REED INTERNATIONAL BOOKS

OXFORD   LONDON   GUILDFORD   BOSTON
MUNICH   NEW DELHI   SINGAPORE   SYDNEY
TOKYO   TORONTO   WELLINGTON

First published 1991

© Caroline Gillies 1991

British Library Cataloguing in Publication Data
Gillies, Caroline
    Business sponsorship.
    I. Title
    659.1

ISBN 0 7506 0012 8

Printed and bound in Great Britain by
Butler & Tanner Ltd, Frome and London

Contents

Contents

Preface

Sponsorship is a versatile medium which transcends all the boundaries of marketing and public relations. But, simply because of its enormous versatility, it is surprisingly often misunderstood. Many executives have a rather blinkered view of sponsorship in which the words 'donation', 'charity' and 'limited budget' feature rather heavily and very inaccurately. Still, it was not that long ago that many company board members felt that public relations itself was an expendable luxury. I doubt that there would be many who would question the value of public relations today.

Jonathan Gee suggests that an industry has arrived and has credibility once it has its own journal. As the editor of *Sponsorship News*, first published in 1981, he should know what he is talking about. 'Sponsorship is no longer a grey area of marketing,' he says, 'people have learnt that if they integrate it into their whole marketing plan, it can be very, very effective.'

Any misconceptions about sponsorship are usually born out of lack of communication and understanding so I hope this guide will help to clear up the mystery. It is principally directed at all those company executives and staff who have some involvement in sponsorship in both a direct and peripheral way. It is also aimed at those who work for specialist public relations, advertising, direct marketing, sales promotion and other consultancies, who may become directly or indirectly involved in sponsorship, so that they may all understand more clearly how to maximize its many benefits. I hope also that it will be a useful reference book for executives in sponsorship consultancies particularly at middle and junior management levels and also for students hoping to get jobs in the communications industry. Sometimes there is so much work and so little time in consultancies that one has to learn on the job and think on one's feet! So I hope this volume may make the thinking and learning process a little easier.

There are also chapters to help those organizations who are seeking sponsorship and those individuals who would like to work in sponsorship.

What I have attempted to do is to look at what sponsorship is all about and where it fits into the marketing and corporate communications plan. And then to look at all the numerous communications options it offers in a simple and logical way. So, if your company or consultancy is thinking of venturing into sponsorship or, if it is currently a sponsor, but you would like to take a long look at what you are doing already and why, then I hope this book will help you make those decisions.

Finally, the English language has the largest and most versatile vocabulary in the world but it has one gargantuan failing. No one has yet invented a word that covers both 'he' and 'she'. Since at least half the people working in sponsorship are female, I ought, strictly speaking, to be using 'she' just as often as I use 'he' but the result would make very irritating reading. So for 'he', please also assume 'she' — I can't find any other sensible way around the problem.

Caroline Gillies

1 The benefits of sponsorship

What is sponsorship?

Sponsorship is a highly effective and imaginative communications medium which uses all the marketing disciplines under one umbrella.

And yet the word 'sponsorship' is frequently misused, often slipped in to disguise the bitter pill of someone asking for a donation or for advertising. Perhaps this confusion is due to the fact that sponsorship is so flexible that people feel they can bend its meaning as well!

Marketing itself is difficult to define in one sentence, sponsorship is even more difficult – but let's try: 'The payment of a fee to another organization (with which the sponsor has no direct connection), the support of which both parties hope to benefit from.' That is an awkward and not very grammatical sentence but it does get over the point. Sponsorship is a sort of piggy-back ride, if you like, where the sponsoring company pays a fee for a multitude of benefits that only the sponsored organization can give and, in return, receives financial and perhaps other support enabling it to operate successfully.

Advertising can buy you space in the *Daily Express* but it cannot buy you the prestige of sponsoring the Grand National.

The vital word in our definition is 'benefit' and yet it is often the missing element in requests for sponsorship submitted by the amateur or inexperienced organization.

Many people when asking for sponsorship actually mean something else: 'Will you sponsor a page in our jubilee programme?' (Will you buy an advertisement?), 'Will you sponsor me in the London Marathon, it's going to Guide Dogs for the Blind?' (Please will you make a donation to Guide Dogs for the Blind?) Consequently, when a serious and major sponsorship proposal comes in to a company, the same managing director who groaned when his daughter presented him with yet another sponsorship form at ten pence a mile, could almost be forgiven for groaning yet again.

So sponsorship should never be confused with donations or patronages which mean the giving of money (or goods or services) with no benefits or public acknowledgement expected. Many major companies make donations to charities and other worthy institutions, and this alone can run into many millions. Marks & Spencer is one of the companies at the top of the donations list, giving around £1.5 million a year – interestingly enough though, you would be hard-pushed to find their name linked with sponsorship and it is well known that they spend comparatively little on advertising.

Nor should sponsorship be confused with advertising. One could argue that a name on a player's shirt or a hoarding inside a stadium is advertising, and, if that is solely what the client is purchasing, then it is indeed advertising. But, if advertising is part of a package of other benefits including entertainment facilities and sales promotion opportunities, then it becomes sponsorship.

Again, sponsorship could very easily be confused with sales promotion. For instance, if Smith's were to 'sponsor' a crisp-eating marathon, would they not simply be promoting the sales of potato crisps rather than genuinely sponsoring another event or organization with no apparent connection?

Finally, sponsorship should not be mistaken for an endorsement. If Nick Faldo is paid a large sum of money to play with certain golf clubs or Steffi Graf paid to wear a particular make of tennis shoe, that is not genuine sponsorship. That is simply a case of someone famous being paid a large sum of money in exchange for promoting a particular product.

'Sponsorship in no longer a grey area of marketing' says Jonathan Gee, editor of *Sponsorship News*. 'It's now an accepted part of the marketing mix and, if used as part of a campaign, it can be very effective. I think, in the early days, a lot of people either made the mistake of thinking it was God's answer to all their marketing problems or they did it on a whim without proper research. That is not the case now.'

The use of the word campaign is very appropriate since, to draw an analogy, no government would want to enter a war with only a navy at its disposal. To stage an effective attack – or defence – on all fronts, it would also need an army, an air force and all the back-up services to help the front line troops function effectively. In marketing, no campaign manager would rely entirely on advertising. He would also use sales promotion, direct marketing, public relations and sponsorship. And the beauty of sponsorship is that, like the marines who can attack from land, sea or air, it is enormously flexible and can reach people in numerous different ways and often when they don't expect it. 'And that,' says Jonathan Gee, 'is something that is unique to the medium of sponsorship!'

The most important question that any potential sponsor should ask of him or herself is: 'Will sponsorship help my company to achieve its objectives? And how?' Those objectives may be marketing (to sell more of the product) or corporate (to give the company a greater profile in the City) or they may be even more tightly defined (to give staff a sense of pride in their company). But the important point is that there should be objectives for the sponsorship to achieve, otherwise the whole exercise is pointless.

So, as we seem to have established what sponsorship is and is not, let's look at what its benefits are in more detail.

Image

Something as simple as a company logo and company colours can help to give an organization an image. The same can be said of advertising and public relations which should all coordinate into building a company's corporate identity.

But all these images are self-created and although the public may be convinced 75 per cent of the time, that isn't necessarily always going to be the case. Sometimes an advertising agency's brilliant idea can backfire. British Rail tried the slogan 'We're getting there' with TV advertisements full of friendly, smiling and helpful staff. British Rail surely should have known that the reality was rather different and it wasn't long before people like 'Disgusted, Tunbridge Wells' were taking delight in writing 'British Rail may be getting there, I'm not!'

A similar situation occurred with one of the big High Street banks (and has no doubt occurred with many similar service organizations). The advertising agency developed a wonderful campaign promoting the bank as the fountain of all knowledge and mother bountiful for blossoming small businesses. Budding entrepreneurs poured in through the doors but, in the enthusiasm of the campaign, no one had told the staff what they were supposed to do with these people and eighteen-year-old counter clerks, when confronted with bright-eyed and bushy-tailed entrepreneurs, simply said 'Er, yeah, small businesses. I think there are some leaflets over on the shelf there' — exit entrepreneur, exit potential business for the bank.

'Sponsorship cannot make a company something it is not' says Richard Busby, chairman of Strategic Sponsorship. 'A food company may look to an active sport tie-in to give it a healthy image but, if doubts start to be cast about the validity of the product's health claims, then the sport may have second thoughts.'

These are prime examples of carrying out segments of your

marketing in isolation. And the same lessons should be applied in sponsorship; it *must* tie in with all your other marketing activities.

Sponsorship can be a very subtle way of creating, enhancing or even changing an image. It is a marriage between sponsor and sponsee and one of its benefits is that the image of the sponsored organization or event should rub off on the sponsor. But both sponsor and sponsee should be absolutely sure that their public images match, otherwise the public may become disillusioned with both.

Image is perhaps one of the most important benefits of sponsorship but one of the unsung benefits since it never appears in the contract of agreement between the two parties.

I shall look at this again when I come to talk about target audiences but it is not difficult to think of examples. Beer images are masculine, comradely, sporty and fun. This obviously calls for a male-orientated team sport with a good following both of participants and spectators. Rugby would probably be a good bet, netball certainly would not. Perfume images aim to be feminine, mysterious, desirable, elegant and sophisticated. This is more tricky than you think since a great deal of perfume is bought by men. Theatre or music would seem a likely choice here. Obviously greyhound racing or pigeon fancying are out.

So, before you start, market research is essential to define exactly what sort of image your company has or desires; from then on, one of the objectives of your sponsorship programme should be either to enhance that image or, if necessary, change it.

Target specific audiences

Market research will also have — or should have — indicated fairly precisely the audience at which the product or service is aimed. This enables the marketeers to pinpoint exactly their targets with advertising, sales promotion and PR — or does it?

Advertising, unless it is carefully targeted, can be extremely expensive. Thirty seconds worth of television time during *Coronation Street* could cost many thousands of pounds, for instance, and although it may reach 18,000,000 viewers, 17,900,900 of them may not be interested in that particular product. Specialist magazines have proliferated in the last few years and may solve a particular problem but equally their readers, who are already enthusiasts, are not necessarily a new market. There are 12,000,000 car owners in the United Kingdom but the top motoring magazine sells to less than 150,000 of them — although it is read by many more.

But sponsorship can offer a targeting that reaches a certain profile of an audience without being too limited by a very specific specialist interest.

For instance, if you happen to be the brand manager of a very expensive sports car which is likely to sell to young men in well-paid professional jobs, where are you going to advertise? There certainly isn't a magazine called 'Young men in highly-paid jobs' and you would have to cover several newspapers to reach the whole market. But if you were to look for a sponsorship to fit the audience you might well pick squash – played by one million people, principally male, middle-class and mostly in good jobs.

Similarly, suppose you were a shoe manufacturer making practical, sensible shoes for adolescent girls. Mums are sold on the brand because it's good for growing feet but their daughters want something more fashionable. Young girls are primarily interested in pop, horses, ballet and boys – probably in that order. So sponsorship of a pop tour, a show jumping team or a TV series on dance could be the way to reach and influence that particular audience.

Target specific areas

It should not be assumed that sponsorship = Great Britain. It does not.

Sponsorship can be local – the High Street supermarket sponsoring the town's netball team is an example of an organization wanting to create goodwill within its catchment area.

It can be regional – a regional water authority sponsoring its regional tourist board's section of the Britain in Bloom competition, for instance, is an example of an apparently impersonal authority wishing to demonstrate that it has the wider interests of the region at heart rather than simply wanting to take the population's money.

It can be national – such as a brewery's sponsorship of a national rugby league, designed to create a national brand loyalty amongst a beer-drinking audience.

It can be international – a cigarette manufacturer's sponsorship of a motor racing team, designed to create worldwide name-awareness and a glamorous image of the cigarette brand in question.

It can link specific areas – by creating sponsorships through competitions and events, it is possible to target specific areas or countries to increase or open up markets. For instance, if a company particularly wanted to increase its overseas sales to countries such as Nigeria, Brazil and India it could, through sponsorship and with the help of an experienced consultancy, organize a televised international athletics meeting involving athletes from these countries.

5

Advertising opportunities

What many sponsors want is simply to see their company's name emblazoned across the country's (or perhaps the world's) television screens. Needless to say, the more coverage they get, the bigger the sponsorship fee is going to be.

The televising of world sporting occasions such as the Olympics and the World Cup has provided a simultaneous global stage for major sponsors. Imagine the problems of arranging TV commercials in 100 different countries across the world and weigh that against the comparative simplicity of being a major sponsor of one of the world's great sporting occasions with your name on the perimeter of a massive stadium and seen by 200 million people round the world. However, enormously high fees mean that this is a league in which only multinational companies such as Coca-Cola and Kodak can compete, but the publicity benefits are huge. Five billion people watched the 1988 Olympics – it's an almost incomprehensible figure.

Sport has always had the advantage over the arts when it comes to having hoardings, banners and perimeter boards within TV view because there are fewer restrictions. Nevertheless, restrictions there are, although these are gradually being eroded. It was not so long ago that there was a great furore about company names on football shirts. First they were not allowed to be seen on television at all, then they were restricted to sixteen square inches and now they are allowed to be thirty-two square inches. Football is generous, tennis allows only four square inches.

Major sponsorships expect to benefit from television coverage but, in the lower echelons, this cannot be guaranteed and the sponsor has to rely on the spectators and the media-reading followers to maximize its name awareness through editorial mentions and photographs.

Sponsors are usually given hoarding and banner sites, poster advertising, programme advertising, and sometimes ticket advertising as part of their package.

Media coverage

Media coverage really overlaps with advertising since much of the purpose of perimeter boards and logos on players' shirts is not so much to be seen by the spectators present but rather to be picked up by a much wider audience. That wider audience may be viewing a game or an event on television and it is the sponsor's intention that his company name should be seen continually as a background to the main event being followed by the cameras.

Television isn't the be all and end all either. Sport, in particular, receives much picture coverage in the national papers and, if a snooker player is seen receiving his trophy with an Embassy banner in the background or a Liverpool footballer is seen celebrating a goal with Candy on the front of his shirt then so much the better.

Those who have the rights to use their name in the title of an event have an extra bonus, too — 'Barclay's League Division 1 ... Arsenal 2 Everton 1 ...', 'Britannic Assurance County Cricket Championship ... Surrey all out for 347, Kent 43 for 1 ...' and so on.

There is a mixed reception from sport commentators to the use of the sponsor's name. Mostly they realize that the sponsor's money can be the lifeline that keeps the sport or an arts event going and are fairly helpful about using it. Sometimes, however, the sheer wordiness of the title makes it an irritation for them and they revert to a shorthand description so that The Barsetshire Equitable Building Society County Lawn Tennis Championships is likely to become the County Tennis Championships.

Some newspapers, notably *The Sunday Times*, refuse to use a sponsor's name at all. Thus the Grand National is not referred to as the Seagram Grand National nor the Derby as the Ever Ready Derby. They were a little flummoxed by the former Benson & Hedges Tennis Championships which, as an event created for B & H, had never been known or even should have been known as anything else. But, nevertheless, they imaginatively renamed it The London Indoor Tennis Championships to the chagrin of Benson & Hedges and the total confusion of their readers. Sports reporters are, on the whole, generous. Unfortunately, the same cannot be said of arts correspondents who, with rare exceptions, see no reason to mention the sponsor's name in connection with an event. Happily, this is just beginning to change.

There used to be mileage in the announcement of a new sponsorship. Liverpool and Hitachi made headline news in 1977 as the first football club to be sponsored. Those days have gone, sponsorship is no longer news unless it is the biggest, the best or the battiest.

Soon the FA Cup will be sponsored and that will make the front pages for the sponsor. Not so long ago it was rumoured that Courage were going to sponsor this famous trophy. It never happened and it didn't need to — Courage received so much more free media coverage through the rumour that they had no need to spend millions of pounds on the reality!

Direct marketing

Once upon a time many, many years ago when even BBC2 hadn't been invented, people used to settle down in front of their televisions and watch BBC1, or ITV which had 'commercials'. And, if you wanted to advertise to a mass market, you bought TV time.

But in the 1990s the media market is becoming more and more segmented. There are four main TV channels (with another on the way), British Sky Broadcasting and many cable channels. There are five national radio channels plus an ever-increasing number of local radio stations. Big cinemas have been closed and multiscreen ones have spawned in their place. There are now nine national daily newspapers, and a handful of women's magazines has turned into a glut with markets clearly defined into segments such as 21–25-year-old single girls with high disposable incomes. You can buy special-interest magazines on every conceivable subject from mountain biking to mortgages.

This means that while the consumer audience is fragmenting, it is possible to target people and their interests much more accurately, and consequently we are seeing the rise not only of more highly targeted media advertising but also of direct marketing.

Direct marketing, in simple terms, is a direct relationship of some sort between the seller and buyer and that usually means the seller knowing the potential customer's name and address. Details of potential customers are commonly compiled from records of enquiries companies have received themselves or by means of a list of names and addresses which has been purchased from another organization.

Direct marketing is a form of advertising which is becoming increasingly popular because it has the potential to target its market so accurately. Personally-addressed letters full of attractive offers now arrive regularly in most households and it's a rare person who won't open an envelope. It's a method which comes in for much criticism but, nevertheless, the enormous success of publishers such as Time-Life and Reader's Digest is more than enough evidence to prove its worth.

Since the market is becoming more and more fragmented, it is much more cost effective to promote to people who are even halfway to being interested in your product, rather than all the world and his wife, who almost certainly are not.

Some sponsorships will offer considerable direct marketing opportunities because the profile of the sponsored organization's audience should match that of the audience you are trying to reach. For instance, a motor cycle grand prix is not only going to be attended by thousands of motor cycle enthusiasts but they are in the main going to be young men between 16 and 25 – a group who are notoriously difficult to reach through conventional advertising. This is an example of an opportunity for a sponsor to give out competition leaflets or run a survey to build a list of names and addresses of potential customers.

Perhaps a list may already exist. Most sports which have a high level of participants as opposed to spectators, such as squash or orienteering, can supply lists of affiliated clubs or sometimes even members for the sponsor's use. Similarly, most theatres have mailing lists which could be used for a direct mail campaign.

Sponsorship is an ideal way of making direct marketing work. Providing the audience of the sponsored event or activity matches the audience that the sponsor wishes to reach, then there is a ready-made, captive and receptive audience waiting to be turned into customers.

Organizations which have members should, for instance, have mailing lists of names and addresses which the sponsor can use in some way. Even unsolicited direct mail is almost invariably opened out of curiosity but, if it has not attracted the reader within the first second, it's fast on its way to the wastepaper basket. But a piece of mail primarily giving information about this year's concert series or this season's cricket fixtures is going to be scanned avidly by the reader, and the sponsor's name on that mailing will be associated with it accordingly. Equally, the sponsor's own leaflet within the absorbing little package is much more likely to claim more than the cursory glance it would have received had it been sent separately.

Sales promotion

Many sponsors, even those with very large budgets, hand over their sponsorship fee, arrange the hoardings and the names on the shirts and then totally neglect any follow-on sales promotion.

And yet a link with a major sport, arts event, tourist attraction, pop tour, or whatever, offers endless opportunities for another angle of attack in the marketing campaign.

Forward planning is essential here, if opportunities are not to be lost. Sponsorships are sometimes arranged at short notice and there simply is not time to key in all the marketing functions that would make it an outstanding success.

Take a major pop tour for example. Quite apart from all the media coverage, there are endless opportunities for sales promotion: on-pack competitions to win tickets to the concerts; on-pack tokens giving priority bookings; special stands selling the product in the foyer of the concert hall; souvenirs and clothing linked to the tour with the sponsor's logo incorporated — to name but a few.

Another example is a major sports sponsorship — again opportunities to win tickets to the events; maybe an opportunity to see behind the scenes and meet the stars; endorsement of the product by the team or individuals; drinks cabinets available for sportsmen on court or on course and so on.

Client entertainment

Some sponsorships are used simply for client entertainment opportunities. For others, it remains a very small or non-existent part of their sponsorship.

Companies who have large dealer networks are likely to opt for sponsorships with entertainment facilities — car manufacturers, electronic equipment manufacturers, breweries etc. Anyone who has to sell to wholesalers, distributors, dealers, shopkeepers etc. will almost certainly go for a sports sponsorship such as football. Those who have to entertain merchant bankers, company chairmen and finance directors are likely to choose an arts sponsorship or an upper class sport such as yachting or polo.

Client entertainment is hard work for the executives concerned and often means that they have to put in a six-day week, but there can be no better opportunity to win friends and influence people.

An invitation to Ascot or Wimbledon, Twickenham or Glyndebourne, Covent Garden or Henley is an opportunity for seller to meet buyer on the strict understanding that this is purely a friendly social occasion and that no pressure will be brought to bear to make the sale. But both know that the invitation is part of a softening-up process where the two parties get to know one another and, as everyone understands, most business is about 'who you know', so every opportunity to widen contacts must be taken.

Prestige

Along with client entertainment and image must come prestige. This can partly come from the type of sponsorship and partly from a particular occasion involving the sponsee.

Few companies would hesitate about the prestige of a sponsorship of the Derby or the Boat Race or an opera at Covent Garden because these are prestigious events in themselves, but the same cannot be said of the 3.15 in the Much Binding Point-to-Point, the Mudsea

Island Rag Regatta or the Littleton Amateur Operatic Society's production of *The Merry Widow*.

So, if it's prestige a company is after, then it has to pick an event of quality, a team or a player that is successful or, better still, going to be successful.

Successful teams, sportsmen and artistes do not come cheaply. Sandy Lyle, Nick Faldo and Ian Woosnam are worth a few million more in sponsorship than they were five or ten years ago. But it takes a shrewd eye and a bit of gambling to spot an up-and-coming star when they're still up and coming. But, all the more prestige to the sponsor if he can also say at the John Player County Cricket Finals, 'Yes, of course, I just had a feeling that Glamorgan would win the trophy this year' or at the FA Cup Final, 'Well, no one ever thought Scunthorpe would make it but here they are.' And if he is entertaining important clients at the same time so much the better.

Corporate goodwill

This might also be termed community responsibility, public relations, community care or something along those lines. Most major organizations are now alive to the fact that a much more sophisticated and well-read public is these days quite as familiar with a company's corporate image as it is with its carefully-created brand images.

This new awareness if of vital importance. Not only can a public, irritated by an organization's well-publicized gaffes, take its custom elsewhere but shareholders, too, are likely to be willing to look more thoughtfully at takeover bids by marauding rival companies.

From a local point of view, a company will want to be seen to be putting as much back into the community as it takes out – particularly if it is a big local employer. It may find difficulty in recruiting staff; it may have a militant workforce; it may sell most of its products locally. Whatever the reason, it will certainly want to show the population in its catchment area that it cares about its local community.

Allied Steel & Wire, who are one of the biggest employers in Cardiff with a workforce of 3000, are a typical example of this. Brian Ford, their Publicity Manager says, 'We have difficulty in recruiting staff with the right technical skills and so we place a heavy emphasis on sponsorships involving young people who may be our future employees. We want to show them that the steel engineering industry is modern, forward thinking and has much to offer in the way of a career.'

Barclays Bank Head of Corporate Affairs, James Poole, takes an even wider view, 'In an environment where the taxation on companies is being reduced, the quid pro quo is that the private sector has to put more back into the community. Now how do we do that? Would we rather have a higher corporate tax rate or have the right to dispose of our own money back to the community which we serve instead. So our sponsorships have to be social – employment, the environment, or industry – we have to be seen to be supporting those areas in which we earn our money.'

Cost effectiveness

Sponsorship can be extremely cost effective. Many companies judge this simply on the number of times that they see their name on television screens or in newspapers. But, when taken together, all of the benefits already listed form an extremely effective communications package which it would be hugely expensive to create from scratch without the benefit of the third party sponsored organization which is going to attract publicity and interest in its own right.

Chairman's whim

Any sponsorship professional reading this heading will, I'm sure, almost have gasped in horror. 'Chairman's Whim' should not really in any way come under the heading of sponsorship benefits but, on the other hand, it is as well to get it out of the way as early as possible. You need to be aware that it exists and, although most PR directors, marketing managers and sponsorship consultancies will tell you that it has virtually been eradicated, I have yet to be convinced.

There are companies who are totally and absolutely professional in their selection of sponsorships. There are chairmen who are passionate about golf but would resist any attempt to persuade them into sponsoring a golf championship for fear of being accused of self-interest.

However, it has got to be a very strong-minded chairman who is not tempted into a sponsorship in which he has a personal interest. I say 'chairman' but it isn't always the chairman. It can be the managing director or the marketing manager, the public relations officer or, worst of all, the chairman's wife. The results of this can be quite extraordinary. I hesitate to name names but I would, for instance, query a brewery sponsoring ice skating or a builder sponsoring opera.

Sponsorship managers are usually given a free hand to choose or reject sponsorships within certain guidelines. But it would be a courageous executive who received a sponsorship proposal via his chairman and then ignored the note attached saying, 'I think we should look at this one *very* carefully!'

Once in that situation, he or she has to spend quite a considerable time working out some justification for this sponsorship and trying to make it work. And who gets the blame if it does not?

That said, there can be advantages to both sponsor and sponsored when there is a personal interest from 'He who must be obeyed'.

From the sponsee's point of view it can often mean a slightly more generous cheque, or added benefits not originally negotiated. It can mean a keen interest in what is going on and regular attendance at events and perhaps the renewal of the sponsorship at the end of the set period. From the sponsorship manager's angle, the interest of the chairman can often mean that doors are opened, budgets found which did not previously exist, and staff in other departments fall over themselves to cooperate where otherwise they might have dragged their feet.

Better to have the chairman's support than not to have it. All I can say is let's hope that his outside interests are channelled into something that also makes good promotional sense for the company.

If they are, then all the more reason to have a properly written sponsorship policy document.

2 Before you consider sponsorship

Set the objectives

No company should enter into a sponsorship programme without first going through a period of setting objectives, targets and a budget.

That may sound too pitifully obvious for words but organizations frequently plunge enthusiastically into sponsorships which are very hard to justify on commercial grounds. Often this is because sponsorships become available or are sold at very short notice so decisions have to be made quickly and there is simply no time for proper research.

The same situation will rarely occur in advertising because there is always another edition of the paper or another television commercial slot coming up.

Most major companies are now in sponsorship in one way or another but let us assume for the sake of this chapter that you are a senior executive in a company which, for some reason, has escaped the sponsorship net so far. You feel, however, that sponsorship is something you should consider seriously as part of the marketing or corporate communications process − or both.

You will almost certainly already be receiving regular proposals from consultancies, organizations and individuals hungry for your money, and it would be very tempting to look at one of these and say, 'That sounds good' and then give yourself all sorts of reasons why it's worth the investment.

But don't let yourself be ruled by temptation, it's better really to go right back to the beginning and think the whole sponsorship question out properly in the context of your company's marketing and communications policy.

Where should the decision be made?

The decision on whether or not to include sponsorship in the marketing and communications package should be made at the top. As you can see, the effects of sponsorship are so wide-ranging that an overall company policy needs to be defined before executives at lower levels start making unilateral decisions to sponsor the local water polo team or the national karate championships which may be entirely inappropriate to the image that the company wishes to portray. Policy should be defined first at board level and then actioned by the appropriate director or head of division.

This is likely to be the corporate affairs department, or possibly the marketing department, and it is the head of that department who should write, or commission the writing of, the sponsorship policy document.

It is probably best for this to be done in-house by an executive who has no axe to grind, no budget to lose, no job to save, no burning interest in golf, opera or saving the whale and who has easy access to executives at a high level. Such a paragon of objectivity is going to be extremely difficult to find, but will probably be the public affairs manager or someone of that ilk. Alternatively, take an objective view from an outside consultancy if you can. But beware again of those with business to lose or gain because their views may be coloured accordingly. Your advertising agency, for instance, might be extremely reluctant to recommend sponsorship if it means losing £1,000,000 of their budget. For this very reason, advertising agencies went through a stage where they were very sniffy about the value of sponsorship, principally because they could see it meant a cut in their income. However, many advertising agencies now have incorporated sponsorship consultancies into their groups and, as a result, are more open-minded.

The sponsorship policy should be looked at in the context of the whole company communications programme − both corporate and marketing. Sponsorship cannot work in isolation. Well, for that matter, no part of a communications programme should work in a vacuum but, if I've seen departments working on their own projects with scant interest or regard for what other departments are doing once, I've seen it a hundred times.

The work of each department should coordinate as neatly as the parts of the human body. Research is linked to product creation, which is linked to design, which is linked to production, which is linked to distribution, which is linked to advertising, which is linked to direct marketing, which is linked to sales promotion, which is linked to public relations, which is linked to sponsorship. If all these departments are functioning with different objectives, themes and timescales, and are rife with internal politics and egos, heaven help the organization!

So, given that your company has some written business mission statement, communications policy, marketing strategy, call it what you will, the sponsorship policy must integrate neatly with this. And half the work of the sponsorship policy will have been done already.

Incidentally, this is usually the point where everyone nods sagely in total agreement that a written policy will save much anguish and expense later. But then a very tasty sponsorship proposal falls through the letterbox and all the good intentions are forgotten in the excitement of getting on with the actual deal.

Very few companies, even major ones, have written policies. 'No, we have nothing written down as such' they say. 'But we are very clear in our own minds what our objectives are.' But the problem is that if this 'policy' is locked in minds rather than written down on paper, not everyone is privy to it and errors will be made; the 'minds' may change jobs, too, and the whole thing is liable to become extremely woolly. Something on paper, however simple, is there for all to see and understand and follow. •

Defining your current situation

This is the first step in the process. 'Where are we now?'

This involves two separate elements: the facts and the research. It is also a jumping-off point for your sponsorship. A policy laid down in 1992 with no relation to the facts of the company's situation in that year may still, in fact, seem to read quite sensibly five years later but may make no sense at all in relation to the company's changed status, public perception and trading situation.

The facts should be quite simple to assemble.

Let's take an imaginary mobile telephone company. The status quo is that the company is the third largest in its field; its profits are 6 per cent of turnover; turnover is increasing slowly but not spectacularly; it used to be one of three in its field and the market leader but more and more companies are getting into the area of telecommunications and therefore the market is becoming highly competitive; and so on.

Factual market research and a perceptions audit are undertaken and reveal some rather disturbing factors. The company, although the third largest in its field, is actually sixth on the list of names recalled by the public. Current customers are less than satisfied with the service they receive and complain of delays in repairs, of breakdowns and of difficulty in getting parts. Potential buyers place its Japanese rivals higher on their priority list because they have a more high-tech image.

From a corporate point of view the company is perceived by its customers as slightly old-fashioned and behind the times. This is not in fact true since the equipment it uses is the most up-to-date on the market but, for some reason, this message is not getting through to the customer.

Clearly a reappraisal and improvement in service is needed in order that the product should be right. But, once that is in place, then the company urgently needs to upgrade its image.

Defining the objectives

In the case of the telecommunications company, the improvement in the service can be dealt with by some hard work and reorganization internally but, at the same time, current and potential customers need to be reassured that the company is efficient, go-ahead and on the ball.

In which case the objectives might look something like this:

1 To be number one in the industry within three years.
2 To improve checks on manufactured instruments to reduce faults.
3 To employ more service engineers to repair faults within a target of twenty-four hours.
4 To establish relationships with current customers who may then recommend to friends and colleagues.
5 To identify and attract a new market for portable telephones.
6 To create an image for the company that will attract both current and potential customers.
7 To change a public attitude that portable telephones are only for yuppies.

Research again comes into play. What, apart from a high quality product and good service, is going to persuade current customers to recommend to friends? What sort of jobs do they have? What companies do they work for? What age, sex, demographic profile are they? What are their spare-time interests and what is their lifestyle? What newspapers do they read and what TV programmes do they watch? All these pointers will help identify the right type of marketing to influence them which may or may not be sponsorship.

The same applies to new customers. Market research can identify the types of jobs and professions which might have use for a portable telephone be they salesmen, farmers, despatch riders or window

17

cleaners. Once again the company would need to have all the information about them to identify the best way of reaching and influencing them.

Given that the company needs a pacier image and that most new customers come from recommendations, it looks as though a sponsorship with a heavy client entertainment element could be a good solution to part of the problem.

Let's take another example:

There is, shall we say, a new type of drink for teenagers called 'Rip'. It looks and tastes a little like lager but is non-alcoholic. The intention is to make young people feel grown-up by ordering it without, of course, breaking the law.

The brewery has carried out much research on this and has established that the market will be young people between 13 and 17, who will be 80 per cent male and 20 per cent female.

The brand manager's objective is to tap into this market and make it as chic and desirable to drink 'Rip' as it is to drink Perrier or Pimm's.

Advertising agency, sales promotion agency and public relations agency have all come up with various campaigns which look very exciting but you are slightly concerned that you are not doing enough to reach young males – they don't watch much television, they hardly glance at newspapers and their main interests, apart from hanging around with the lads, are football, motorbikes and girls – in that order. They'll certainly have tried smoking and drinking.

The brand manager and his team sit down and confirm that their objectives must be to make 'Rip' into a drink that young teenage boys aspire to, that is seen as masculine and a proper man's drink. That message will come across in the advertising but they come to the conclusion that sponsorship may well be a solution to giving the drink a credibility and a prestige it otherwise would not have had.

These are mythical examples of situations where sponsorship could very well be an entirely suitable solution to an image problem.

As I said earlier, every company's objective is, almost certainly, ultimately going to be to sell more of its products or services more profitably. But there will also be any number of secondary objectives for which sponsorship may be a solution.

These objectives may be marketing or they may be corporate. For example:

Typical marketing sponsorship objectives

- Soap powder – to reinforce name awareness.
- Tobacco – to persuade smokers to change their brand.
- Beer – to attract a younger market.

- Sherry – to aim at a more sophisticated market.
- Scotch – to aim at a new foreign market.
- Soft drink – to keep position in world market.
- Breakfast cereal – to attract wider share of market.
- Chocolate bar – to relaunch ailing product.
- Motor car – to launch new model.
- Bank – to attract student market.
- Building society – to encourage first-time buyers.
- Insurance company – to increase number of house insurances.
- Newspaper – to increase female readership.

Typical corporate sponsorship objectives

- Bank – to be seen to have a community responsibility.
- Brewery – to be seen to have a responsible attitude to drinking and driving.
- Scientific instrument manufacturers – to attract graduate employees.
- Petrol company – to be seen as environmentally conscious.
- Construction company – to maintain a high profile with government contract managers.
- Builders – to maintain a high profile with local government planners and specifiers.
- Utilities supplier – to maintain a caring image with the consumer.
- Major industrial group – to keep loyalty of shareholders.

Those are just a few examples of the sort of secondary objectives that a company might set itself over a particular period and, in fact, virtually all these examples could very well be achieved by use of the right sponsorship as part of the communications package.

This is not a book on market research but, as I have said several times already and will probably say several times more, you need to understand what your current situation is and how people perceive you before embarking upon any method of improving it. Gut feeling and nous may give you a pretty good idea but don't make assumptions. Hard facts are what you need. Consequently, comprehensive market research including lifestyle research and perceptions research is something that you will need in order to plan your sponsorship programme.

This applies to any type of company and any type of organization from giant conglomerates selling millions of pounds-worth of soap powders to financial institutions lending money to developers; from small clothing manufacturers to even smaller specialist computer bureaux.

The target audience

Is it to be a shotgun or a high velocity rifle? Well, as in reality, you can't do too much damage to an elephant with a shotgun and you are likely to miss a pigeon with a rifle.

So, it's important to define your targets and match your objectives and your possible sponsorship accordingly. You will see from the previous examples that, almost in the same breath, the objective and the target audience are listed together, i.e. objective — 'to attract'; target — 'prospective graduate employees'.

In fact, it's quite difficult to know which should come first on the list — the objective or the target (like the chicken and the egg).

Here are some examples of some of the many different audiences you may be trying to reach in one way or another:

1   *Consumers*   The great mass market out there who buy your goods or services, or who are potential buyers.
2   *Current business customers*   You want them to keep buying. You want them to buy more. You want them to buy other products or services that you can also offer. You want them to recommend your product to their friends (remember the adage — a happy customer will tell three people about you, an unhappy customer will tell ten).
3   *Potential business customers*   Obviously current customers represent a finite market although you may be able to sell other goods or services to them. You have to look for new customers in new markets, maybe in new areas and in new countries. All these people need to be persuaded that you have something worth buying.
4   *Government and local authorities*   There are 630 MPs at Westminster and 52,000,000 people out there who would like to influence them. Parliamentarians receive sackfuls of promotional mail, hundreds of invitations to meetings, lunches and receptions and specialist consultants are employed to lobby them. It all costs a great deal of money and takes a huge amount of time. Local councillors don't have to put up with such pressure but, nevertheless, considerable power rests with local government, particularly the planning committee. Incidentally, civil servants and local government officers often wield a great deal of power and are responsible for very large budgets and can certainly influence decisions, even if they don't actually always make them. They are, strictly speaking therefore, business-to-business contacts.
5   *Employees*   The sales force is a particularly important element

of staff relations since their success or failure has an immediately recognizable effect. Much thought is usually put into motivating the sales representatives and giving them incentives to perform even better. But the backroom staff are an often forgotten but vital element in any communications programme. An uninformed and disgruntled staff can do an organization a great deal of hidden damage whereas a motivated workforce that feels it is playing a part in the company's future can, by its very enthusiasm, put extra time and energy into improving results.

6 *Potential employees* Despite the unemployed millions, attracting employees is a very real problem for many companies, particularly in the high-tech and engineering fields, and the problem is increasing because of the dip in the birth rate in the 1970s. There now aren't enough very highly-qualified students to meet the demand. If a company has a dull, stolid image and a reputation for poor pay and prospects for promotion, it will find that students are going to look elsewhere.

7 *Wholesalers, distributors and retailers* Very few companies sell goods direct to the public. Consumer goods are mostly sold through a chain that involves a wholesaler and retailer or a distributor. The success or failure of your product can depend very heavily upon the goodwill of these links in the chain. Canned fruit stacked in a dark corner or a TV dealership shared with a younger more aggressive manufacturer is the quick route to poor sales. So good relations with the middle men are vital.

8 *Suppliers* Similar but less obvious are relationships with suppliers. One might assume that if you give a company an order it will be falling over itself to get you the goods or parts on time. But if you are in a situation where you have to rely on a number of suppliers, you will already know that this is far from the case. Bigger orders, more demanding customers, cash payers, indifferent staff can all play a part in your urgent order being pushed further back on the schedule and that will then affect your production or your sales.

9 *Shareholders* Once a company goes public, it becomes a target for a takeover. And, if shareholders are being wooed by generous outside offers, then there has to be a pretty strong argument for them not to take the money and run. So it is important for a company to establish a good relationship with its funders.

10 *The City* Funders include the big City financial institutions who lend huge amounts of money for investment into plant, production or buildings. Those who invest vast sums in buying shares can make or break an organization.

21

11 *The public* This includes everyone listed above and the rest of the population who cannot be so readily defined.
12 *The press* The press are not last on this list because they are the least important – in fact probably the reverse. But the point is that they are not a target audience in themselves, they are merely a vehicle to reach any one, or all, of the above targets. However, this vehicle is so powerful and influential that it should always be placed high on the priority list.

There are twelve different target audiences listed above. You may be able to identify others which are particularly relevant or important to your business or you may wish to exclude some and to break others down into even smaller groups such as:

Business customers

● Major customers spending over £200,000 per annum.
● Middle rank customers spending over £25,000 per annum.
● Small customers spending up to £20,000.
● Occasional customers.
● Potential customers.

What is the message?

You will almost certainly be reading this book straight through but, if you were to follow the thought process, you might by now be defining your major company objectives and setting out a list of target audiences coupled with secondary objectives on these lines:

● Major objective – to be number one in our field by 1995.
● Current customers – to increase business from this group by 10 per cent within the next two years.
● Potential customers – to attract 100 major new customers in the next two years.
● Suppliers – to speed up delivery from all suppliers by an average of two weeks.
● Distributers – to persuade dealers to display our products more prominently.
● Staff – to raise morale and encourage a company esprit de corps.
● Press – to attract positive press coverage.

These are very simple examples but in a sense you don't need to make them wordy or complicated. The simpler the message the more likely it is to be understood by all parties. But it does need to be carefully and logically thought out and, above all, it must integrate with the whole communications policy.

Once you have the targets and the objectives, you need to define the message you want your audiences to receive in order to achieve those objectives.

Again, there may be a general message that you wish to implant in the minds of all those audiences and it needs to be unique and to the point (i.e. Avis car hire – 'We try harder'). This is a good message in the form of a slogan since it implies to customers that they are going to get good service and to staff that they have something to live up to.

But the secondary messages may need to be slightly different for each group.

Take a fictitious car hire company:

- Corporate message – 'The customer comes first.'
- The public – 'We're the first car hire firm you can name.'
- Current customers – 'You'll get extra fast service.'
- Potential customers – 'You receive many additional benefits from us.'
- Counter staff – 'Be polite and helpful no matter what.'
- Service staff – 'Don't take short cuts, they'll be noticed.'
- Press – 'We're always ready to respond to situations in an innovative way or with a suitable quote.'

Overall the message is very similar for all those groups: 'the price is the same as other car hire companies, the cars are the same but we offer better service.'

Advertising, direct mail, sales promotion and public relations will all play an important part in this car rental company's marketing plan but sponsorship could give it an additional bite by enhancing an image, promoting name awareness, giving the staff something they can identify with, offering opportunities for direct marketing to target audiences, for sales promotion opportunities and for account customer entertainment.

If you have a look at your own company's marketing policy, you'll probably come to very similar conclusions.

Is sponsorship the right vehicle?

Once you have identified objectives, targets and messages, it makes sense at this stage to stop and consider whether sponsorship is the right vehicle to promote your company image or product. Perhaps it would be better to go down the route of advertising, direct marketing, public relations or a combination of these. In practice, it is actually quite difficult to think of any company or organization that could write off sponsorship as a communications aid.

In Chapter 1 we looked at some of the benefits of sponsorship so maybe now is the time to stop and look at some of the reasons people give for not using it:

- *'We can't be seen to be spending half a million pounds on sponsorship when we've just closed our Sunderland factory.'* Someone is afraid that the workforce will react badly. But would they object if the same sum were spend on a TV advertising campaign? It's really down to a lack of understanding of what sponsorship is all about and the mistaken assumption that it is giving money away for a huge jolly for the sales staff. But if the sponsorship is a genuine vehicle to boost sales, and can be justified as such, then it's really a question of communicating that message properly to the workforce.
- *'If we sponsor one thing, we'll be flooded with requests for more.'* True. But would a company stop advertising to save itself the trouble of being badgered by advertising agencies and newspaper sales representatives?
- *'We only have a small staff. We wouldn't have the time to manage it properly.'* Then use a consultancy.
- *'We can't afford it.'* If there's no money for marketing, presumably there isn't going to be a business to promote for very much longer.
- *'Chairman doesn't believe in sponsorship.'* Chairman's whim in reverse. But has anyone explained properly what sponsorship is all about or is the chairman firmly convinced that sponsorship simply is a pseudonym for donation?
- *'We only have four major customers. There wouldn't be any point.'* In that case those four customers could be entertained very successfully on an individual basis without recourse to a major sponsorship involving an entertainment package. But this statement assumes that the only audience is the customer. This is a company which may need heavy investment from the finance houses; it may have a poor record of industrial relations; its heavy delivery lorries may cause a real traffic problem in the town; it

may find it difficult to recruit skilled staff and so on. In which case, sponsorship may help to solve any of those problems.

- *'Our articles of association forbid us to advertise.'* Fair enough, but rules for professional organizations are changing very rapidly. Solicitors, accountancy practices, chartered surveyors and even doctors and dentists can now spend money on promoting themselves within certain guidelines. So it makes sense to keep abreast of the changing times and be one of the innovators rather than one of the also-rans.
- *'We are not allowed to promote this product by law.'* Again, fair enough. There are products which genuinely can't be promoted to a wide audience, such as drugs which can only be obtained on prescription. The same does not apply to over-the-counter drugs or to the companies which manufacture them, however.

I would suggest that you now look at all your target audiences and the message you want to get over to them and, if you cannot see a role for sponsorship for any of them for one reason or another, then forget it. But I think you'll find it an almost impossible task!

Here is a brief checklist to save you a little time. But use your own headings as you prefer.

Checklist

Where are we now?

1   Company name and details.
2   Company business. (Be sure. Are you in the business of running a railway, manufacturing cigarettes, selling perfume? I think not. You're more accurately in the business of providing people with transport, supplying them with a stimulant/relaxant and helping women smell attractive.)
3   What information do you have about your various audiences – public, customers, staff, suppliers, distributers, shareholders, City, press? These may include facts and figures, demographic profile, likes and dislikes, lifestyle, perceptions and attitudes?
4   Likewise, what further information do you have about particular audiences relating to your group companies or brands?
5   What is your annual turnover?
6   What is your annual profit?
7   What growth do you expect next year?
8   How much are you investing in marketing to achieve that growth?

9   How much are you investing in corporate relations?

10   Do you expect any major problems in the coming five years (such as factory closures, discontinuing brands, takeovers)?

11   Can you forecast any major innovations in the next five years — (such as new factories, branches, products, takeover)?

12   Is there anything else that is important and relevant to mention?

The objectives

1   Do you wish to enhance the company's current image?

2   Do you wish to change it?

3   What image do you wish to portray?

4   Do you need to change a public attitude to your company or brand?

5   Do you want to increase its name awareness? What is the target?

6   Do you want to increase your share of the market? What is the target?

7   Are you happy with the current profile of your customers? If so, what is it?

8   Or do you wish to move into a new area? If so, what or who are the targets?

9   Are you launching a new initiative (such as privatization, share flotation, takeover, new product) which needs a massive publicity campaign? Who are the targets?

10   Do you want to improve staff relations and communications? If there is a problem, what is it?

11   Do you need to motivate sales representatives and other staff? If there is a problem, what is it?

12   Do you want to provide better incentives than your rivals in terms of staff and customer incentives? What are the restrictions of this and how could they be circumvented?

Target audiences

1   Who, in terms of sponsorship, do you see as your most important target audiences? (Try placing these in some kind of order.)

2   What are your objectives in terms of each target audience and what message do you want to get over to them?

      Consumers
      Current customers
      Potential customers
      Staff and sales representatives
      Suppliers
      Wholesalers, distributors and retailers

        Shareholders
        The City
        The public
        The press
        Others
3   In the case of your most important target audiences what is their
     profile:
        Demographic profile
        Age group
        Sex
        Employment
        Spare-time interests
        Lifestyle
        Where do they live?
        How do they perceive your company or its brands?
4   How do you want to reach them?
        Through name awareness advertising?
        Through positive publicity and editorial coverage?
        Through face-to-face contact such as client entertainment?
        Through direct mail?
        Through special offers and promotions?

Sponsorship limitations

1   What are your budgetary limitations; is it to be a defined annual
     sum or will directors, heads of department and brand managers
     have a free choice of how to spend their marketing budgets
     including sponsorship?
2   Do you wish to impose further limitations appropriate to the
     company's stated objectives i.e. do you wish to exclude spon-
     sorship of individuals, charity sponsorship, sponsorship involving
     bodies with which you might be at odds such as pressure groups,
     dangerous sports, religion, politics etc?
3   Do you wish to encourage any particular sponsorships, i.e. staff-
     involved sponsorships, educational sponsorships, community-
     based sponsorships.
4   Which sponsorship vehicles will you consider or exclude and
     why (see Chapter 3)? For instance, bad publicity or cynical press
     coverage could arise from an unwise choice: tobacco or alcohol-
     sponsored children's events; a record attempt or expedition where
     life is at risk; a star who is the subject of press attention because
     of his private life, etc.
5   Where client entertainment is involved, is there a constraint on
     certain days of the week or times of the day, e.g. retail customers
     may only be available in the evenings or on Sundays?

6   In terms of client entertainment, do you wish simply to entertain the client himself, or should you also include his wife and family to increase the goodwill?

There may be other questions you may wish to ask yourself but those listed above should enable you to write a simple and sensible sponsorship rationale. This document can be expanded into a sponsorship policy at a later date, once suitable sponsorship vehicles have been identified and the sponsorship management structure worked out.

3 Sponsorship opportunities

This chapter gives an overview of the basic advantages and disadvantages of each sponsorship vehicle or opportunity. It also gives
a star rating from one to five for each in terms of target audience,
client entertainment possibilities, media coverage and so on. But
please don't analyse these too closely. They are intended to be a
rough guide only. You can always devise a more refined scheme of
your own if you need to assess the benefits of, say, sponsoring a
symphony orchestra as opposed to sponsoring a litter clean-up.

Sport

Sport comes first on the list of sponsorship opportunities simply
because it is, at the moment, taking the lion's share of the sponsorship
cake. I say 'at the moment' because this balance may well change
in the next twenty years to a yet untapped market – sponsored
broadcasting for instance.

Sport is an excellent choice for sponsorship. It is enjoyed by almost
everyone, if not as a participant, then as a spectator. Even the woman
who groans every time her husband switches on the football or
the racing, may sit glued to the television for a fortnight during
Wimbledon.

Sport has high visibility. Not only does it fill our television screens
and the back pages of our newspapers in one way or another every
day of the week but sports stars are now in some cases bigger
celebrities than film stars, so their activities (usually off the field!)
often reach the front pages as well.

Sporting audiences can be targeted very accurately. Marketing
directors aiming at adolescent girls know that show jumping and
gymnastics are good bets. If they're promoting expensive motor cars
then squash and yachting are likely to be the right choices.

Not only can you target the audience but also the area — town, county, country, continent and world are all readily achievable markets through sports sponsorship.

Sport offers considerable scope for name awareness. It can be incorporated into the title of the event — the Seagram Grand National, the ADT London Marathon; or a league — the Barclay's League, the Heineken League, the Courage League; or a club or participant — Cadbury's Kingston, Everest Naughty Boy and so on. This means constant broadcast mentions and listings on the sports pages.

Televised sport means that perimeter boards, banners, hoardings and players' kit all appear on millions of TV screens all over the country or even the globe. Different regulations apply to different sports — on clothing, for instance, this can range from thirty-two square inches in football to four square inches in tennis but, although the message is often subliminal, the name is registering in millions of minds.

And not only does TV coverage promote the company or product, the general public, too, are often more than happy to become walking billboards for sponsors such as Candy or Sharp. No Arsenal supporter wants a replica shirt without JVC on it, which is all good publicity for JVC. The sale of clothing and equipment in some sports is worth a huge amount in its own right. In simple terms it can be regarded as free advertising but many sponsors have set up extremely profitable merchandising deals of their own. In the early 1970s it was chic for motor racing fans to be seen wearing the black and gold John Player rally jacket, nowadays it is more likely to be a stylish sweatshirt in the red and white of Marlboro or yellow and blue of Camel.

Sport is a wonderful way of entertaining clients. In an informal atmosphere with plenty of colour and excitement, it is an excellent way of making friends with customers, both existing and potential. There is a mutual pleasure in seeing a try scored, a race won or a new champion crowned. And a pleasure shared is often the moment when friendships are formed and friends make better customers than acquaintances.

Table 3.1 will give you an idea of the wide variety of sports and activities which are available and a feel of whether they are mainly participatory or spectator sports. But for a much more detailed analysis, buy a copy of The Sports Council's *Digest of Sports Statistics* which gives you a great deal of information about each sport and is a good starting point for a potential sponsor.

The ratings in Table 3.1 are necessarily very general and will vary widely from event to event. For instance, the Grand National is one of TV's most popular sporting events and cannot in any way be compared with the 2.30 at Much Binding. Similarly, the ratings for

Table 3.1

Sport	Participation (non-competitive)	Watched live	Watched on TV
American football	—	*	***
Angling	*(***)	—	—
Association football	***	***	***
Athletics	*	**	***
Badminton	*(***)	—	*
Ballooning	*	*	—
Baseball	*	—	*
Basketball	*	*	*
Bowls	**	*	***
Boxing	*	*	***
Camping and caravanning	(**)	—	—
Canoeing	*	—	—
Caving	(*)	—	—
Cricket	***	***	***
Croquet	*	—	—
Curling	*	*	—
Cycling	*(**)	*	**
Darts	*(**)	—	***
Equestrian sports	**(**)	***	***
Fencing	*	—	—
Fives	*	—	—
Flying	*(*)	***	—
Gaelic ports	*	*	*
Gliding	*(*)	—	—
Golf	**(***)	***	***
Gymnastics	**	*	**
Handball	*	—	—
Hang gliding	*(*)	—	—
Hockey	**	*	**
Hunting	(*)	*	—
Ice hockey	*	*	*
Ice skating	*(*)	*	***
Judo	*	*	—
Karate	*	—	—
Lacrosse	*	—	—
Land yachting	*	—	—
Lawn tennis	*(***)	**	***
Martial arts	*	—	—
Model aircraft flying	(*)	—	—
Motor cycle sports	**	**	**
Motor sports	**	***	***
Mountaineering	(*)	—	*
Netball	*	*	*
Orienteering	*	—	—
Parachuting	*(*)	*	—
Pentathlon	*	*	*
Petanque	*(*)	—	—

Sport	Participation (non-competitive)	Watched live	Watched on TV
Polo	*	**	*
Rackets and Real Tennis	*	—	—
Roller hockey	*	*	—
Roller skating	*(*)	*	—
Rounders	*	—	—
Rowing	*	**	**
Rugby	**	***	***
Shinty	*	—	—
Shooting	*(*)	—	—
Skateboarding	*(**)	—	—
Skiing	*(***)	*	***
Snooker, billiards and pool	**(***)	*	***
Squash	*(**)	*	*
Sub-aqua	(*)	—	—
Surfing	*(*)	*	—
Swimming	*(***)	*	**
Table tennis	*(*)	*	*
Tenpin bowling	*(*)	—	—
Trampolining	*	—	—
Tug-of-war	*	*	—
Volleyball	*	*	*
Walking	*(***)	—	—
Water skiing	*(*)	*	*
Weightlifting	*(*)	—	—
Wrestling	*	*	*
Yachting	*(**)	*	*

Key:
— minimal
* small
** good
*** excellent

participation refer to those who partake in sport competitively rather than those who just do it as a pleasant form of exercise such as walking, swimming, angling or cycling. Where there is a high level of non-competitive participation the star ratings are in brackets.

If you plan to sponsor your local hockey club or the regional tug-of-war league, presumably you will be doing it partly for reasons of community goodwill. But for a major level of expenditure, the marketing element will almost certainly take the highest priority.

Sport these days is very big business so it seems hardly possible that any company would step straight from a sponsorship programme of zero into a major international sports sponsorship (although I am assured that it happens). So, one hopes that if your company decides to tread the world sponsorship stage, then it will have gained some experience of sponsorship at a regional or national level. If not, then you should certainly work with one of the major international sports sponsorship consultancies or agencies.

Many of the international sports, tournaments and players these days are handled, indeed owned, by sports marketing agencies. In one sense this is hardly surprising because the likelihood of an individual sports star or even a sports governing body having the degree of expertise required to market itself on a global stage is remote. Creating or managing events, negotiating TV coverage, guaranteeing which players will participate and for how much, and negotiating worldwide sponsorships are formidable tasks. Knowledge, expertise and contacts are all needed and there are only about seven or eight sponsorship consultancies in Britain capable of doing these things effectively.

If this leaves you feeling somewhat fazed, take heart. There is a Sports Sponsorship Advisory Service run by the Central Council for Physical Recreation and funded by the Sports Council. Their advice is impartial. (Perhaps I should qualify that by saying it is impartial once you have made up your mind that it is sport that you wish to sponsor.)

The Sports Sponsorship Advisory Service functions on three levels.

First, it is works with the various governing bodies of sport in order to help them to professionalize their sponsorship marketing and management.

Second, it has set up a series of sponsorship workshops on particular sports in order to help potential sponsors assess the benefits of a particular sport on an uncommitted basis. 'We've just run a motor sports workshop down at Brand's Hatch' says Peter Lawson, the CCPR's secretary. 'It was extremely successful. We had seventy companies there, they were able to look at the different motor sport options, ride in the cars, talk to the drivers and the organizers and just get a picture of what was on offer without in any way feeling that they were under any obligation.'

Third, it will offer individual advice to any company thinking about sports sponsorship but undecided. 'We'll gladly talk to potential sponsors and point them in the right direction. We also offer a detailed research and advisory service if a potential sponsor requires more information about a sport or sports before committing himself. But we charge a fee for that, dependent upon how much time is required.'

Also run by the CPRE is the Institute of Sports Sponsorship. For a fee of £500 a year, the company becomes a member of the Institute, receives all literature and mailings, is invited to the various events and can seek advice as and when required.

Sports score rating

Image match	*****
Target audience	*****
Target areas	*****
Name awareness	*****
Media coverage	*****
Direct marketing	****
Sales promotion	*****
Customer entertainment	*****
Prestige	***
Community goodwill	*

Note: These markings will obviously vary from sport to sport so should be taken as being based on the top ten sports.

Further information

Numerous directories, yearbooks, guides and books have been published on all sports. Each sport also has a ruling body but if you are starting from scratch try the following:

Useful organizations

The Central Council for Physical Recreation
Francis House
London SW1P 1DE
Tel: 071 828 3163
(Also Institute of Sports Sponsorship and Sports Sponsorship Advisory Service)

The Sports Council
16 Upper Woburn Place
London WC1H OQP
Tel: 071 388 1277

The Sports Council is responsible for administering government grants to governing bodies but also has a helpful information department and produces many useful publications.

Useful publications

A Digest of Sports Statistics in the UK published by the Sports Council.

The arts

If sport offers a wide range of opportunities to the would-be sponsor then the arts must come a close second.

Companies sponsoring the arts tend to take a slightly different view from companies who sponsor sport. A company sponsoring an international golf or snooker tournament will probably be doing so because of major TV coverage. Arts events fare pretty poorly in the name awareness and advertising stakes. Logos may appear on a racing driver's overalls but you won't find the second violin sullying his evening suit with the sponsor's name. Advertising hoardings may be sprinkled prominently round the golf course but you won't find them in the scenery of *Macbeth*.

It is rather a matter of taste. The day has yet to come, fortunately, when a sponsor overwhelms an arts event with his corporate identity or forces changes to suit his own publicity purposes. As Prince Michael of Kent once said, 'I personally hope we never see an opera called − The Hair Stylist of Seville − even if it is sponsored by a unisex hair salon.'

Sport is on the whole brash, bold, commercial − the arts are generally considered to be tasteful and restrained.

But in spite of these disadvantages, a huge number of companies contribute over £30 million a year towards arts sponsorship.

One of the major reasons is that sponsorship of the arts is well organized. I do not mean that individuals, theatre companies or string quartets seeking sponsorship are necessarily any better at it than anyone else. They do, of course, have the benefit of some public funding through grants from the Arts Council but additionally they have the support mechanism − Association of Business Sponsorship of the Arts − which was formed in 1976.

The arts also has the Business Sponsorship Incentive Scheme. This scheme was originated by Lord Gowrie in 1984 when he was Minister for the Arts and is administered by ABSA on behalf of the Office of Arts and Libraries. In simple terms, the government will match pound for pound the amount contributed by any first-time arts sponsor. This is subject to a minimum investment of £1,000 and a maximum contribution of £25,000 from the BSIA. It does not stop there either. A new sponsorship signed by an existing arts sponsor will be matched in the ratio of one to three subject to a minimum of £3,000 and again a maximum BSIA contribution of £25,000.

The sponsor does not benefit from this but it is a wonderful incentive for arts organizations to go out and sell themselves to industry knowing that if they can find a new sponsor who will contribute, say, £25,000 then another £25,000 is almost guaranteed.

35

I say 'almost' because, apart from having to fulfil certain application conditions, the grants are distributed through an annual fixed sub-vention from government to the BSIA and those applying late in the budgetary year may be disappointed.

Commissioned works, festivals, concerts, exhibitions, buildings, refurbishment and the purchase of equipment and many other activities are eligible. Not eligible are the funding of appeals, donations, sponsorship in kind, entertainment expenses and investment in commercial entertainment.

ABSA's staff have done a hugely successful job in bringing business and the arts together. Not long ago the Association launched a new scheme called 'Business in the Arts' and one of its objectives is the placement of company executives, on a short-term project basis, into certain arts organizations. 'Young ambitious managers will be asked if they will give up perhaps two hours a week to help a local arts organization' says ABSA's deputy director Caroline Kay. 'Better still we'd like their firms to give them up for half a day a week on the grounds that it will add an extra dimension to their work. With the forthcoming drop in the birthrate, companies will find it more difficult to attract staff in some areas and so it's going to be important for firms to make their employees' lives interesting, fun and motivating. It could also be used as a credit towards their managerial careers.'

ABSA also hopes to persuade businesses and universities to open up a few places on management training courses to arts organizations to give senior staff an added professionalism. 'Arts people are incredibly committed, motivated and bright but undertrained' says Caroline Kay. 'So a scheme like this one will mean that they don't simply have to learn on the job.'

The arts have got their act together in terms of seeking sponsorship, but often they have to work under a handicap because there is a reluctance on the part of arts reviewers and correspondents to mention a sponsor's name in editorial copy. Somehow it's seen as infra-dig to state that the concert was sponsored by Whitbread or the art exhibition by Lloyds Bank. Not surprisingly many sponsors are considerably put out by this.

But Caroline Kay suggests that that is one area in which ABSA is, after much hard work, beginning to make inroads. 'For some time, we've been trying to persuade the media to mention the sponsor's name and we now have the arts organizations backing us on this too. I think that the press are beginning to understand that, in some cases, if it weren't for sponsors, some events simply would not exist, in which case they would also lose because there would be nothing for them to write about!

'Naturally, no journalist wants to do a story on an exhibition or a concert and be obliged to put in the words "which is sponsored by the Nottingham and East Midlands Mutual Friendly Insurance Society". It's too wordy and would be the first thing to be crossed out by the sub-editors anyway. But one or two papers have discovered a new way of solving the problem and that is to use a drop-out sentence at the end of the article. *The Independent* did this recently with an exhibition at the Tate. They simply inserted a sentence in italics at the end of the article which read – The Paul Klee Exhibition is sponsored by BP – and everyone was happy.

'Arts sponsors should be comfortable with the area that they are sponsoring' says Kay. 'New art and music is always hard to get sponsored simply because it's difficult to understand. Companies don't want to invite customers along with the net result that they feel bored or inferior because they don't understand the contemporary art exhibition or don't like the contemporary music. It tends to be those companies who want to be seen as innovative and on the edge who sponsor this type of thing – computer companies, for instance, who are in a fast-moving technological environment.

'But similarly, companies can pick something that they think is safe and still get it wrong. One company wanting to impress its clients and upgrade its image chose a Shakespeare production at the National Theatre and had a lot of seats to fill. Now the thing about the National is that it's very informal and most of the sponsor's guests turned up in black tie and consequently looked very overdressed. The company also made the mistake of giving the women boxes of sweets with the result that there was much rustling of cellophane during the performance. All this might have gone unnoticed had they not chosen the night that the critics were there and naturally they ripped into them.

'However, there are instances where what you might consider to be rather unlikely companies have successfully sponsored the arts. In Wales, there's an example of a garage which sponsored an exhibition of six young artists. They bought twenty of the paintings outright and then gave them away to people who bought cars. If you bought a car you could take the painting of your choice. It was a very original and highly successful sponsorship.'

One thing we should avoid doing is thinking of the arts as middle-class highbrow. No less valid than symphony orchestras, operas, or Royal Academy exhibitions are jazz, folk, country music and old-time dancing.

Companies may not be queuing to sponsor modern jazz bands but there is one area of the music industry which is already beginning to attract millions of pounds worth of sponsorship and that, of course, is pop.

37

Pepsi-Cola's Stacey Clark says, 'I do not need to dwell on how well targeted contemporary music is, if you want to talk to 12 to 24-year-old cola drinkers. Music is what these young people live and breathe. It forms a substantial part of their social lives, conversation and spending.'

Pepsi invested millions in Michael Jackson's world tour in order to promote Pepsi to a worldwide audience through a star and a medium with a huge international following.

'The key to success is understanding the areas of common ground,' says Clark, 'notably the mutual desire for publicity, to generate sales and to build artiste stature alongside brand personality development. Don't forget the artiste or event manager is not only interested in the fee. He is also concerned to promote his image and increase sales.

'Michael Jackson provided the vehicle for a great international advertising campaign but we, at Pepsi, consider that our success in music marketing is due to the fact that we attach great importance to organization of a fully-integrated programme.

'To use the Jackson tour as an example, in the UK five million consumers received a free Pepsi Jackson poster with a coupon to try the product and win concert tickets. Across several trade sectors, point of sale was placed advertising the competition to win the tickets. Frequently these were tailor-made to individual customers. Additional widespread media coverage was solicited such as a competition in *The Sun* and a massive campaign linked to the ITV Telethon. The public relations effort continued throughout the tour including coverage on the national news.

'There was substantial branding at Wembley seen by half a million people and 1800 guests were entertained in the VIP suite at the stadium. The impact of this hospitality proved to be far greater than anticipated and probably paid for many of the UK costs itself. Far better to entertain at your own event rather than someone else's.'

Does it work? 'It's difficult to prove the value of a sponsorship programme exactly,' says Clark, 'but I can prove the media value obtained and I can show you many indicators which have shifted. Volume sales went up by 30 per cent and the market share by two points on the previous year.'

Like sport, you can sponsor arts at any level from a few hundred pounds for a local sponsorship up to the million pound level such as the sponsorship by Royal Insurance of the Royal Shakespeare Company. The opportunities are very wide as you can see from the following list.

Opportunities

Dance   Ballet, contemporary, ballroom, old-time, Scottish and other folk, ethnic.

Theatre   Theatre companies, theatres, productions.

Classical music   Orchestras, concert series, performances, performers, choirs, ensembles, recordings.

Popular music   Concerts, tours, bands, performers, performances, recordings.

Festivals   Classical, jazz, pop, folk, country and western, poetry, dance.

Literature   Fiction, poetry.

Visual arts   Exhibitions, galleries, painters, paintings, films, video, photography, sculpture.

General   Competitions, grants.

Performing arts score rating

Image match	*****
Target audience	*****
Target areas	****
Name awareness	**
Media coverage	**
Direct marketing	****
Sales promotion	***
Customer entertainment	*****
Prestige	****
Community goodwill	***

Visual arts score rating

Image match	*****
Target audience	****
Target areas	****
Name awareness	**
Media coverage	*
Direct marketing	***

Sales promotion   **
Customer entertainment   ***
Prestige   ****
Community goodwill   ***

Further information

Useful organizations

Association of Business Sponsorship of the Arts
Nutmeg House
60 Gainsford Street
Butlers Wharf
London SE1 2NY
Tel: 071 378 8143

The Arts Council
14 Great Peter Street
London SW1P 3NQ
Tel: 071 333 0100

Broadcasting

'Everyone says that sponsored broadcasting is going to be big,' says Jonathan Gee of *Sponsorship News*, 'but nothing much seems to be happening at the moment.' He's right. This is the wrong time to be writing about sponsored broadcasting because changes are now being made and boundaries pushed back and consequently any information I give now will almost certainly be out of date within months. So my advice is to keep yourself up-to-date with what is happening and try to anticipate sponsorship opportunities ahead of the crowd.

The industry is indeed in a state of flux with more channels to come on stream in the 1990s and satellite and cable TV becoming more widely available, in spite of the merger between British Satellite Broadcasting and Sky Television into British Sky Broadcasting. The former regulatory bodies – the Independent Broadcasting Authority and the Cable Authority – no longer exist in name and have spawned two new bodies, the Independent Television Commission and the Radio Authority which both have their headquarters at 70 Brompton Road, London SW3.

Television broadcasting corporations and companies used to be bound by two Acts of Parliament – 1981 and 1984 – but these have now been superseded by the 1990 Act and anyone seriously interested in sponsored broadcasting should obtain a copy of this Act for reference. The BBC is bound by its own charter which forbids it to accept any form of advertising or sponsorship for programmes — although it may cover sponsored events and is also seeking and receiving sponsorship for some of its own events such as the 'Young Musician of the Year' competition. This charter comes to an end in 1996 and will no doubt be suitably amended to take account of changing attitudes to sponsorship ready for the next century. As if that weren't enough, the arrival of cross-frontier television means that there also has to be a more international set of regulations and the European Directive on Television Broadcasting is effective from October 1991.

The ITV channels and direct satellite broadcasts were formerly governed by the IBA under the 1981 Act but cable broadcasts and BSB satellite TV were governed by the Cable Authority under the 1984 Act which has much fewer restrictions. Cable and satellite television currently offer the most opportunities and freedom for potential programme sponsors but, as yet, they have not built up an audience of any substantial number. Licences for cable networks are currently being negotiated and some fifty cable TV companies should be up and running in the next few years. They will each have forty channels available for use so can key into transmissions by BBC, ITV, British Sky Broadcasting, overseas broadcasts and also run their own local channel, if they wish.

ITV, cable and satellite will now all be governed by the 1990 Act and regulated by the ITC. The ITC has issued a *Sponsorship Code* which may well be honed and improved over the next few years. Chris Quinlan, former advertising controller of the Cable Authority thinks, 'It will be very difficult for the ITC to remove, with one exception — the news — any sponsorship freedoms which have been enjoyed under our code from cable and satellite channels because there is no evidence that this has caused anybody any harm. There's no public detriment. In fact you could argue the opposite because it has helped create a pool of resource for more programming and more revenue.'

Robin Duval, chief assistant (television) of the former Independent Broadcasting Authority, says, 'The first and most important point that any potential programme sponsor should remember is that sponsored broadcasting is not the same as a sponsored event within a programme. If you are sponsoring a golf tournament which is being televised then, within certain agreed restrictions, your company name may appear on hoardings and clothing or be mentioned in the title of the tournament. If, however, you sponsor the broadcast of the tournament, then that is an entirely different matter and you will probably be restricted to a credit at the beginning and the end of the programme and before and after the commercial breaks.'

This slightly anomalous situation used to mean that if you sponsored an event, your company or product name could be seen rather more frequently and prominently than if you had sponsored the broadcast. However, the ITC's *Sponsorship Code* will now allow the same sponsor for both event and programme.

Robin Duval explains the previous restrictions for the ITV networks and Channel 4. 'Until the new Act came into force, you could sponsor the weather, instructional programmes, arts review programmes or elements within programmes where the proceeds were going to charity. Programmes such as the Telethon, for instance, come under that last heading and an arts review programme such as London Weekend Television's *South Bank Show* would be classed as an arts review programme. But the greatest opportunities lie with factual coverage. This means that the events being recorded must have an existence independent of television – sports, arts and so on. Documentaries have also been sponsorable but not current affairs programmes or the news which obviously must be seen to be free of any type of sponsorship.'

However, although it comes at the end of the ITN news, the weather forecast has been seen as a different matter and completely separate from the news. It is currently being sponsored by Powergen to the tune of almost £2,000,000.

Nevertheless, as a precautionary measure, the Powergen logo was removed from TV screens during the period that the share offers in the regional electricity companies were being advertised. Whether the sight of the Powergen logo would have persuaded any more viewers to buy shares in twelve individual electricity companies is doubtful but Powergen concurred and simply donated the space to five major charities.

Many more TV and radio channels will come on stream in the next few years which means that the number of broadcast hours available for advertising and sponsorship will increase dramatically. But conversely, unless we are all doomed to watch television or listen to the radio during every waking moment, the listening and viewing audience will simply split down into smaller slices of cake. The net result will be that there will be many more programmes available for sponsorship but the audiences may be comparatively small and therefore it is important that the sponsorship is correctly targeted.

Many TV companies and independent producers are looking for sponsors for programmes that they already have in mind. But there is nothing to stop a commercial company being pro-active and going to a television company or an independent producer with an idea which may be suitable for television. For instance, a paint company might create a series on decorating the home; a supermarket might do a series on cooking with exotic vegetables; a motor manufacturer might produce a series on the history of the motor car. Provided the programme is good enough, and there is a market for it, then the opportunities are there. It must, however, conform to the ITC Code which states that there must be no reference to the advertiser who is supplying the programme within the content except in the case of programmes of unusual historical or cultural value. It would, one imagines, be rather ridiculous to produce a history of the motor car without mentioning the Model T Ford but quite unnecessary to mention Sainsbury's in a cookery programme. However, the advertiser, or sponsor, must be credited at both the beginning and the end of the programme and may also be credited at the breaks. The spin-off from these short credits may be comparatively minor but considerable opportunities for further explanation of the sponsorship lie in the production of linked videos, leaflets, books, in-store promotions, competitions, on-pack promotions, exhibitions, conferences, and so on and this is where the sponsorship of a broadcast programme could really become effective.

Chris Quinlan says, 'We've carried programmes made by companies and by charities. For instance, Guide Dogs for the Blind made a feature on how guide dogs are trained. And the programme was labelled at the beginning and the end as being produced by the Guide Dogs for the Blind Association. We've carried a programme on the history of writing materials through the ages. This was made by Parker and eventually they went into a factory and showed how fountain pens were made. And again that programme was very clearly labelled as being made by Parker and we saw no problem with that. We didn't consider that there was undue emphasis on Parker within the terms of our code and that was fine.'

At the moment programmes tend to be made either by the broadcasting companies themselves or by independent producers who sell programmes on to the broadcasters. Sales are invariably agreed in advance simply to ensure that the costs of making the programme are covered. So a commercial company interested in programme making and with money to spend has several options – to go direct to the broadcasters such as BSkyB with a concept for a programme, to go to an independent producer, who will not only make the programme but negotiate the sales, or to employ a specialist consultant or in-house expert who knows their way round the broadcasting world and knows how to strike a deal. It is also possible, of course, for major companies to set up their own production units but is probably more cost effective to employ independent producers.

In terms of finance, the deal may be that the programme is shown for nothing – particularly by cable channels with a large number of hours to fill – or there may be a fee involved. That may mean the TV company paying a fee to the programme maker or sponsor, or the sponsor paying a fee for time in the schedule, in which case he may also use the advertising slots for his own advertisements or sell-on the time to other companies. It is up to the programme maker and sponsor to strike a deal and this is not an area which should be attempted lightly by a novice in the business because there are many traps for the inexperienced. For instance, provided the sponsor retains the rights to the programme, then there are opportunities for further sales from repeats, sales to other channels, sales overseas, sales of videos, sales of publications, in-store promotional opportunities and advertising and PR possibilities, which all have benefits far beyond the original showing.

One area about which the old IBA used to be quite touchy was that of programmes which were made for TV where the sponsor's visibility has been somewhat heavy-handed. These include programmes such as Kellogg's *Magic Mirror* and the Anchor *Go-getters*.

Robin Courage, director of broadcasting of the Rowland company was the man behind the Anchor Go-getters Challenge where teams of starlets were sent off to perform a series of tasks ranging from milking a cow to collecting a pop star's underwear. He has become an expert in the field of sponsored broadcasting and says, 'The frontiers are being pushed back all the time. The problem is that it is an absolute minefield of contradictory information and decisions. The official line may be – The law states that you cannot ... – but producers and promoters will prove that, in practice, you can get away with a lot more than is allowed in theory. It's just a question of continually testing the water.'

There is no doubt that television is a powerful medium and it is quite right that there should be some sort of regulatory system to prevent its exploitation. This includes product placement which is not allowed. You cannot purchase the right to have your box of washing powder put in an episode of *Coronation Street* (soap or no soap) although naturally it is impossible for programmes to be produced without showing all the paraphernalia of modern life. But the choice of purchase, hire, beg or borrow of such items is down to the production team and continuity staff and it seems an unlikely scenario that someone seeing Persil in Vera Duckworth's kitchen, will immediately be driven to rush out and buy a packet.

Equally we can't live in a vacuum as far as location is concerned – not so much a question of product placement within the programme, more a question of putting the programme in a place! I wonder how much the visitor figures to Jersey have been affected by *Bergerac* or the Yorkshire Dales by *All Creatures Great and Small*. These types of programmes must be a godsend to those who depend on tourism and a nightmare to those who don't. I think if I were the tourist officer looking to increase the number of visitors in a small Lancashire town like Rochdale, I wouldn't half wish that some nice producer would want to make a series on the life and times of Gracie Fields. Now there's an interesting thought!

Of course, broadcast sponsorship does not simply mean television. It very much relates to radio, too, and there are forty-six independent radio stations with the potential to reach 91 per cent of the population and more coming on stream all the time.

Radio sponsors have much more freedom than television sponsors and can either sponsor existing programmes or create a completely new one. The package will usually include programme credits to the sponsor plus advertising slots, and the choice of programme can be highly appropriate to the sponsor. Chris Field of Independent Radio Sales gives some examples of LBC programmes which have attracted sponsors: 'Slazenger sponsored Wimbledon reports, the Bank of Ireland sponsored the *Family Money* programme, Alitalia have sponsored the air traffic news and Texas Homecare have sponsored the 'Fix-It' do-it-yourself phone-in.

'But we have created features, too. For instance, Sun Alliance's medical insurance arm, Health First, sponsored a series called *Sound Advice* by Claire Rayner. Listeners could write in for a complementary fact sheet on each subject and, of course, this enabled Health First to include their own marketing literature and they were able to build up a mailing list as well as having broadcast mentions of their name at regular intervals.'

If you can digest all the information you collect about sponsored broadcasting, then you will probably come to the conclusion that it is almost certainly going to be the sponsorship medium of the future. Changes are happening all the time but it is inevitably going to be the mid-1990s before there is a noticeable difference in the market.

If you want to be ahead of the pack, then you would be wise to either employ a specialist or a sponsorship consultant who is absolutely up to date with what is happening and how to use the medium to best effect. Some of the bigger advertising agencies, PR consultancies and sponsorship consultancies have already gathered some expertise on sponsored broadcasting. The other option is to build up your own expertise by getting in touch with the sponsorship managers or the sales directors of the TV channels and networks, and with independent producers, to gather information and opinion on what is currently available in terms of programmes seeking sponsorship or what might be available in the future.

The ITC's *Sponsorship Code* is very useful and is so clearly worded that it has been reproduced in the Appendix at the end of the book.

Sponsored broadcasting score rating

Image match	*****
Target audience	****
Target areas	****
Name awareness	****
Media coverage	*
Direct marketing	****
Sales promotion	****
Customer entertainment	*
Prestige	**
Community goodwill	*

Further information

Useful organizations

The two former regulatory bodies – the IBA and Cable Authority – have now merged into the Independent Television Commission and the Radio Authority.

The Independent Television Commission (formerly Independent Broadcasting Authority, television section)
70 Brompton Road
London SW3 1EY
Tel: 071 584 7011

The regulatory body for anything broadcast on independent television.

The Radio Authority (formerly the IBA radio section)
70 Brompton Road
London SW3 1EY
Tel: 071 581 2888

The regulatory authority for anything broadcast on independent radio.

The British Broadcasting Corporation
Wood Lane
London W12 7RJ
Tel: 081 743 8000

Provides public service television and radio broadcasting.

The Producers Association
162–170 Wardour Street
London W1V 4LA
Tel: 071 437 7700

The trade association for producers of films and TV programmes etc.

Independent Programme Producers Association
50–51 Berwick Street
London W1A 4RD
Tel: 071 439 7034

The trade association for independent producers of TV programmes, commercials, videos, training and corporate films, as well as feature films.

Useful publications

Blue Book of British Broadcasting – an analysis of around 140 UK TV and radio stations, executives and presenters. Published by Tellex Monitors Ltd.

Directory of British Film and TV Producers – published jointly by the Producers Association and IPPA and lists members of both organizations. It also gives considerable detail of their areas of interest and programmes they have produced and also those for which they are seeking sponsorship.

Broadcasting Act 1990 – will give you some guide to what can and cannot be sponsored. Published by HMSO.

Broadcasting in the 90s: Competition, Choice and Quality – the white paper on broadcasting was published in November 1988 and outlines the government's plans for broadcasting in the 1990s. It is rather more readable than the Acts and is a useful insight into the possibilities for the future. Published by HMSO.

47

ITC Sponsorship Code – the definitive guide to sponsored broadcasting on independent television. Reproduced at the end of this book but also available from the ITC.

Books and publications

Books were one of the first sponsorships. The earliest I can think of is *Wisden's Cricket Almanac*. But who or what is Wisden? (in fact a gentleman's outfitters in Worcester).

Some sponsorships have been going for so long that they simply become integral with the name and by-pass the publicity benefits. It isn't difficult to think of examples. *Pears Cyclopaedia* and the *Guinness Book of Records*, for instance, are linked with company names which have become synonymous with the books themselves.

Many companies use books as sales promotion aids – cookery books are a prime example of this (Sainsbury's and Marks & Spencer to name but two) – all designed to persuade you to buy the product. The same applies to the sponsorship of road maps and guides (The Michelin maps, Shell guides etc.) which encourage you to use your car, which uses petrol and runs on tyres.

But there are more genuine examples of book sponsorship. The *Rothman's Football Yearbook* has become to football what *Wisden* is to cricket for instance.

Book sponsorship only uses some of the elements of sponsorship benefit. It's not high on client entertainment for instance. But it can, at the launch, attract considerable media publicity and, if a long-term regular seller, bring about sustained name awareness and offer a number of sales promotion opportunities.

In the main we are talking about non-fiction, directories, guides and instructional booklets. As far as I'm aware no one has yet sponsored a fictional work. *From Russia with Love* sponsored by Smirnoff Vodka or *The Nylon Pirates* sponsored by Pretty Polly do not somehow seem easy mixes but no doubt the day will come.

Beyond books, there are a number of opportunities for the sponsorship of other types of publication such as maps, leaflets, brochures and guides. Most of these can be very highly targeted. For instance, three quarters of a million tourists use the London Tourist Board's visitor map every year so a natural sponsor was an organization seeking to attract this market. Marks & Spencer, high on the list of 'musts' on the tourist route, became the first sponsor of this publication and not only had their name prominently on the publication but also their shops featured on the map itself.

One company which has specialized in sponsored publications is Columbus Press which publishes the *World Travel Guide,* a huge directory of travel information on every country in the world and an invaluable reference for trade and business alike. The information contained in the guide is all on a massive database which can be pulled out and used in other publications – not least by many of the national tourist offices for their British promotional brochures. Using the database, Columbus produced a *Travel Guide* to six popular destinations for National & Provincial Building Society to promote their new Holiday Saver account.

Columbus specialize in producing similar pocket booklets which are sponsored by companies and then given away as incentives such as *Stay Healthy While You Travel* sponsored by Kodak and given to customers in Boots the Chemist when they buy double packs of Kodak film.

Nigel Barklem, managing director of Columbus, says 'These days many of the goods and services you buy are identical in price. Take travellers cheques, for example, where a bank might offer something extra to give added value and added service to the customer – such as Barclays Bank who gave away the *Traveller's Guide to Spain.* Another example is Pan Am who gave away *Driving in the USA* with their airline tickets. But it has to be more than a simple question of a sales incentive. To give credibility, all our booklets are endorsed by official organizations such as the Royal Institute of Health and Hygiene or the Association of British Travel Agents. Another version of *Stay Healthy While You Travel* was sponsored by the Confederation of British Industry for use by their members. And a major conference was arranged in conjunction with the launch which received considerable national publicity.'

Apart from being a semi-permanent reminder of a sponsor's name, a sponsored book can be used in a number of other ways such as a peg for media stories, a conference or a give away. But its major advantage is that it puts the sponsor's name very firmly in the hands of its target audience.

Books and publications score rating

Image match	*****
Target audience	*****
Target areas	**
Name awareness	**
Media coverage	*
Direct marketing	****
Sales promotion	****

Customer entertainment	*
Prestige	**
Community goodwill	*

Further information

If you are interested in book sponsorship, then publishers will certainly also be interested in you but it is a question of finding one in the appropriate market. There appears to be no organization willing to advise the potential sponsor which leaves you with little option but to look along the shelves in book stores. There are, however, two directories which are a useful source of leads.

Useful publications

Cassell Directory of Publishing – details all UK and Commonwealth publishers and government agencies, associations and societies promoting the publication of books. Published by Cassell Ltd.

Publishers in the United Kingdom and Their Addresses – a list of 2000 of the most active publishers and the types of book they publish. Published by Whitaker & Sons.

Competitions and prizes

Companies love sponsorships which involve awards and prizes because media coverage is virtually guaranteed. Winners and losers make good copy – it's as simple as that.

In order to make a competition into a sponsorship rather than simply an aid to sales promotion ('Win a fabulous holiday in our lucky draw!'), there should be a third party involved – an independent organization to administer and give authority to the competition. And in this case, the benefits to you as the sponsor are just as likely to be in terms of publicity and prestige as they are in terms of promoting sales.

Obviously you will wish to match the audience of any award scheme with your own target audience but, if you decide to sponsor a prize or a major competition, then you should also think very carefully about the administration before you go ahead. For instance, how will it be publicized? Does the organization you are sponsoring have the mechanism to reach potential entrants directly though a membership, mailing list or publication? Will people or places nominate themselves, will they be nominated or will you simply find them by some other means?

If the competition is already in existence, it will almost certainly have both these criteria well organized. For instance, the Civic Trust Awards are made to local authorities, builders, architects, planners etc. to recognize outstanding architectural merit. The awards have been in existence for thirty years so the channels for entry and administration are well established. And since the entrants, the judges and the administrators are precisely the audiences that the current sponsors, Steetley, who manufacture bricks and aggregates, are trying to reach, the sponsorship of the awards not only brings them prestige but also, through printed material and presentation ceremonies, puts them in close contact with potential customers.

Entrants for the Civic Trust awards nominate themselves. But in the case of the Booker Prize, the most coveted prize for literature in the UK, entries are nominated by publishers. The hefty cheque for £20,000 plus is nice for the author but the prestige and publicity are of far greater value, as are the vastly increased sales of the book. But what of Booker? I have yet to meet a member of the general public who has any idea of who or what Booker is. They are, in fact, a multinational company in the food business and their sponsorship of the Booker Prize is very much to do with influencing their business customers and shareholders. Christine Shaw, head of publicity for the Book Trust which administers the Prize, says 'Booker have been sponsors since 1969 and have built up considerable prestige and name awareness in that time. They wanted to be seen to be supporting something worthwhile that was outside their own business and encouraging works of good literature has been outstandingly successful for them.'

Finding a common denominator for a bigger target market can be more difficult. Calor Gas also looked at their customers carefully before deciding to sponsor the Best Kept Village Competition. 'The buyers of liquefied petroleum (bottled) gas were mainly in rural villages so it was an excellent way of keeping the name of Calor in the public profile and gaining considerable local publicity to boot' says Michael Palmer, the marketing consultant who conceived the sponsorship and administers the scheme for Calor. 'In practice it is a complicated scheme to run,' he says. 'Counties all have their own individual competitions which may be administered by a variety of organizations ranging from branches of the Council for the Protection of Rural England to local voluntary service councils. So it was a question of contacting each one individually and fitting in with them or helping them develop the competition.'

The administrators receive a small grant to run the competitions and the prizes, too, are small but the villages are delighted with the honour and the glory and there is always considerable local press publicity. The name Calor also appears on all the village hall notice-boards and printed publicity and involves them directly with influential people within the community.

But some awards don't want to sell themselves to sponsors. One of the most successful schemes around is the *Woman's Own* 'Children of Courage' awards. It could hardly fail really. A combination of children, plus stories of daring rescues and brave fights against illness, are such that the press lap it up. This is an interesting point since newspapers appear to be happy to mention magazines but will never name a rival paper as a sponsor. 'But in spite of this,' says Tony Warner, the magazine's publicity manager, '"Children of Courage" has become an event in its own right and *Woman's Own* is frequently left out of the title.

'Readers nominate children but we also seek out nominations from the police and fire services amongst others so we end up with a variety of winners. The presentation ceremony in Westminster Abbey is always performed by a member of the Royal Family and there are many celebrities present at the lunch in the House of Lords afterwards.

'Our other scheme "Women of Achievement" is sponsored by Bachelors but we prefer to keep the "Children of Courage" awards to ourselves rather than sharing the publicity.'

If you have an idea for a totally new award scheme and are seeking a particular audience for it, then you would be wise to approach one of the official bodies to which your chosen audience belong or relate. This will give it status and respectability and enable you to work with an organization which can set sensible criteria, appoint reputable and respected judges, and so on.

Competitions and prizes can be enormously successful for sponsors but make sure that your competition is a credible one within the group from which you hope to attract entries. It also makes sense to make the sponsorship a long one, like Booker, in order to build up reputation and name awareness. Creating a competition one year and dropping it the next will achieve neither of these objectives.

Competitions and prizes score rating

Image match	*****
Target audience	*****
Target areas	***
Name awareness	**
Media coverage	***
Direct marketing	***

Sales promotion   ****
Customer entertainment   *
Prestige   ****
Community goodwill   *

Further information

Useful publications

Directory of British Associations — a complete guide to all national and some regional organizations with details of spheres of interest, categories, membership, activities and publications. Published by CDB Research Ltd.

Expeditions

The British are an adventurous race. They love exploring. They love adventure. Any major company involved in sponsorship will tell you that a sizeable proportion of sponsorship proposals come from those who seek adventure. The problem is that it is extremely difficult for a sponsor to relate any kind of marketing or corporate objective to yet another expedition to climb Everest.

Alan Preece, formerly the Public Relations Controller of Asda, says, 'I once had a request for sponsorship from a couple of guys who wanted to canoe up the Yangtze. I can't imagine how they thought that this was going to do anything whatsoever for Asda.' Well, the point was that they hadn't thought. Like many adventurers, they were so caught up in the excitement of the expedition that they had only considered their financial needs rather than any possible benefits to the sponsor.

However, sometimes a sponsorship proposal can land on a marketing manager's desk at just the right moment. In 1986, the Fuller's Brewery were looking for a name for a new lager they were to launch the following year. A proposal came in from climber John Barry asking Fuller's if they would be interested in sponsoring the first all-British expedition to climb K2. 'We were looking for a modern and memorable name for the new lager. We liked the name K2,' says Fuller's director Charles Williams, 'since the link with a cold snow-clad mountain and high achievement fitted very well with the image we wanted to create. Yes, we could have just called the lager K2 without sponsoring the expedition but we wanted a genuine connection and it was important to us that the expedition was all-British and so decided to sponsor it.

'All the climbers' clothing and equipment bore our logo and they even used our umbrellas as sunshades for the first part of the climb. I know it sounds ridiculous but there is about a fortnight's hike to get to the bottom of K2 and it can be very hot, so they were quite grateful for them.

'We built up story-boards of the expedition in our pubs but it was rather traumatic in the end since the leader of the expedition, Alan Rowse, was killed. On a personal level it was very upsetting since we had built up a good relationship with the climbers. And from a business point of view it was also difficult to know whether to go ahead with the launch or not. But Alan's relatives assured us that they wanted it to carry on. In the event it was launched in the spring of 1987 and, from a marketing angle, we feel that the sponsorship of the expedition undoubtedly helped to build brand awareness.'

Shane and Nigel Winser who run the Expeditions Advisory Centre for the Royal Geographical Society help something in the region of 600 expeditions a year. The Centre is sponsored by Shell International. 'It's an appropriate sponsorship,' says Shane. 'First, a company like Shell receives many, many requests a year from people wanting to undertake expeditions and they can't help all of them. But what they can now say is that they sponsor the Advisory Centre rather than sponsoring individual expeditions. It also makes sense from the PR angle as their name appears on all our literature which is seen by a very wide audience of people undertaking both adventurous and scientific expeditions. And those are precisely the sort of people Shell are seeking as potential employees for jobs overseas. For instance, if you are an exploration geologist and are likely to be sent to some remote part of the world, then you will need to have the resourcefulness and respect for the host country you probably learnt on your first undergraduate expedition. If you also met your wife on an expedition up the Orinoco, then there's less chance that she'll want you to come home to the comforts of England.'

Expeditions attract a high proportion of their funding in gifts and equipment and rather less in sponsorship at the moment, although this is growing.

The problem is that expeditions to obscure places tend to attract little in the way of media interest unless some disaster strikes and that is going to bring negative rather than positive publicity to the sponsor.

Virtually all of the globe has now been explored but the opportunities now go beyond Earth — if you have the budget. The Juno project was set up to raise funds to put the first Briton into space via a Russian spacecraft. Curiously Interflora were one of the first sponsors to sign up for the initial televised publicity programme which announced the names of the two short-listed candidates — Helen Sharman and Tim Mace. But in practice, the sponsorship was a clever one and a prime example of creative thinking.

'First,' explains Howard Park, Interflora's head of marketing, 'we wanted to emphasize the international aspect of Interflora. And particularly that we now have outlets in the main Soviet cities. We also wanted to create a more modern high-tech image for the company, which might be perceived by some people to be old-fashioned, but in fact is very modern. Virtually all our orders are sent down the line by computer these days. And finally, we were able to decorate the studio with flowers to create an image in the viewer's mind.'

Unfortunately, but perhaps not surprisingly, Juno failed to raise the £9,000,000 required. But happily the Russians have agreed to go ahead anyway.

Expeditions score rating

Image match	****
Target audience	**
Target areas	**
Name awareness	*
Media coverage	**
Direct marketing	**
Sales promotion	**
Customer entertainment	*
Prestige	****
Community goodwill	*

Further information

Useful organizations

Expeditions Advisory Centre
Royal Geographical Society
1 Kensington Gore
London SW7 2AR
Tel: 071 589 2057

Record attempts

The sponsorship of a record attempt is a totally different animal from the sponsorship of a football team or a concert orchestra.

Its sponsorship value lies almost entirely in its newsworthiness. It may achieve an enormous amount of publicity for a few days and then it will be gone, probably for ever.

If you are approached by an individual (and it almost inevitably will be an individual) attempting to break this record or that – you should, above all else, look at its news value and the ability of your sponsee to attract the media.

You will almost certainly be approached by people wanting to travel from Land's End to John O'Groats by some crazy method or other. But the people of West Cornwall barely give a second glance now to the caravan of strange people passing down the A30 – people roller-skating backwards, riding penny-farthing bicycles, or dressed as pantomime horses. And the media, I'm afraid, are even less interested. You need to be an Ian Botham to get journalists to turn out in numbers.

Sadly the same almost applies to round-the-world attempts. People have sailed single-handed round the world, cycled round the world, driven London buses round the world, and even travelled round the world from North to South. And I bet if you think very hard you could remember the name of the leader of that particular expedition (Sir Ranulph Twistleton Fiennes) but could you name the sponsors?

A record attempt needs to fulfil several criteria if it's going to make headlines, so ask yourself these questions before you hand over the cheque:

- Is it genuinely newsworthy? (Ask a journalist if you want a candid opinion.)
- Will the record-breaker involved make news in his/her own right, either because he or she is a well-known personality or for some other reason such as overcoming a physical disability.
- Does the attempt have national prestige value?
- Is there a risk or possibility of death involved?
- If so, could this bring bad publicity to the sponsor?
- Will the sponsor's name be prominently displayed?

I can think of no better example of a five-star record attempt – several five-star record attempts in fact – than Richard Branson's attempts to cross the oceans in a power boat and then in a balloon. They could not have been better scripted by a film producer.

First, an attempt to beat the record for crossing the Atlantic – a genuinely newsworthy record attempt.

Second, to attempt to win the Blue Riband of the Atlantic back from the Americans – national pride at stake.

Third, a household name – Richard Branson, chairman of Virgin.

Fourth, a 'yes' to danger was proved when the first boat sank.

Fifth, Richard Branson is, of course, chairman of Virgin, not only a record company but also an airline carrying thousands of people across the Atlantic.

Branson made worldwide television, radio and press with the *Virgin Challenger* and then went on to surpass himself with the *Virgin Flyer*, the balloon record to cross the Atlantic.

What more could a sponsor want, albeit Branson's own company, than its name splashed across a 100 ft balloon seen bravely crossing the Atlantic and then high drama as the balloon ditches in the sea and the two heroes are rescued from almost certain death. It was a brilliant piece of publicity.

Branson has set a benchmark which I doubt that anyone will better for some time and, when they do, it will require an investment of millions. So bear in mind that if you want to sponsor a record attempt you will be likely to get what you pay for.

Timing can be crucial too. Branson flew the Pacific in 1991. And if you don't recall the feat, it would be because the Gulf War broke out that week.

As far as the media is concerned, the sponsor's name is of very little importance so is very likely not even to get a mention unless it is incorporated into the name somewhere, for example had Richard Branson called his balloon the *Flyer* sponsored by Virgin, the last three words would certainly have been deleted but the balloon was called *Virgin Flyer* which meant a mention for the sponsor in every other sentence. So a sponsorship involving a record attempt almost invariably needs a vehicle of some sort which can bear the sponsor's name in its title and on its livery. A human being attempting a feat of endurance presents a smallish site for a billboard and he certainly won't be able to change his name. Boats, aeroplanes, airships, balloons, parachutes, and so on, all present suitable backcloths for advertising – two-wheeled transport, animals and human beings aren't so good. But there again, vehicles are expensive to build, human beings are not!

If you can find the right record attempt to sponsor and have a big budget to back it up, then from a publicity point of view, the rewards can be equally huge.

Record attempt score rating

Image match	*****
Target audience	**
Target areas	***
Name awareness	***
Media coverage	***** (on major attempts)
Direct marketing	*
Sales promotion	**
Customer entertainment	**
Prestige	**** (on major attempts)
Community goodwill	*

Further information

If the record you want to attempt is a sport or activity which has a recognized governing body, you should contact them in the first instance. Alternatively, Guinness Superlatives will usually be able to supply information and authentication notes for any record attempt your sponsee wishes to break or create. They also produce *Record News* six times a year giving details of various record attempts which have either been made or are to be attempted, which should be useful to potential sponsors. Contact the Press Office at Guinness Superlatives Ltd, 33 London Road, Enfield, Middlesex EN2 6DJ (Telephone: 081 367 4567).

Useful publications

The Guinness Book of Records published annually by Guinness Superlatives.

Education

Some years ago there was something of an outcry about foreign students in the UK – thousands of students from Third World countries preventing our own nationals from taking up their rightful university places, was the complaint.

But what a short-sighted view that was. Perhaps now that we live in a better-travelled society, people are more aware of the importance of international trade. And hopefully the same people who moaned about Nigerians and Malaysians being allowed to study at our own institutions, now realize that this ultimately results in other countries having a well-educated and influential stratum of society which speaks

English with easy familiarity, is British-educated, familiar with British life and products, feels at home here, and is therefore highly likely to order British-made goods when the chips are down.

The same criteria can be applied to education and research at any level. It is really an investment in the future and in the near future. Because of the drop in the birth rate in the 1970s, there is going to be a parallel drop in the number of school and university leavers in the 1990s. Highly-talented young people are going to be able to pick and choose their jobs, and those companies who haven't thought what to do about this are going to find themselves desperately short of engineers, scientists, computer programmers, accountants, and professionals for all those other specialist fields where the jobs vacancies outnumber the people available to fill them.

There could be a number of reasons for considering an educational sponsorship of some sort or other:

- Sponsoring the local school or higher education college in some way, if not with cash then with equipment, specialist staff or facilities and buildings. Local companies who need to attract a regular influx of young school leavers can find this a very good entrée. It creates goodwill and is a soft introduction to potential staff and, indeed, to potential customers.
- Sponsoring equipment at a college or university again is an entrée to potential recruits and in areas of really short supply a generous bursary can be tied in with the offer of a guaranteed full-time job at the end of the course which can be extremely attractive to a student setting out in the world. The services have this one pretty well taped; they offer school and university scholarships well in excess of the average grant in exchange for a period as an officer in the Army, Navy or Air Force – a tempting thought when you're a penurious student.
- Sponsoring a complete college or school. A surprising number of high-tech companies do find it difficult to attract staff and sponsorship can help this, not only in the case of offering a bursary but because of a company's image or lack of it. A well-known firm in the defence industry had precisely this problem. A survey conducted amongst students placed it very low on their list of first places to work because it was perceived as dull and uninspiring. There was no great kudos in working there and, if the world is your oyster, there is much more cachet in saying that you work for Rolls-Royce than for Dodd's Dumper Trucks.

So, if recruitment is a problem for your company, then your first

59

step should be to find out why by talking to potential high-fliers. A bursary to get their commitment at an early stage might be one way of doing it and, if it's an image problem, then an appropriate image-building sponsorship may tip the balance.

Many companies look at educational sponsorships from a different angle because they want to attract potential customers. Children are very impressionable and receptive and the seeds of an idea germinated at an early age can reap many long-term benefits. That's why banks and building societies are keen to promote young-saver accounts. A few free goodies today could mean a millionaire tomorrow.

If you want to sponsor something to do with schools or young people, seek advice first. Do not do what many companies do and conceive a painting competition, spend a fortune on mailing to heads of 35,000 schools and receive three entries.

Talk to school heads and teachers, talk to the advisors attached to the local education authority and talk to children. School staff are greatly overworked and are not to going spend their valuable time promoting a sponsored competition where little Johnny might win a new bike but the school receives nothing.

I was once given the advice by a local authority education advisor to bear the following in mind:

- Head teachers receive piles of mail so your package needs to be quick and easy to read.
- Send a second copy of the material to the teacher responsible for history/art/cricket/home economics or whatever. Their enthusiasm may be greater than the head's.
- There must be some benefit in it for the school. Why should they want to act as your sales promotion agent for no reward? Schools always need money and capital goods. So do not put all your eggs into the prizewinner's basket. 'Every school entering will receive a Natsuhishi video recorder' is going to be a difficult one to resist.
- Enlist the help and support of local education authorities who may do the mailing for you and act as useful sounding boards.
- Try to develop something that fits the syllabus. The national curriculum is now in operation and again the local authority will advise you on what is appropriate and useful to education. Arts competitions are very popular with sponsors because they have a visual result and are easy to judge, but you may find that sponsorships involving maths and sciences are actually better received by the schools.
- Do not overpromote your company name or it may cause enough

irritation for all your expensive printed material to be tipped straight into the dustbin.

- Do give enough lead time for the sponsorship to be organized. Companies who mail schools in July and ask for a response in August are not even worthy of a reply. If you want a project to start in the autumn term, start planning a year ahead and get the material to staff in the summer term so they can plan to incorporate it in their syllabus for September.

Of course, schools are not the only organizations patronized by young people. There are others including the Scouts, Girl Guides, Cubs, Brownies, Boys Brigade, National Association of Boys Clubs, youth football teams, marching bands and more. The opportunities are endless. But again, seek advice from those who know first and remember that the success or failure of your sponsorship will ultimately depend upon the enthusiasm of the individual group leader and how your sponsorship is going to make his or her task easier. Get that one right and you'll be received joyously.

The latest development in education is the City Technology Colleges where a partnership with industry is not just welcomed, but is essential. The idea of the CTCs is to develop a school leaver who is industry-orientated and who understands the business ethic, so the whole school, corporate identity and method of studying are very much related to outside industry as opposed to being structured along the formal academic lines of traditional education.

Several CTCs exist already and have been part funded by industry – 10 per cent is the minimum requirement but even this can mean an investment of £1 million plus.

Educational establishments are always seeking money. Companies are always keen to reach this highly attractive audience of the future. But to make the marriage work, each party needs to understand precisely what will motivate the other.

Education score rating

Image match	****
Target audience	*****
Target areas	*****
Name awareness	**
Media coverage	*
Direct marketing	***
Sales promotion	*
Customer entertainment	*

Prestige   ***
Community goodwill   ****

Further information

Useful organizations

If you wish to do something on a very local level, then it is appropriate to contact the head teacher of the school, the principal of the college or the vice-chancellor of the university concerned.

On a wider scale, if you wish to sponsor something on a regional level, contact the director of education at the appropriate local authority.

Information about sponsorship of the City Technology Colleges can be obtained from The Chairman, CTC Trust, 15 Young Street, London W8 (Tel: 071 376 2511).

For national schemes which might involve all schools or higher education colleges go to the top. Contact the Secretary of State, Department of Education and Science, Elizabeth House, York Road, London SE1 7PH (Tel: 071 934 9000). For Scotland contact the Scottish Education Department.

Useful publications

The Education Yearbook – lists all local authorities and gives a complete list of all secondary, middle and specialist schools but not primary and infant schools. There is also extensive coverage of higher education. Published by Longman.

British Universities Guide to University Study – lists all universities and the courses they run. Published by the Association of Commonwealth Universities.

The environment

A few years ago nobody wanted to know about the environment. But suddenly, and happily, it has became hot news. Oil spillages, holes in the ozone layer, disappearing tropical rain forests, the protection of rare animal species, the recycling of waste and the rise of the Green Party have all become extremely topical and many causes worthy of support have emerged as a result.

One of the merits of an environmental sponsorship is that your company cannot be accused of doing it so that the chairman gets tickets for Glyndebourne or Twickenham. Any self-interest on the part of senior executives can only be put down to the support of a very worthy cause.

Environmental sponsorships are perfect for companies who need to put forward images of being caring, concerned, responsible members of the community. For this reason, those companies who go for environmental sponsorship are sometimes those who, boot on the other foot, tend to be damaging it in some way. So you must be very careful, if this is the case, not to be seen to be trying to buy yourself out of trouble. Most environmental organizations tend to be cautious about who they'll allow to sponsor them and the very 'green' could give you a reason for finding almost every company in the land totally unacceptable – they use too much packaging, they have interests in some politically unacceptable state, they want to build an oil terminal in a famous beauty spot, they want to introduce forty-tonne trucks, and so on.

So, if you have an image problem because of some major or minor damage to the environment, try to see your company through the eyes of your worst critics and think carefully about the best way to redress the balance.

Sometimes it is better to sponsor something that is not in the field in which you are doing the most damage because you will almost certainly have it flung back in your face otherwise. For instance, it would be ludicrous for a tobacco company to sponsor a cancer research campaign since, although it would undoubtedly attract a high level of publicity, it would almost inevitably be cynical publicity.

On the other hand, although it might appear a little risky for a cigarette company to sponsor a litter campaign, it does have certain merits. It would need to be a carefully thought-out campaign since even those smokers who do not throw their wrappings and packets on the ground, almost certainly never give a second thought to dropping spent matches or cigarette butts. A tobacco company managing an anti-litter campaign which married advertising, sales promotion and sponsorship could do its image the power of good. Litter has nothing to do with the contentious issue of health but it affects and annoys everybody.

The other way of looking at it is to develop a sponsorship to create an environmentally-conscious image for your company. Thus, even though you may not have in mind to build a factory extension on the local playground, or put up a string of electricity pylons across a national beauty spot, the right sponsorship does create within the population, national or local, the feeling that you are, on the whole, a caring and community-conscious organization. This type of sponsorship is very definitely PR orientated and can often help to soften an unexpected blow.

For instance, disaster may never strike your company but you should never take that chance. You should always have a plan of action to cope with unexpected eventualities just as the emergency services practise in advance for major air disasters, motorway crashes, floods and fires.

If this were a book on public relations, I would be recommending very strongly that you practise and prepare for crisis management. It is not a book on PR, but nevertheless I still recommend that you do just that. Your company may not be another Townsend Thorensen or London Underground, but even the most unlikely of organizations can be struck by a totally unforeseen disaster which results in very damaging bad publicity, made worse because of poor crisis management.

Who could have foreseen the salmonella eggs crisis, BSE or mad cow disease, Legionnaire's disease and air conditioning, glass in Heinz baby food, ninety-five people crushed to death at the FA Cup semi-final at Hillsborough? It may not happen to you on that scale but even comparatively minor events such as making people redundant, closing a local branch, an employee being maimed because of laxity of safety regulations, a child being killed falling through your factory roof, or your kitchens being closed by the Department of Health can be very bad publicity.

I'm not suggesting that sponsorship is the answer to these situations. What I am saying is that, if a particular type of sponsorship helps to build you a sensitive and caring image before trouble strikes, then those who write about the problem and those who read about it may be more inclined to throw pebbles and not bricks.

One organization which has invested a great deal in environmental sponsorship is British Telecom. BT's Head of Corporate Advertising, Robert Evans, says 'We're very much involved in corporate sponsorship as opposed to marketing sponsorship and, as far as the environment is concerned, we sponsor Environment Week and the Community Pride Awards. We also sponsor the Recycling City project which is already established in Sheffield and Cardiff with UK 2000 and Friends of the Earth. This is a model scheme which will be used as an example and a catalyst for other similar projects all over the country.

'The reason we have decided to sponsor the environment is not that we necessarily damage it in any way but simply because we have a high presence in the environment. We have a very large staff; we have the largest fleet of vehicles in the country; and we have a fairly obvious presence through our telephone boxes, and of course we are a significant user of paper and other materials. So we feel that we are very much part of the community and therefore should be seen to be putting something back into it.'

Environment score rating

Image match	***
Target audience	****
Target areas	****
Name awareness	**
Media coverage	**
Direct marketing	**
Sales promotion	*
Customer entertainment	*
Prestige	***
Community goodwill	*****

Further information

Useful organizations

There are literally hundreds of environmental organizations seeking sponsorship of one type or another. If you have no fixed ideas, then you can short-circuit a certain amount of time in research by contacting:

World Wide Fund for Nature
Panda House
Weyside Park
Godalming
Surrey GU7 1XR
Tel: 0483 426444

WWF seeks to protect the green environment both in the UK and worldwide but with a particular emphasis on plant and wildlife. It has nine participating conservation organizations in Britain and is one of twenty-three similar worldwide national organizations.

Useful publications

Civic Trust Environmental Directory – lists 300 environmental organizations in the UK. Published by the Civic Trust, 17 Carlton House Terrace, London SW1Y 8AW. Tel: 071 930 0914. Price £3.00.

Directory for the Environment — lists 1000 organizations including government departments, statutory bodies, research institutes, and voluntary organizations and pressure groups. Published by Routledge & Kegan Paul.

Community affairs

There is often an overlap between community sponsorships and other types of sponsorship but the whole raison d'être of a community sponsorship is to do exactly what you would expect and that is to benefit the community and usually the local community at that.

Community sponsorships are ideal for companies which have their main customer base and their main workforce in a particular locality and consequently rely heavily on local goodwill to trade successfully.

Cheltenham & Gloucester Building Society, for instance, has its base in Gloucestershire and therefore all of its sponsorships are concentrated on that locality to build up a feeling of loyalty and togetherness. They cover a wide range of grass roots sponsorships which reach every stratum of society from sports, such as the local Sunday football leagues, to productions at the Everyman Theatre in Cheltenham, but they have also undertaken a very interesting community sponsorship in conjunction with the Rural Development Commission.

Jerry Angrave from the C & G's marketing department explains: 'We've encouraged applications from any of the rural Gloucestershire villages for community projects. The awards are fairly small sums designed to start people off. For instance, we've helped set up a parent and toddler group at Whittington, we've funded a pensioners' tea dance at Newent, a Gingerbread single parent group at Wydean, a history society at Sheepscombe and a village appraisal at Painswick. People apply to the Rural Initiative Fund in Gloucester. A representative of the C & G sits on the committee and decides on the grants and for every £1 we put in the Rural Development Fund matches it. Usually we're talking about small sums of £50 to £150 but we always make a presentation which gets publicity and, of course, creates goodwill for the society.'

Cheltenham scores highly in the area of community sponsorship. The Cheltenham and District Health Authority is the first health authority to talk seriously to local businesses in terms of commercial deals.

'We didn't want to do anything that would affect our donations income,' says the district general manager James Hammond, 'so we decided that it would be a business-to-business arrangement in which we would approach local companies to see what we could construct with them on a four or five year basis.

'We put together a business package including a video and the response was very enthusiastic. In fact, our problem has almost been to find sponsorships to suit the businesses. Interestingly enough, their main concern has been to be seen to be doing something for the community but in a fairly restrained way. Nobody has asked for a ward to be named after them or to have doctors walking around with their company logos on their gowns. Some have given us money, others material and goods such as vehicles. One company, Silent Gliss, has got together with a number of sub-contractors and is going to refurbish the whole of the Cirencester Hospital for us.'

One might assume that anyone with goods or services to sell would have an eye to the main chance in that they would see a local health authority as a big spender. However, Hammond denies this. 'No, it doesn't work that way. Any of our contracts are constrained by all sorts of formalities and invariably go to the lowest tender. Our sponsors actually want to show that they are putting something into the community in which they work. After all, they employ people and their families who will at some time inevitably use our medical services – the notion of the good company citizen in other words.'

It is not only health authorities which are going into partnership with local companies. Councils, too, are looking for ways of bringing local businesses into their own community projects which might be education, health, environmental or indeed anything that might benefit a local community.

But beware of any company that does this with the intention of winning friends with the local council. Any national or local government officer is bound by stringent rules and any whiff of a suspicion that a company is sponsoring a council with the intention of winning a big contract or easing the passage of a planning application would do that company more harm than good. Elizabeth Smith, a South Bucks District Councillor says 'Both councillors and officers are bound by the Pecuniary and Other Interests Act and it would simply be out of the question to accept a sponsorship for a company which was going to tender for a local authority project. There are all sorts of checks and balances to stop this happening.

'However, we are, I believe, a genuinely philanthropic race, and if any company wanted to offer financial assistance to a local council simply in order to feel that they were being the good citizen, and perhaps for the press and public relations benefits, then I would recommend that they talk to the chief executive of their local authority and ask how they might help. It might be anything from a major tree planting project, to simply sponsoring a litter bin in their local High Street, to the printing and distribution of a new town guide. I think most local authorities would welcome discussions of this sort.'

Many companies like to have friends in parliament, if only as a useful source of information and advice. It is very difficult to get your message across to parliamentarians simply because they are so bombarded with information. Direct mailing an MP with circulars is a highly ineffective way of getting your message over since each receives a huge postbag of material which is divided by long-suffering secretaries into 'must reply', 'possible interest' and 'wastepaper basket'. And I need not tell you which makes the largest pile.

Advertising isn't going to be much of a choice so the lot of lobbying MPs falls, not surprisingly, mainly to those consultancies which specialize in parliamentary PR. The most effective way of getting through to an MP is a personal letter but it is possible to sponsor events which MPs are involved or interested in giving the sponsor a friendly link into the House of Commons.

It is useful for any company to know what is going on in Westminster but if you have a particular cause to fight or axe to grind, then it is worth finding out which MPs are interested in what. Most major companies have forged links either with their local MP or with members who they know have an interest in their field. If you haven't already done so, you could use a specialist PR consultancy or invest in some of the books which will tell you what you need to know such as *The Times Guide to the House of Commons* or *The Register of MPs' Interests*. And an MP's main interest is likely to be his constituency, so sponsorship offered for some local project dear to an MP's heart should be listened to with close interest.

Community sponsorships are all about creating friendly relations and goodwill. There is no massive TV coverage, there are no sales promotion opportunities, you can't usually entertain clients but, in terms of your organization being seen as responsible and caring, it rates very highly indeed.

Community sponsorships score rating

Image match	***
Target audience	***
Target areas	****
Name awareness	*
Media coverage	**
Direct marketing	*
Sales promotion	*

Customer entertainment	*
Prestige	**
Community goodwill	*****

Further information

Useful organizations

Business in the Community
227a City Road
London EC1V 1LX
Tel: 071 253 3716

BIC was set up to encourage business and industry to become involved in the community. It can offer advice, training, briefing papers and contacts. It also coordinates the Percent Club which aims to encourage companies to pledge more resources to charities, community involvement, job creation and training.

Action Match
81 High Street South
East Ham
London E6 4EJ
Tel: 081 472 6652

Funded by the Home Office, this project aims to develop social sponsorship by companies mainly at a local level.

Useful publications

Directory of Local Authorities. Published by Longman.

Municipal Yearbook and *Public Services Directory.* Published by Municipal Publications.

Vacher's Parliamentary Companion — lists all members of the Lords and Commons and senior staff of government offices and public bodies. Published by A. S. Kerswill.

Dod's Parliamentary Companion — similar to the above but with photographs and biographies.

The Voluntary Agencies Directory — lists the objects and activities of

1400 voluntary bodies. Published by Bedford Square Press and the National Council for Voluntary Service.

Charities

Many of the sponsorship vehicles previously mentioned are run by organizations which are already registered charities or trusts, and this includes many arts organizations, environmental organizations and community groups. So if ever there were going to be an area of confusion about the difference between sponsorship and donations, then this is it.

Charities, which once relied solely on donations, are now expanding their fund-raising activities to include sponsorship, sales promotion, merchandising and events. However, the confusion often arises when some charities still expect something for nothing, and equally many companies automatically assume that any approach from a charity means nothing for something.

This misunderstanding is further compounded by the fact that many of the bigger companies and corporations have community affairs departments which dispense funds for both donations and sponsorships.

It's as well to clear up this confusion from the start of any relationship because, from the company's point of view, sponsorship in conjunction with a charity can have numerous advantages. Most of them have now professionalized their fund-racing activities to the extent that they can offer some extremely good schemes.

The benefits of charity sponsorship include publicity which should enhance the company image as good, caring and responsible, thus improving relations with customers, suppliers, staff, government and shareholders.

Furthermore, the link with a charity can open doors which would not otherwise have opened with a more commercial sponsorship. Personalities, who would expect a large fee for opening a supermarket, will be more inclined to give their time free to charity fund-raising functions (for their own corporate image as much as anything!) and there is always a good chance of the attendance of a member of the Royal Family. Most of the big charities have royal patrons which is a help – though no guarantee of attendance.

Some charities and trusts have huge mailing lists of members or donators which can be very attractive to sponsors. For instance, the National Trust has a membership of over 2,000,000 and the Royal Society for the Protection of Birds nearly half a million.

Charities also often have armies of volunteers they can call on to distribute literature or organize events. But be cautious about the use of large numbers of volunteers because you cannot expect them to be at your beck and call in the same way as paid employees.

It won't be difficult to find a charity to support. The major ones will certainly find you and provide you with information packs bulging with ideas on how to spend your money.

Help the Aged is a prime example of one of the big successful charities and it raises over £2 million a year from the world of commerce and industry. It offers a wide variety of business packages and, ironically enough, in an ever-growing market.

One of the many tailor-made sponsorship packages that Help the Aged has developed is the Gala Charity Preview of the Chelsea Flower Show, which it has done in conjunction with the Royal Horticultural Society. 'The RHS had an existing event, which we felt offered enormous potential for development and extension,' says Head of Commercial Development, Tony Elischer. 'We not only had the expertise in event management and organization, but also the contacts with the commercial world to create unique corporate hospitality opportunities. The other major strength of the charity is its public relations department, with access to numerous celebrities and our Patron, HRH The Princess of Wales.

'In 1990 the preview was sponsored by Enterprise Oil who not only had the benefits of profile and association with such an event, but the opportunity of entertaining 250 key customers, potential customers and decision makers. Enterprise Oil were so delighted with their commercial association with Help the Aged that they have now sponsored the charity's ongoing Schools Programme that reaches over 750,000 children a year.

'Amongst the many other unique and tailor-made sponsorship packages that the charity offers is the Golden Awards for Elderly Achievers. In 1990 this is sponsored by Tunstall Telecom whose main product is a community alarm for the elderly, so the sponsorship is a natural for the company. In its first year (1989) the event attracted extensive media coverage and interest, particularly as the charity's Patron was able to present the awards personally. We are obviously hoping to build on this and develop it this year, for the benefit of our overall sponsors, Tunstall Telecom.'

One company which also looked at its target audience carefully was Pentland Industries who produce sports footwear. They were approached by the Scout Association and agreed a package which includes the sponsorship of two of the scouts' badges — the Athlete Badge sponsored by Matchstick sports shoes and the Mountaineer Badge which is sponsored by the Chris Brasher brand of mountain boot.

'We managed to persuade the former Prime Minister to present the cheque and launch the sponsorship,' says Scout Association commercial manager Mark Thatcher, who is no relation to his namesake. 'Pentland is in Mrs Thatcher's Finchley constituency so that was how the connection was made,' he explains. 'But the sponsorship is ideal for Pentland since we have a membership of more than half a million boys in the Scouts, Beaver Scouts, Cub Scouts and Venture Scouts who all wear training shoes these days.'

Another intriguing Scout sponsorship is by Reckitt and Colman who, through their Cherry Blossom Handy Shine brand, sponsor 'Job Week'. Their £30,000 deal involves the branding of all job week literature and scouts set up shoe shine stalls on the High Street during Job Week using Handy Shine packs.

A totally different type of fund-raising organization is The Sports Aid Foundation which gives grants to athletes to help fund their training. (All but two of Britain's medal winners at the Seoul Olympics were helped by the SAF at one time or another.) They also run the Sports Aid Trust which has charitable status and gives grants to young athletes still in full-time education.

From a hard-nosed sponsor's point of view an organization such as the SAF has a lot to offer. It is not as emotive as Oxfam or Save the Children but the public's interest in sport, and particularly the interest in winners, is so great that any sponsorship or promotion undertaken will attract maximum interest. It's also an open door to many famous sports personalities from Seb Coe to Fatima Whitbread who will give their time free to support a cause which has supported them in the past.

'TDK, the audio and video tape manufacturers, sponsored a wrapper promotion through the SAF,' says Jack Maddison, the Foundation's marketing manager. 'For every audio wrapper sent in, they guaranteed a donation of 30p and, for every video wrapper, £1.50. The promotion raised £100,000 which went immediately to support thirty teenage athletes.'

As with any sponsorship, you will get the best value for money when working with charities, if you are clear about your objectives and target audiences. But the charity, too, will want to make sure that you are an appropriate company with which to link, in order that it should not be seen as selling itself to the devil!

Charity sponsorships score rating

Image match	****
Target audience	***
Target areas	****

Name awareness   **
Media coverage   **
Direct marketing   ****
Sales promotion   ***
Customer entertainment   ***
Prestige   *****
Community goodwill   *****

Further information

Useful organizations

Charities Aid Foundation
48 Pembury Road
Tonbridge
Kent TN9 2JD
Tel: 0732 771333

CAF operates two schemes to aid company giving. The first is to act as a half-way house for companies' charitable payments so that companies avoid administrative problems but still benefit from the tax advantages. The second is the Give As You Earn scheme for employees. From a sponsorship point of view, the CAF has information on most national charities and publishes a series of small directories of organizations active in particular areas such as cancer, drug misuse, disabled sport and so on.

Charity Commission Registry
57 Haymarket
London SW1Y 4QX
Tel: 071 210 3000

The Charity Commission keeps a register of the thousands of charities in this country and can therefore verify that an organization has charitable status.

Useful publications:

Donor's Directory of Registered Charities – this guide gives details of over 1000 charities classified under areas of activity. Published by Trade & Technical Press.

The Corporate Donor's Handbook by Michael Norton – an invaluable guide to all types of company giving, including sponsorship. It is published by the Directory for Social Change which specializes in books of this type.

The Charities Digest – lists 1200 carefully-selected charities and gives details of their work. Published by the Family Welfare Association.

Tourist industry

This is an interesting one. The tourist industry has hardly dipped its toe into the water yet as far as sponsorship is concerned but I predict that a change is on the way.

Since businesses are trying to pin-point their markets more and more accurately these days, and at the same time trying to find more original ways to reach potential customers, it follows that an attraction which is visited annually by hundreds of thousands of people, who form a captive audience for anything from an hour to a whole day, is worth looking at.

I can think of no major museum which is currently sponsored, save for the Guinness World of Records which is not a true sponsorship since Guinness, the brewers, haven't paid a fee to sponsor the World of Records. It is simply a title owned by the separate company Guinness Superlatives Ltd.

There are galleries or collections at museums sponsored by commercial firms but, as yet, no one has come up with 'The Big One'. But I think the first company that does may reap the benefit of being just that – the first.

National museums such as the Science Museum or the V & A are not likely to be able to rename themselves after a commercial sponsor, although new wings often take the sponsor's name – for example, the new extension at the National Gallery has been funded by Sainsbury. But the Tetley's Tea Tate Gallery doesn't have quite the right ring about it. However, I don't see the same constraints applying to every attraction, particularly those which are wholly privately-owned collections, museums, stately homes or other visitor attractions.

Many manufacturers are now running their own museums and guided tours as public relations and sales promotion exercises. The pottery manufacturers have done this for years but others have followed suit, principally as public relations exercises. Nuclear power stations, for instance, have encouraged visitors for obvious reasons and with some success. But to be a true sponsorship, the museum or attraction should not be for the direct promotion of a company's products, although it may be so indirectly.

Kodak, for instance, sponsor the cable ride at Alton Towers. It is not called the Kodak ride and the name is simply lettered on the car's exterior in a very subtle manner. The arrangement is all part of a deal which gives Kodak the sole rights to sell film on the site — over two million visitors a year and prime opportunities for photography make it a sound investment.

Kon-Tiki Travel, a company which runs European camping tours for young people, sponsors 'The Rock Tour of London'. Will Birch who created the tour explains: 'We run a twice-daily tour round all the historic rock and pop sites in London, from Abbey Road to the pub where the Rolling Stones made their first recording. It's very popular with the 18-to-30 market. The double decker bus has been redecorated in the Kon-Tiki livery, their name appears on all our posters and publicity material and, as part of the deal, they have the use of the bus every evening to run a tour of London for their own clients. So in that way they provide an added benefit for the people who take their holidays, but are also publicizing themselves to a new market in precisely the age group they want to attract.'

One comparatively new tourist attraction raised nearly £2,000,000 from sponsorship in its first year. In Manchester, the Granada Studios tour which features, amongst other things, the set from *Coronation Street*, has nearly twenty major sponsors ranging from Coca-Cola to Kelloggs.

'We tailor packages to the sponsor,' says marketing manager Alan McGregor. 'That can include anything from advertising space on the set of a New York street, to a range of corporate hospitality packages including the use of the whole site for the day to entertain 2000 people.'

Another major tourist attraction, the National Motor Museum at Beaulieu, is run as a charitable trust and has made strenuous efforts to raise funds though sponsorship. 'We have a number of exhibits and stands which have been sponsored,' says curator Michael Ware. 'For instance, we wanted to set up an old-fashioned motor accessory shop so we approached Halford's. They now have their name on the shop in a prime site in the centre of the exhibition which is visited by 500,000 people a year.'

There are going to be many opportunities in tourism in the future. The market is wide open for imaginative and creative thinking.

Tourist attractions score rating

Image match	****
Target audience	***
Target areas	*****
Name awareness	**
Media coverage	*
Direct marketing	****
Sales promotion	*****
Customer entertainment	****
Prestige	**
Community goodwill	*

Further information

Useful organizations

English Tourist Board
Thames Tower
Blacks Road
Hammersmith
London W6 9EL
Tel: 081 846 9000

Scottish Tourist Board
23 Ravelston Terrace
Edinburgh EH4 3EU
Tel: 031 332 2433

Wales Tourist Board
Brunel House
Fitzalan Road
Cardiff CF2 1UY
Tel: 0222 499909

Northern Ireland Tourist Board
River House
48 High Street
Belfast BT1 2DS
Tel: 0232 235906

The above four national tourist boards in the United Kingdom have a wealth of knowledge and research available on tourism in this country and should be able to supply a wide range of ideas to any company interested in sponsorship from particular new museums, publications, publicity campaigns and competitions. Contact the marketing director at the appropriate board. The British Tourist Authority is responsible for the promotion of the whole of Britain overseas and therefore is the appropriate contact for any company interested in reaching audiences in other countries. The British Tourist Authority can be contacted at the ETB address.

People

There are two distinct types of people sponsorships. The first is the sponsorship of a personality, often a sports star in return for benefits which usually include the wearing of the sponsor's name on clothing, personal appearances, after-dinner speeches, presence at exhibitions and customer events, endorsement of products etc. This naturally brings the sponsor publicity, prestige, name awareness, good public and customer relations and sales promotion benefits.

The second people sponsorship is more low key. This involves the sponsorship of a person in a job. This normally means the secondment of an expert into a charitable organization for a defined period of a year or two. The benefits to the sponsoring company are that the seconded executive gains useful lateral experience but at the same time the sponsorship offers an opportunity for the company to show and prove corporate responsibility and good citizenship on a very practical scale.

A prime example of a personality sponsorship is Courage's sponsorship of Steve Davis which is worth £1 million to the snooker champion. For that he is required to turn up at forty events a year for Courage, usually demonstration matches.

'He's brilliant,' says Courage's sponsorship operations manager Sue Roberts. 'He's totally reliable, never lets us down, is always charming to the guests and is a wonderful ambassador for us. Yes, it's a lot of money but how can you put a value on a key account such as Butlin's. The fact that Steve Davis goes to a holiday camp for a demonstration match is not simply a matter of him being seen by several thousand members of the public, but it helps maintain extremely good relations with some of our very big customers.'

One might assume that for £1 million, anyone should be reliable and charming but unfortunately this is not necessarily the case. I know one famous pop star who is also famous for promising faithfully to turn up at events and then phoning up with an hour to go having 'developed a sudden cold'. Well, at least he phones!

So, if you are considering investing a huge sum in a personality sponsorship of this type, do a little research on his or her reliability first and meet the star a number of times, too. A tendency to arrive late, or continually to rearrange meeting dates at the pre-contract stage, should cause you to hesitate.

Be clear about how this sponsorship will work and exactly what is expected on both sides. Get a lawyer to draw up a very tight contract. A handshake and a 'We're both honourable people' is not enough.

Think very hard about the person you are considering sponsoring:

- Are they going to be here today and gone tomorrow or will they be consistently in the limelight like Steve Davis?
- What happens if they suddenly get bad publicity because they are involved in a changing room brawl or found in bed with the barmaid?
- Can they actually attend functions on the dates you want or are they likely to pull out because of a major competition?
- If impressing clients is the main purpose of your sponsorship, is your sponsored star a likeable sociable person? The friendly handshake, warm smile and merry quip don't come naturally to someone just because they're good at running or singing. Try a test run with your own directors or staff first.
- Does he or she have a theatrical temperament, stage walk-outs, have hysterics, or become 'tired and emotional' after half a lager?
- Is the star committed to anyone else? Is he or she a walking billboard with dozens of engagements and commitments to fulfil?

If the star is very well known, they will almost certainly have an agent who will be constantly seeking out lucrative deals for their protégé. Agents usually receive between 10 and 20 per cent of the personality's earnings so it's in their interests to make sure that the contract works and ensure that it is fulfilled to the letter. Most of your negotiations are likely to be with the agent but, I repeat, get to know the star first before you commit yourself.

The alternative to sponsoring someone very famous is to invest in someone who has talent and potential and may one day be a top sports star or artiste. This is a gamble which calls for a 'nose' and a lot of research.

I was once in a similar situation, as a photographer for a small photo-feature agency. My job was to photograph pop stars and the pictures were then syndicated worldwide. Of course, the big stars weren't interested in peripheral publicity. The nonentities were enthusiastic, willing and instantly available, but the press wouldn't buy the pictures. So the trick was to try and pick someone who was about to have a hit record and get the photographs out just at the time when the press were desperate for them. Notable gambles which paid off were Englebert Humperdinck, The Troggs and the Tremeloes — notable failures are rather too many to mention!

So picking a star of the next decade is going to be a similar lottery. You will need to know your sport or artistic area pretty intimately (or find someone who does) to be able to pick a winner of the future.

But imagine the pleasure and the publicity of spotting a budding Steve Cram or Jonathan Brundle or Nigel Kennedy or Victoria Wood.

There is no guarantee that your protégé will ever become famous but you could lessen the odds by investing in several potential stars of the future.

Take British tennis, which seems to have taken a dive into the doldrums in the last twenty years. One company has, however, invested several million pounds in its future. Pilkington Glass sponsor the ladies championships at the Eastbourne Championships, pre-Wimbledon each year. They also sponsor Jo Durie but their involvement in tennis goes right back to the grass roots.

Clifford Bloxham is the client services manager for Advantage International, the consultancy which manages the Pilkington sponsorship. 'Part of the arrangement with Jo is that she runs about a dozen tennis clinics for youngsters each year,' he says. 'These can be in conjunction with local schools or tennis clubs and we also often have some of our customers' children there as well.

'They receive a two-hour coaching session, advice on steps to improve their game and, if they are very exceptional and between 15 and 20, Pilkington Glass may sponsor them individually. They sponsor about four each year.

'Sometimes the gamble pays off, sometimes it doesn't, but we ask the youngsters to take part once a year in a mass coach-in for 6500 children at a Hertfordshire school. Along with Jo, our four sponsored players and about twenty coaches we have a very enjoyable and busy day and encourage a lot of youngsters to take up tennis.'

Pilkington Glass also sponsor tennis coach Alan Jones to enable brilliant young tennis players to receive free coaching from him.

'Pilkington Glass sponsor tennis because it's a sport enjoyed equally by men and women,' says Bloxham. 'And this is particularly important since women have the major influence on household spending, double glazing, conservatories and so on. But the important thing is that Pilkington Glass see this as a long-term sponsorship and have invested at all levels. It's not simply been a flash in the pan.'

Young talented people are hungry for success. Sometimes literally hungry, too, and are prepared to make huge sacrifices for their ambition to be a star. Sometimes the odds are too great even so. One of the most imaginative sponsorships I can recall is that of Nottingham City Council's support of Torvill and Dean, then struggling to make their way in ice dance against huge financial odds. But the council's sponsorship of the couple paid off. Torvill and Dean became Olympic and World Ice Dance Champions and Nottingham got all the good publicity it well deserved.

At the other end of the scale is the sponsorship of a person into another job, usually in a charitable organization which needs expertise of one sort or another but can't fund a salary. The sponsoring organization simply seconds the executive for a year or two into the charity and pays their salary.

For the sponsor this has two advantages. First, they are seen as the good citizen – they are making their contribution to the community. But second, they are giving their staff member broader work experience.

Many big companies do this already. Shell usually has some ten middle management secondees out at a time. One of these is Brian Veasey who was a marketing manager with Shell UK Oil. He is currently associate director with the Involvement and Participation Association which seeks to encourage industry to involve staff in decision taking at all levels thus increasing their motivation and consequently the performance of the company.

The IPA is his second secondment. His first was with the Civic Trust, a charitable organization which tries to preserve and improve this country's architectural environment.

'Shell UK has always supported the Civic Trust,' says Brian, 'and Sir Bob Reid, the former chairman, who is also a trustee was concerned with implementing a consultancy report which recommended that the Trust give much more attention to marketing. So Sir Bob decided that Shell would make someone with marketing expertise available to the Trust on a two-year secondment. 'At Shell I had been used to a structural, hierarchical, goal-orientated way of working. At the Trust, I was given total freedom to act – starting with a clean sheet. I realized very soon that my goals and priorities needed to be realistic and attainable. The challenges faced were very varied and, whereas in a Shell world I would have been able to call on specialist help, at the Trust it was a question of finding my own solutions and taking the decisions. But I received tremendous support from the staff. At Shell, resources, particularly money, were not a real problem provided you could show a return. I expected to come to the Trust and be given a budget to manage. But it wasn't like that, I spent a lot of time actually trying to raise money rather than trying to spend it. So I've certainly seen a different side of life and it's given me a much broader appreciation of smaller organizations.'

But although it broadens a secondee's experience, which can be invaluable to a sponsoring company, it can have disadvantages, too, admits Brian. 'I think some people realize that there is life after the company and become rather unsettled. Then, from the charity's point of view, one has to consider what they are going to do when the secondment finishes. It doesn't make sense to start up a wonderfully efficient marketing operation, membership scheme or accounts system and then leave it high and dry after two years with no one to run it. I think both the sponsor and the sponsee should have this very much in mind when they decide to go ahead.'

People sponsorship score rating

Famous people

Image match	****
Target audience	***
Target areas	*****
Name awareness	*
Media coverage	**
Direct marketing	*
Sales promotion	*****
Customer entertainment	*****
Prestige	***
Community goodwill	*

Secondments

Image match	***
Target audience	*
Target areas	****
Name awareness	*
Media coverage	*
Direct marketing	*
Sales promotion	*
Customer entertainment	*
Prestige	**
Community goodwill	*****

Further information

Famous sports stars generally have agents who negotiate sponsorships. You can generally obtain a lead to the right person by contacting the sports personality's club or official governing body.

Actors, musicians, film stars etc. also all have agents. If you have no immediate source of enquiry such as the *BBC Artists' Index*, record company or theatre, then try the appropriate magazine for the industry concerned – *Melody Maker* for pop stars, *The Stage* for actors and so on.

Useful organizations

Action Resource Centre
1st Floor
102 Park Village East
London NW1 3SP
Tel: 071 383 2200

If you do not want to make a direct approach to a voluntary organization, the Action Resource Centre acts as a clearing house for secondments, providing advice to companies and matching executives to suitable secondment opportunities. They also publish a guide to secondment.

Useful publications

Who's Who published by Adam & Charles Black lists the worthy famous and their contact addresses, but not the lightweight famous.

Spotlight – lists all major actors and actresses and their agents.

Who's Who on Television – gives brief details on many of the famous faces on TV and their agents' addresses. Published by Independent Television Books.

Other opportunities

There seem to be very few subjects which have not been covered in the preceding pages. Everything that can be sponsored already seems to have been sponsored but then, a few years back, who would have thought of sponsoring an art exhibition or a school? All you need is the inspirational idea and a willing partner and the door is open.

Buildings and stadiums, open spaces, plants and flowers, exhibitions, shows, conferences, inventions, teachers, public transport, roads, footpaths, research, and a hundred other opportunities are all out there for the taking, if you have the creativity to make the most of them.

But if none of the vehicles listed here or on the earlier pages really seems to hit the nail quite on the head, then perhaps this is the time to go back to the beginning and look at your objectives and your target audience and find the common factor.

The common factor is almost certainly going to be that the audience is very difficult to reach for one reason or another. For instance, you may be trying to reach high-flying City finance directors. They leave home early to get into London, arrive back late, bring work home, hardly have time for television, and don't play sport or have any hobbies. There appears to be no way to reach them. But there must be common factors to be exploited – they mainly travel in by train, they use the Underground, they travel a lot by taxi, they always forget their wives' birthdays, they hate buying clothes, they are all high achievers, they eat out a lot, they mostly have children of university age, and so on. There are, in fact, many avenues by which to reach them but you need to do some lateral thinking to discover an unexplored method.

Lateral thinking resulted in one sponsorship which almost every person in this country could name. 'The time sponsored by Accurist is two forty-five precisely' announces the speaking clock. Andrew Loftus, Accurist's managing director says 'Our name is mentioned 8640 times a day and we are now well past our one billionth call.

'It would be difficult to assess exactly how this sponsorship has affected our sales because, of course, it is only part of our marketing activities. Our turnover has, in fact, increased ninefold over the last seven years so we were doing very well at the time we announced the sponsorship in 1986. But in a sense, even if you are already successful, you have to seek new ideas to keep in the lead. This sponsorship certainly gave us a very high profile, not only with the public but also within the trade. We were able to link in advertising and sales promotion campaigns and it was very much a talking point in jewellers' shops.

'British Telecom were very conscious that they might be seen as selling a public institution for commercial gain. They were very, very cautious about it and almost pulled out of the deal at one point since they were quite concerned that they would attract bad publicity.

'It did, in fact, attract considerable publicity but we managed it very carefully. We knew that it was a big story but front page stories tend to be sensationalized so we consciously waited until there was a piece of news that would make the lead – the engagement of Prince Andrew to Sarah Ferguson – before releasing our story. We ended up making the second page lead in most papers and the item was written without any sensationalization and both BT and Accurist were very happy with that.'

Further information

It is difficult to recommend any useful sources of information such as the Association of Lateral Thinkers or the 'Directory of Creative Ideas'. Inspiration is one of those things that seems to strike either in the bath or during a night of insomnia. Sometimes it happens when a group of people get together to bounce ideas off each other and that is probably the obvious way to start.

4 Managing the sponsorship

The in-house team

If you and your company decide to take sponsorship seriously and include it in your communications programme, you will need to consider carefully who will manage the sponsorship internally.

It may be that there is an obvious answer to this question but there certainly seems to be a trend for sponsorships now to be managed within corporate public relations, corporate marketing or corporate advertising departments, particularly where companies may be part of larger groups where it makes sense to have central services units such as advertising and design. This is perhaps more true of organizations providing services than of those selling consumer products but, since every company seems to be structured in an entirely different and often unfathomable way, a specific recommendation is virtually impossible.

However, in general, if the intention is to promote a product, the sponsorship should almost certainly be managed by the marketing department. If the aim is more to do with the presentation of a corporate image, then the sponsorship may be better dealt with by the corporate affairs department which may well report direct to the chairman and not the marketing director.

This choice can be a slightly ticklish problem in companies where there is a certain inter-departmental rivalry. Sponsorship, as we have already established, traverses many areas and, if it is to be beneficial to the whole company, then it is vital that all departments work together.

The final choice will almost certainly depend upon which department has the sponsorship budget and then it is sensible to appoint an executive at a fairly senior level to be responsible for all sponsorships either at director level or reporting personally to the appropriate director.

In practice, even very large organizations seem to run very tight 'sponsor' ships. Usually there will only be a sponsorship manager at middle or senior management level who reports to a head of marketing or director of corporate affairs. He or she will then probably be able to call on other departmental assistance and secretarial help but is — in the main — the coordinator.

But one person cannot know everything and be everywhere so the coordinator will have to call on expertise from other departments to help in the management of the sponsorship programme.

Since sponsorship does cover so many areas, it is essential for departments who are going to have staff involved in the sponsorship to feel positively about it right from the start. This may necessitate preparing a presentation on sponsorship policy to staff in the communications field but it will be time well spent.

The sponsorship manager will obviously be the lynch-pin, but his best plan of action to make the sponsorship function smoothly is to set up an inter-departmental project group and this group may well vary from sponsorship to sponsorship. A cricket sponsorship involving much client entertainment is not necessarily going to involve the same project team as a community sponsorship which is for goodwill purposes only.

The team should not be unwieldy but these are the sort of departments and/or their agencies which may be involved:

- Head of corporate affairs
- Sponsorship manager or sponsorship consultancy
- Marketing manager or marketing consultancy
- Advertising manager or advertising agency
- Sales manager or conference and event planners
- Direct marketing manager or direct marketing agency
- Sales promotion manager or sales promotion agency
- Press officer or public relations consultancy
- Designer or design group
- Minutes secretary
- Representative/s from sponsored organization

You will notice that the various other agencies have been listed because their particular expertise may be necessary where there is no in-house executive with that responsibility. Similarly, the words 'sponsorship consultancy' appear near the top of the list as their all-round expertise may be an essential factor if your sponsorship programme is likely to be an extensive one. It will also probably obviate the need to bring in a multitude of other consultancies.

Using a sponsorship consultancy

Virtually all big companies tend to use consultants and agencies to supplement their own staff. It makes sense to buy in expertise when it is needed rather than setting up huge departments which have to create yet more work for themselves in order to perpetuate their existence.

Barrie Gill, chairman of the sponsorship consultancy CSS International Limited says 'I used to be the marketing manager of Ford and they employed fifty-six people. Then I went to Detroit to see my opposite number and I found that he employed three people. 'Bring in the consultancies' he would say and it was made obvious to me at that time that companies were perfectly willing to spend money but head count was something else.'

Do you need to use a specialist sponsorship consultancy for your sponsorship programme? If it is a major sponsorship, the answer should almost certainly be 'yes', just as you will use an advertising agency for your advertising campaign. If it is a minor one, then you will need to make your own judgement as to whether you handle it in-house or use your current advertising agency or PR consultancy or design partnership to do the extra work.

Sponsorship is, as I have already said, a combination of many facets of marketing and corporate relations and therefore whoever is running your sponsorship both internally and externally will need to be someone who has a wide and varied range of marketing experience – someone who won't simply see the sponsorship in terms of press coverage or advertising boards, but who has the knowledge and ability to judge all the benefits of sponsorship without bias towards one element or another.

A sponsorship consultancy can make life very much easier for you. Whereas you may be new in the sponsorship field, they know their way round the business and can avoid all the pitfalls that are likely to catch you out. If you are an experienced sponsor, you are just as likely to use an agency, too, simply because you'll need someone to do a lot of the seasonal work and to do some of the million things for which you may have neither the time nor the in-house expertise. Sue Roberts, sponsorship operations manager for Courage says 'We tend to use a number of different sponsorship consultancies according to the sponsorship. If it's rugby then we use a consultancy which has expertise in rugby. If it's tennis, then we'll use one which has good contacts in tennis and so on.'

First of all, a sponsorship consultancy will be able to assess for you whether you should be in sponsorship at all.

If you have not already worked out your sponsorship policy

document, they will be able to work on it with you and, with their experience in the business, arrive at exactly what should and should not be included by asking the same sort of questions that I have already suggested you ask yourself.

They will be able to do extensive research for you on suitable sponsorships. They are likely to have many files of potential sponsorships available and will try to match these with your criteria. They will also talk to likely candidates and find out what else is on offer for you.

They will help you negotiate all the sponsorship benefits you require. And again, their extensive experience will enable them to include things that you probably never would have considered.

They will negotiate with the media. If television is involved, then they will arrange the best possible deal for you within the restrictions given by the medium for each particular sport or event. They will negotiate the fee and the timing, and they will set up the contract and make sure that it is legally sound.

They will manage the sponsorship for you – the announcement, the publicity, the advertising, the client entertainment, the sales promotion, and so on. They will keep their eyes open for new opportunities for you and be ready to act at very short notice. They will have enough staff so that when you need twenty people, to entertain 500 competition winners, you don't have to look to your own company, you can use the consultancy staff and simply pay for the hours they work. In fact, your sponsorship consultancy can be used for all or any single aspect of your sponsorship.

All companies, however small, will be using consultants of one sort or another whether they be designers, advertising agencies, PR consultancies, direct marketing or sales promotion experts, exhibition planners or conference organizers. Some corporations may use a dozen different consultancies with very specialist knowledge in specific areas.

It may well be that if you want to dip a toe in the sponsorship water that you are already asking the advice of your advertising or PR consultancy. If it's one of the big players in the game then the chances are that it has some expertise in sponsorship or has a sister company or a connection of some sort with a sponsorship consultancy. If the consultancy is quite small, then you need to be sure that they have the necessary expertise.

There are something like 150 specialist sponsorship consultancies in Britain – some employing fifty or sixty people, some one-man bands. Some tackle anything, some specialize in sport or the arts, some work for a limited number of clients, some represent particular athletes or organizations, some charge fees for managing sponsorships, some take a percentage from the sponsee for finding a sponsor. It is bit of a minefield so you need to know your way around before making a choice. You would not, for instance, want to go to a consultant for some independent advice on a sponsorship and then later discover that he had sold you a sponsorship and received not only your fee but a 15 or 20 per cent commission from the sponsored organization as well.

Before you use any consultancy or agency, and this applies just as much to advertising and PR, you should understand their raison d'être. Although they will tell you that their loyalty is to you, the client, and although they may even believe that their loyalty is to you, the client, in practice their loyalty must be to the consultancy and to build business for it. So the more ideas they can put up to you which you accept, the more fees they gain for the consultancy which means more money and safer jobs for the executives concerned.

But do not let those few words of wisdom put you off using an outside agency; they are merely there to add a note of caution and to stop you blindly accepting every word of advice your consultancy gives you on the grounds that they are the experts and therefore that they know best. You may have a wonderful relationship with them but never forget that, deep down, they would much prefer to sell you a project which involves their time and therefore earns them fees than to recommend that you do nothing.

However, if you build up a good relationship with your consultants so that you trust each other and if you are a valued client paying a high level of fees, then they will want to keep you at all costs. This means that they will want to do their best for you and are quite likely to 'overservice' your account which means putting in more hours than you are actually paying for.

Most people reading this book will know how to go about finding a PR consultancy or advertising agency and exactly the same principles apply to sponsorship.

A survey I once conducted revealed, not surprisingly, that most people find their PR consultancy through recommendation from friends or colleagues or because they know one of the consultancy executives from previous acquaintance. So, if you are looking for a consultancy, one of your first tasks should be to ask around to find out who is using whom and to get an honest opinion.

Incidentally, my same survey also revealed that most companies had been with their PR consultancy for less than a year and that, on the whole, the level of satisfaction was not high. So it is all the more important to get it right from the beginning.

Your second source of information should be the directories, magazines and organizations concerned with sponsorship – namely

Sponsorship News, the *Sponsorship Yearbook,* and the *Hollis Press and Public Relations Annual.* The Central Council for Physical Recreation also publishes a *Register of Sponsorship Agencies* listing those consultancies which specialize in sport.

If you can find the time to look through all these directories and magazines, it will be time well spent, because a picture will begin to emerge of who are the well-known names in the business, who their clients are and what their specialities are. You may want to look at those who are particularly sports orientated or have an arts speciality or, if you are out of the London area, you may want to look at consultancies in your own region. Big does not necessarily mean best, because ultimately it is all down to the staff who will be working on your account and their experience and expertise. At a big consultancy you could end up with a very junior executive being assigned to your account whereas at a small one, you are likely to be working with one of the directors. On the other hand, the executive at the big consultancy has a multitude of in-house resources to back him up but the smaller consultancy will have to buy in other experts.

Shop around to find the best and make time to do so. Don't necessarily pick the first consultancy that is recommended, they may not be suitable.

Make a shortlist from your directories and contacts and write or phone each and ask to speak to the director in charge of new business and see what happens. You will get an immediate feel for the company from the way your are handled by the switchboard and the way your contact responds. If they falter at the first hurdle, you can knock off a few brownie points straight away.

You should ask first of all for a company brochure (or a letter detailing their services and current clients). This is likely to be a shiny publication telling you how wonderful the consultancy is, and after reading it, having read twenty similar such publications, you may be none the wiser. Company brochures are designed to promote the consultancy and not necessarily give you answers to all the things you need to know. What the brochure will do, however, is give you a feel of the organization and some of the background information you need. If a consultancy is unable to produce good material for itself, then don't assume that it can do better for you!

Beyond the brochure, you will also need to have the following pieces of information:

1   Are they a pure sponsorship consultancy or part of another type of agency such as PR or marketing?
2   If they are not solely a sponsorship consultancy, what other expertise can they offer under the same roof – design, advertising,

perimeter hoardings, legal expertise, sales promotion, direct marketing?

3 How many staff are actually working on sponsorship? Can you have pen pictures of those staff?

4 How long has the consultancy been in existence?

5 What clients do they have and what sort of work do they do for them?

6 Have they any clients in a competitive market?

7 How do they charge? What are their hourly rates for different executive levels? Do they have a minimum monthly fee level for clients? What are their charges for items such as photocopying and postage? Do they add a handling charge for out-costs such as printing?

8 Do they accept commission from those seeking sponsorship?

9 Can they give you any references?

Get the information sent to you and note how long it takes and how well it is presented. Pick ten or twenty, or as many as you can reasonably cope with, and then start weeding out.

Any consultancy worth its salt is not, however, going to let you get away with it that easily. Once the initial contact has been made, the whisper of a possible new account will mean that the new business executive will certainly phone you again to ask if you would like to come and look round their set-up, or if they can come and talk to you about your requirements, or if they can give you a presentation — anything to get face to face with you.

But unless you really want to trek round twenty different offices, you will need to be firm at this stage and say that you are looking at a large number of consultancies to start with and want to make a shortlist from this information and that you will let them know.

Hopefully, you will be able to whittle the pile of information down to a long shortlist or even a short shortlist. It should be fairly obvious which should be included and rejected but certainly reject those which either do not come up with proper answers to the questions you asked them or try to waffle their way round them. You may also want to exclude consultancies who already have clients in the same business since there may be a conflict of interests.

Do write to the rejected consultancies to tell them that they have not been included in the shortlist. It will save you time in the end because otherwise they will almost certainly ring to find out for themselves.

If you have a PR consultancy, sales promotion or advertising agency which you feel may have some of the right expertise in-house, it would be reasonable as a matter of goodwill to give them an opportunity to 'pitch' as well. They may refuse on the grounds that they have no expertise in this area but they will appreciate being asked and may be able to make recommendations.

Most client companies shortlist up to seven or eight and then ultimately cut this down to a final two or three. If you decide to go this route, then allocate about three days to the first selection and one day to the final one. Take one or two colleagues with you for another opinion.

On the first run, when you visit, simply ask for a credentials presentation and a quick tour of their offices. Do not allow this to take more than an hour and do not visit more than three in one day. Do not be led into time-consuming lunches at expensive restaurants or invitations to Ascot. Keep it on a business level at this stage so that you are under no obligation to repay the hospitality!

A credentials presentation should mean that you are shown some of the work that has been done for other companies. This may be in the form of a presentation folder, an exhibition, flip charts, a slide show, a video or whatever can be mustered. Particularly ask to see anything that is relevant to your own field. It is also useful to try and find out who they have worked for in the past but are no longer working for now.

Actually looking round the offices themselves may prove to be very revealing. Are they run down and shabby or high-tech, is the place buzzing with activity, or are the staff too busy gossiping about the last office party?

Talking of staff, the chances are that the presentation will be given to you by the managing director and the new business director. Not surprisingly, these are people who are good at presentations and therefore, without a doubt, you will be suitably impressed and get on famously with them. But, even if you do not do it at this first stage, you absolutely must insist on meeting the people who are likely to be doing the work for you. You may get on wonderfully with the managing director and be bowled over by the new business director but, in a big company, they certainly will not be working on your account, whatever protestations they may make to the contrary. In a small consultancy, they may well act as account directors and work on your account but, in a big company, you will not see them more than once or twice a year. So it is vital that you meet the staff who would actually be doing the work.

Going back to my survey, virtually all the people who responded said that they chose their consultancy because they liked and trusted the executives they met. Chemistry is so important that you must make sure you get on well with the people you will actually be working with.

As you go round your long shortlist of consultancies, make notes or one will begin to fuse into another towards the end of this marathon tour.

As soon as you have seen all the likely candidates, allocate an hour or so to sit down with your colleagues and short shortlist. Most people shortlist to three as a manageable number but that is not a hard-and-fast rule by any means.

It may be blindingly obvious which are to be the chosen few. But if you are unable to make up your mind, then it may help to phone up one or two of the consultancies' current clients and ask some pertinent questions. Better still, phone up some of their ex-clients and ask why they went elsewhere. The explanations may be reasonable but, if you catch a whiff of mismanagement and disaster, then your question is answered.

Once you have a short shortlist, you can ask these consultancies to do a final presentation to you and tell them that you will be making your choice based on these presentations. You will probably be asked who the other consultancies in the frame are and, unless you have particular reason to keep it secret, there is really no reason why you should not let them know who their rivals are. It honestly does not make any difference to their presentations, they just feel happier if they know who they are up against.

Many companies do not give a proper brief or a budget when asking consultancies for presentations. They then get irritated when they are badgered for further information and say things like 'You're supposed to be the experts. We'd like to know what *you* think we should be spending.' There seem to be two main reasons for this. First, clients don't want to be made to feel foolish if they say to a big agency 'We have a budget of £2,000' and then see the agency staff collapse in hysterical laughter; second, they feel that, if they don't quote a figure, they may get a bargain.

This is a most frustrating thing for consultancies who have to guess what they think the client can afford, besides being a short-sighted ploy on the part of the company who then may not be able to compare like with like. One consultancy may come up with a programme at £100,000, another with a programme at £10,000 and then it is impossible to make a reasonable comparison.

All consultancies charge on roughly the same basis so you will not get a bargain by being secretive about your budget. This is one of the reasons for asking your potential consultancies if they have a minimum fee level. If you are thinking in terms of a fee budget of £5,000 a year and their minimum fee level is £1,000 per month, then you do not need to waste each other's time. But equally no big agency will try and make you feel foolish if you have only a small budget to work with. They are much more likely to be helpful and offer the names of some smaller consultancies that they know will be happy to work with small budgets. After all, if they register in your mind as helpful and informative today, you may come back to them as a big-spending client tomorrow.

If you are in some doubt about what you should be spending on sponsorship, ask your shortlisted consultancies to come up with three different options at different budgets, and to justify them.

If you want to make a true comparison between consultancies make sure that they all have exactly the same brief, the same information, the same budget and the same amount of time to prepare their presentation. I have often been in situations where Consultancy A has had three weeks to prepare their presentation and poor Consultancy B has had a mere three days. Parkinson's Law seems to have dictated that I have always been working for Consultancy B!

But to return to the brief. This should include a short statement about where you are at the moment and where you want your company to be in the future and exactly what you want your consultancy to do.

It can be as short or as long as you want it to be. If you make it too short then you are bound to be asked, quite rightly, for more information. On the other hand, it is quite useful to see just how much initiative your potential consultancy shows in finding out about your market.

Greville Waterman, managing services director of Strategic Sponsorship, says 'Companies frequently write muddled briefs and it's up to us to sort out this muddle. Many don't know what makes their customers tick. But others know which ones go on foreign holidays, which ones entertain at home, which ones dine out and so on. But few companies offer that information in their initial brief. We need to know as much as possible right down to their favourite TV programme. After all, sponsorship is about lifestyle interest and detail like this is important and crucial for developing a successful strategy. Once this is sorted out, we need to develop communications channels appropriate to those lifestyle interests and to convey the sponsorship messages to the consumer.'

Here is a very simple example of the sort of brief you might give a potential consultancy, which should be backed up with any other information you can supply such as brochures, press cuttings, research, consumer survey results, a list of contacts at other agencies and consultancies you use, and so on. If you have followed my earlier advice and already written a sponsorship rationale document, then you will help the shortlisted consultancies by enclosing it. But alternatively, you might seriously consider leaving it out just to see

whether the consultancies come to the same conclusions as your own staff. If they do, then you obviously are going to work well together.
Here is an imaginary example of a sponsorship brief:

Sleepwell Bedding Company Ltd – brief for A to Z Sponsorship Ltd

Background

Sleepwell is an old-established bedding company, the second largest in Britain. A recent consumer survey shows that our products have an extremely high reputation but that our name awareness is very much higher in the 44 + age group than in younger age groups. This is borne out by the fact that most of our purchasers are over thirty. Our sales have remained steady but our share of the market has declined slightly.

Intention

We intend in the next five years to invest in marketing to a younger age group and are particularly keen to reach newly-weds and to increase the name awareness of Sleepwell within the age group who are most likely to get married within the next five years. We are looking at a number of marketing options at the moment and this may or may not include sponsorship. Should we appoint a sponsorship consultancy, we would require that consultancy to research, assess and completely manage all aspects of Sleepwell sponsorship in conjunction with our marketing director.

Brief

An information pack has been included with this brief which includes the consumer research programme completed in May, some samples and details of our current advertising, sales promotion and PR programmes, our annual report and also some information about the bedding market in general. No further meetings may be arranged between now and the presentation date but, if you require further information, please telephone John Daws in the marketing department who may be able to help.
From this information we should like you to assess the following:

1   Would you recommend Sleepwell uses sponsorship as part of its marketing mix? If not, what other options would you suggest?

2 If the answer is positive, what benefits should the company look for from sponsorship?
3 What would you recommend as the most suitable sponsorship vehicle or vehicles for Sleepwell?
4 Assuming that you have a notional budget of £250,000 per annum for five years to include all sponsorship fees, consultancy fees and out-costs, please give a brief example of what you see as being a suitable sponsorship package for Sleepwell and outline how the company should maximize its potential. Please note that this is for example purposes only. However, within this example we would particularly like to know what you would assess to be a suitable amount for fees and exactly what your methods for charging would be.

Presentation

Please be ready to present your proposal at 10.00 a.m. in the boardroom at the above address on Thursday 15 October. You will be presenting to marketing director, Jim Hobbs, corporate affairs manager, Mary Reynolds, and four members of their staff.

Contact Fred Adams in the corporate affairs department to discuss any visual aids you may wish to use and let him know how many will be in your team. Please ask for him when you arrive. The room will be available for you to set up from 9.00 a.m. and coffee and biscuits will be arranged for you on request.

You will have no more than one hour to present your proposal and should allow at least fifteen minutes within this for questions.

Please note that we would particularly like to meet and hear from members of the team who will be working on our account should you win it.

*   *   *

Allocate a day at your own offices for the presentation. Give each consultancy at least three (and preferably four or five) weeks' in which to prepare.

I would suggest that you allow an hour including questions (and don't be generous with extra time). Consultancies should not be allowed to overrun their hour but you would be wise to allow half an hour at the very least between each presentation in order for your company executives to have a break, answer urgent telephone messages, have coffee and a chat and generally wake up before the next group comes in. Run on one after the other and you will have managers dashing out to take phone calls and falling asleep in the final session.

What you should be looking for during this hour is a professional presentation from the consultancy team. There is a difference between professionalism and slickness. After all you do not want to feel that you are simply another audience in the consultancy's presentation road show. As I said earlier, the managing director or new business director (who may be called something like client relations director or some other such title) will probably lead the presentation because that is his or her forté. But do make a point of listening to, and asking questions of, the people who will be managing your account. It really is vital that you establish a rapport with the people you will be working with since they will effectively become members of your staff.

During the presentation, take particular note of whether your brief has been followed or whether they have gone off at a tangent and done their own thing. 'We know you only asked for one example but in fact we've put in four' may indicate a tendency at a later stage to do what they want and not what you want.

Everyone will of course be on their best behaviour during a presentation in which case it can be quite difficult to judge the real characters behind the smiling faces. Try throwing in a few difficult questions or getting one member of your team to say that they think some statement that has been made is 'nonsense' just to see what the reaction is. The situation should be dealt with smoothly, calmly and politely.

I once worked for an organization which used a consultancy where one of the partners simply could not bear it if we expressed doubts about any of his ideas. He would argue his case strongly and with great vehemence, while at the same time implying that he was the 'consultant' and that we were mere clients who were paying for his expertise and should therefore almost be seen and not heard. Faced with this tirade, it became easier to give in eventually and let him have his way. The strange thing was the company still continued to use him on the grounds that anyone who felt that strongly about his work must be good. Yes, he was good but not so good that, given the choice, I would have continued to use such an obnoxious man – consultants who treat clients as though they are ten bricks short of a load do not rate very highly in my book.

Creative ideas are important but do not get led down the path of becoming thrilled about a brilliant idea without first considering whether it will actually do the job it is intended to do. You may get so caught up in the enthusiasm of sponsoring a world record attempt for resting on a bed of nails that you lose sight of the fact that the public may well draw the conclusion that Sleepwell Beds are extremely uncomfortable.

So do make sure that what is being said has been well researched, well thought out, makes good common sense and – most important – will help achieve your objectives.

However, be fair in your expectations of the presentation. If your budget is £5,000, it really is not reasonable to expect consultancies to invest weeks of work into an all-singing, all-dancing extravaganza. On the other hand, if your budget is £500,000, then you should expect an appropriate amount of time and effort to be put into the meeting.

Sometimes clients feel that consultancies' fees are very high but at the same time are quite happy to see a consultancy pitch for their business, investing hours of time and effort into researching and preparing for a presentation completely free of charge and then receiving nothing in return. It is a hard life as a consultant – you give away all your best and most creative ideas completely free and then a client purses his lips when confronted with a large bill for stuffing envelopes!

It seems to me not unreasonable that consultancies should be paid if they are expected to put a lot of creative work into a presentation – the research, the artwork, the slides and the document are all going to cost them money. But it is such a competitive business that you will hardly ever be asked for a fee to cover costs. But don't react with distaste if you are. Simply ask for the reason for a fee to be justified and consider it on its merits. Look at it from the consultancy's point of view – if you were unscrupulous, for instance, there is nothing stopping you asking four consultancies to pitch, copying all their ideas for nothing and putting them into practice yourself. The new business director of one of the biggest consultancies in the business confides, 'We have stopped giving people very detailed proposals before they become clients. Now we give them perhaps two sheets of paper.'

And two sheets of paper may be perfectly adequate if the strategic thinking is right. If it is patently obvious that the consultancy has assessed your needs and formulated a sensible plan to meet your objectives that is fine, and it is much better than 100 pages of waffle which miss the point.

If you are still in doubt after seeing all your potential consultancies' presentations, it is not a bad idea to arrange to have an informal lunch with just the account director and account executive of your two final choices to get a more intimate feel of the consultancy and its staff before you make a final commitment. If the managing director seems anxious about this, then you should wonder why.

Your final decision should be based on a number of factors including the chemistry with the account group staff you will be working with, the quality and experience of the directors they report to, their understanding of your business objectives, the consultancy's back-up organization, its track record, what other people say about it, its creativity, its professionalism and its honesty and integrity.

You should also be very clear about what you will be committing yourself to before you make a final decision. In other words, how much it is going to cost you. This is why it is sensible to define the budget first, but it would be interesting to see what proportion of this money each consultancy sees as being allocated to the sponsorship fee, to out-costs and to its own fees.

Consultancies make their money from selling their time plus their expertise to you. It is going to be a very remarkable sponsorship consultancy which tells you that sponsorship is not for you (if you do meet such a body, take note for future reference!) simply because they would be turning away business. It would almost be like going to a car showroom and the salesman telling you that your old Austin was perfectly adequate so there was no need for you to buy a brand new Rover.

As I have said before, consultancies earn their fees by selling their expertise and the more work they can generate from you, the better it is for business. So it is as well to understand this from the start and remind yourself of it from time to time, however friendly your relationship with your consultancy staff may become.

Sponsorship consultancies work very much as other consultancies. They charge for their time, usually by the hour – sometimes by the day. And the hourly rate can range from roughly £30 for a very junior executive up to around £180 or more for the managing director.

What will usually happen is that the consultancy will work out a sponsorship management programme for you, estimate the number of hours a month they think it will take to action that programme and quote you a fee accordingly. Alternatively, they will charge you by the hour up to an agreed monthly ceiling fee.

The hourly rate for a sponsorship consultant varies as much as the hourly rate for a solicitor or accountant. So you will pay a lot more for the services of a director of a London consultancy than you will for an account executive in a provincial agency. In practice, most of the work will be done by account executives at the lower end of the rate scale. They will be managed by account directors of middle management rank and a board director will probably have overall responsibility for the strategy and for overseeing the account (the titles may vary but the principle is the same). Your fees, therefore, will be calculated on variable proportions of three or four executives' time.

It is virtually impossible for a consultancy to estimate exactly what sort of time they are going to have to spend on a project but an experienced organization should be able to make a fairly close approximation. In their own minds they will work it out over a year something like this:

Board Director	6 days x £900 per day	= £ 5,400
Account Director	25 days x £500 per day	= £12,500
Account Executive	50 days x £300 per day	= £15,000
		£32,900

But they will rarely quote it in this manner to you. What they will actually say to you is more likely to be that they will charge you a monthly fee of £2,750 to cover their time on the sponsorship. I have quoted a fee of £32,900 merely as an example but the same principle applies whether the fee is £2,000 or £100,000.

Do not be hesitant about asking a consultancy for their exact fee level for each executive and how much time they estimate each will put in on the account, if you really want to know in detail. When the sponsorship is working, you are quite entitled to ask for a regular total of these hours, if you wish. Some consultancies will even offer to show you their staff timesheets, if you ask for them.

In practice, clients are strangely reticent about discussing fees in detail. However, if you want to know, ask. It's your money after all.

An all-encompassing fee is the easiest way to work with a consultancy unless you require them to do a very small amount of work. If you pay by the hour, you can become very conscious that every exchange of pleasantries and remarks about the weather is costing you £1 a minute and it suddenly seems hugely expensive. But remember that it's swings and roundabouts. £1 a minute is a very costly way of discussing this morning's rain storm but it's very cheap for that inspirational idea which got you on the front page of every national newspaper. Consultancy fees are on the whole pretty fair, with a fairly low profit margin so you are getting value for money.

So do not be too paranoid about time apparently wasted or you will be looking at your watch every five minutes and making everyone nervous. But there are one or two practical points to consider as well as strategic ones.

First, where is your consultancy in relation to your office? If you are in Bow and your consultancy in Kensington, then each meeting is going to involve an hour and a half's travelling time. It is your time if you go to them, but you will pay for their travelling time if they come to you and that could mean a notional charge of £200 simply for three people to get to you!

Second, the more people the consultancy involves in the sponsorship, the higher the charges will be. Obviously, meetings involving six people can be very expensive. If it is a question of experts such as copywriters, designers and lawyers needing to be involved it is better that you go to the consultancy so that they can come in and out for a few minutes as necessary, rather than sitting though a two-hour meeting just to do one five-minute presentation. However, it is advisable that at least two people work on your account and that both know what is going on. One-man accounts can cause problems for both clients and consultancies. If the one-man account executive breaks a leg, goes on holiday or leaves suddenly, you could be left high and dry.

I suggest that before a contract is signed you are clear, not only about fees, but also about other costs. It is reasonable that you should be charged for photocopying, postage, deliveries and other office charges, but ask for a list of these charges before you come to an agreement. Check their policy on charging for travelling and subsistence expenses and agree a level, especially if entertaining other people is involved. Many clients are astonishingly sloppy about this and then complain bitterly that they 'didn't know we were going to be charged for all these extras'.

Don't spoil the ship for a ha'p'orth of tar, however. I once knew a client who became extremely annoyed that a consultancy board director travelled to client meetings by taxi. It was a two-mile journey and he obviously felt that it was outrageous to be charged £5.00 for a taxi fare when a 70p bus fare would have sufficed. However, the taxi took ten minutes and the bus journey more like twenty-five minutes and, at £100 an hour for the director's time, the client's meanness actually would have cost him another £50 a meeting!

Ask also if your consultancy adds a 'handling charge' for any out-costs they order and pay for on your behalf. It is almost certain that they will. Once upon a time agencies used to add a 10 per cent handling charge, but now it can be anything up to 20 per cent and this can add a huge amount to your invoice. A print bill of £30,000 could become £36,000, for instance, so it could cost £6,000 for someone else to send out an order and pay a bill for you!

Finally, still on the financial side, be blunt and ask your shortlisted consultancies if they accept commission from organizations seeking sponsorship. You may already have an inkling of this by looking at their client list. If names such as the International Wellie Throwing Authority and the English National Musical Comedy Society appear, then the chances are that this question will not be out of place. Do not necessarily let it colour your judgement if they do accept commission – some of the most well known and reputable companies accept commission or even own sponsorship properties themselves which they sell. Others make a point of making it clear that they do not.

For instance, Barrie Gill says 'There are rare occasions when you can make a sale for a client organization that is something you actually own, where you can get paid by both parties. But these are the exception rather than the rule and nobody would last very long in this business if you as a client came to me with a brief and I said 'Have I got something for you!'. But to give you some examples – we sold the Football League to Canon and they then hired us as a consultancy to run it. We sold the Football League Cup to Milk and the National Dairy Council hired us. Take Alan Pascoe, for example, who acts on behalf of athletics. For every athletics sponsorship he sells, he also offers a servicing package and it's up to the client whether he wants to take it or not. When you are a consultant you have to be absolutely scrupulous that the property that you're selling is right for the client otherwise you lose both times.

'Often the best people to manage a sponsorship are the agency which sold the sponsorship in the first place because they know it so well,' he says. 'When you buy a car it's always best to go back to the garage you bought it from to have it serviced.' (A clever analogy, I think.)

Robin Ford, managing director of Option One Sponsorship, takes the opposite point of view. 'I would be concerned that our credibility might be called to account,' he says, 'if we were discovered to be taking a fee from an organization for selling a sponsorship and then recommending it to one of our clients who are paying us for our knowledge and expertise.'

I suppose the difficulty lies in knowing whether the agency you are dealing with is on a commission or not. If sponsorship worked in the same way as advertising where agencies buy media space and automatically receive a commission, then everyone would be quite comfortable about it.

Once you have chosen your consultancy, you should work very closely with them and invest some of their time (which you will be paying for of course!) in learning about your business, meeting the appropriate executives and touring your offices or factories, because the more they know about you, the better the job they can do for you.

The working structure

With sponsorship manager and/or project team and/or consultancy in place, now is the time to look again at the sponsorship policy document and perhaps fine tune it.

I hesitate to suggest yet more paperwork when all everyone really wants to do is to get on with the enjoyable bit of seeking out and organizing the sponsorships. If there is nothing in writing, it's amazing how people can manage to justify the most outlandish projects and sweep everyone else along in their misplaced fervour.

'It'll be wonderful for client entertainment!' enthuses the sales manager. And it isn't until later that someone realizes that the clients are all in their forties and fifties and not many of them seem desperately keen to travel to Penge to watch the finals of the London area disco-dancing championships. Be warned, I have seen it happen all too frequently!

The budget

Budgets for sponsorship don't suddenly materialize. Someone is going to give a cry of anguish if their budget is cut and handed to another department.

Ideally, once it is decided which department is going to handle the sponsorship, then it is best that the budget is allocated for the next financial year and incorporated into the grand departmental budget. In other words, if it is marketing, then it is up to the marketing director to allocate a slot for sponsorship within his marketing budget. The sum, in the first instance, may be a fairly notional central budget of £100,000 in year one but before long he may need to shuffle money in and out of this budget as he will certainly be doing for other departments and campaigns anyway.

This is why it is essential for all those departments involved to feel positively about any sponsorship since they may wish to put in further sums where they can see particular benefits. The advertising department may be able to use the sponsorship in some creative way in a particular brand campaign, for instance, or the sales division may wish to use the sponsorship as an incentive for their sales force, both of which will need extra budgets.

In the past, many companies have made the mistake of thinking that once they had paid their sponsorship fee, that is it. Far from it. You need to allocate at least the same sum again to making the sponsorship work, and probably more. Some companies allocate two or three times the fee but this will depend greatly on the size and scale of the sponsorship. One sponsoring brand was reputed to have spent £300,000 on a sponsorship which cost them £30,000. This is highly unusual and one can assume that the sponsorship was either too cheap or that the sponsors went absolutely overboard. Equally, I know a company who in their first year of a £75,000 league sponsorship allocated a mere £20,000 to making it work. They were quite put out to find that the public were still using the name of the previous sponsors!

I would advise that the overall budget includes not only the sponsorship fee but also the cost of making it work and that includes sponsorship consultancy fees, design, advertising hoardings, promotional gifts, hospitality, and so on.

If this sounds like a minefield, it gets worse. Multinational companies involved in international sponsorships need to have global budgets for sponsorship because the concept of going round to each national company or division for a quota would be out of the question. It would take far too long and, by that time, the sponsorship on offer may have gone. Similarly, many major companies and organizations have regionalized themselves; consequently, their local sponsorships often come out of regional budgets and the decision is made by the regional manager.

Sort out the management structure and the budgetary control as early as you can in the sponsorship; it will pay dividends later on.

5 Identifying the right sponsorship

Receiving an approach

Any big company or corporation, in fact almost every organization from ICI down to Bloggs Butchers will, at some time or other, be approached for sponsorship. The vast majority of applications will be ill-considered and probably inappropriate but there will be others which will appear very tempting and you may be rushed into a decision in order 'not to miss the opportunity' before you have really considered the proposition thoroughly.

Most of those seeking sponsorship will leave it to the last minute. Rare is the sports or arts organization, expedition or record attempt that actually talks to sponsors two years before the event. You are more likely to be approached with a month to go and not a hope of gaining the maximum publicity under such circumstances.

That is one of the reasons why it is important to have your 'sponsorship policy' document to hand so that you can weed out all the non-starters without much effort. Don't be swayed by a personal interest in origami or underwater polo. Your job will be to find sponsorships which match your objectives, not to indulge your spare-time hobbies. But, that said, it's a rare sponsorship where a little bit of self-enjoyment is not involved. I've been to a number of conferences and listened to hard-nosed sponsorship managers lecturing on the importance of keeping to corporate objectives one minute and then, in the next sentence, talking with almost misty eyes about the joys of listening to Pavarotti in full voice.

Many big organizations employ a full-time member of staff to scan all the sponsorship applications and requests for donations which, unfortunately, in the eyes of some people, appear to be one and the same thing. And if you, as the sponsorship manager or public relations officer or marketing executive, find yourself receiving a pile of letters every day on this subject, then it may be a necessity for you, too.

Sponsorships will come in addressed to all sorts of people from the chairman to the personnel officer but it should be company policy that all applications eventually are filtered through to one desk. The choice of that desk really rests with the objectives of your sponsorship programme as discussed in Chapter 2. What you don't want is the corporate affairs department and the marketing department all 'doing their own thing' and agreeing to all sorts of sponsorships which contradict each other.

So the sponsorship manager (even if he or she does not use that title) should be the lynchpin for the vetting and management of all sponsorships, even if he or she does not make the final decision to go ahead.

Once your name appears in print as sponsorship manager for your company, expect the floodgates to open. Every post will bring a bizarre collection of proposals – some expensively printed, some photocopied, some even handwritten.

Mostly, you will be able to tell at a glance whether they are suitable or not but the 'sponsorship policy' document will assist you to weed out the wheat from the chaff. For example:

- Will it help meet our objectives?
- Does it match the image we want to create?
- Will it reach our target audience?
- Is it within our target area?
- Is it going to receive TV coverage?
- Will it create goodwill locally?
- Will we be able to entertain clients?
- Is it within our budget?
- Is the timing right?
- Is it unique?

Once you have said 'No' to the first three questions, you really need go no further and then it's simply a question of writing a polite letter of refusal.

And do write. The proposal may be badly worded, idiotic and without a hope in hell of getting a sponsor but the person who has written it may be a customer and the fact that they do not receive a reply or even a curt refusal may rebound on you at some point.

Many years ago, when I was a very amateur autocross driver, I wrote to Duckham's Oil and naively ask for £500 in sponsorship. They sent me a gallon of oil, some stickers and a nice letter and I have bought Duckham's oil ever since.

So be kind and helpful without actually encouraging further correspondence. If you're *too* helpful you may end up spending a lot of unproductive time as a free advice centre for round-the-world cyclists and schoolgirl gymnasts!

The wonders of the word processor should enable you to have several letters in stock for use as appropriate with minor adjustments. For instance:

Dear Mr Snailspace

Thank you very much for your letter of 19 January telling us about your project to ride on a camel from Land's End to John O'Groats. It sounds like a most original idea and I'm sure you'll attract considerable attention en route.

However, I'm afraid the North of England Bank has a very firm sponsorship policy, and any sponsorship that we undertake has to match very strict criteria. One of these is that we do not sponsor individuals or groups, only competitions, leagues or events. So I'm afraid that we will be unable to help you in this instance.

However, if you are finding it difficult to raise money from a corporate backer, may I suggest that you talk with your local North of England branch manager in Rotherham, Mr John Kindheart, who would be happy to discuss some other options with you such as a short-term loan which may solve the problem.

Wishing you the very best of luck in your most exciting venture.

 Yours sincerely

Mary Jones
Sponsorship Manager

The letter is short but friendly, gives a good reason for saying 'no' and is promoting the bank's own services, too. Mr Kindheart in Rotherham should receive a copy of the letter and, while he may or may not be able to arrange a loan for Mr Snailspace, it's all good PR for the bank.

If your company offers a service such as banking, insurance, or where your relationship with your customers is a big selling point, don't lose the opportunity to promote your own services to the sponsorship seeker. Make it a soft sell even if it's only to enclose some leaflets with your letter.

If you're selling products, then a small gift will cost very little but achieve much goodwill (as with my Duckham's experience); a pack of chocolate bars, a company T-shirt or a voucher, along with the nice letter, is all you need to do for individuals. Major sports organizations, orchestras etc. will probably survive on the nice letter alone.

Asda receive around 500 sponsorship proposals a month, almost all of which will receive a polite letter of rejection. However, they do hold a monthly draw for 'the losers' — two of whom each receive a cheque for £50 which is a very much appreciated gift and a nice PR gesture.

Not everyone will write, of course. Many will phone believing that it is much more difficult to say 'no' to a voice than to the written word. They are quite correct in this assumption. It *is* much more difficult to say no to a personal approach so you must decide whether you are going to speak to every single caller or not. A very rare number of sponsorship managers make time to speak to everyone on the grounds that if they don't they may just miss the whizzo idea. Others are more difficult to get at than Fort Knox.

It can be extremely tedious and time-consuming listening to an enthusiast waxing lyrical about the joys of sponsoring the Penge Drum Majorettes Troupe when you know that there isn't a chance in a million that your company could be interested. The traditional method of getting rid of people is to say 'Can you put something in writing?' (More than one secretary, trained in this mould, didn't listen to what I was saying and insisted that I write in to gather information for this book.) Some callers probably won't even have a proposal available and will come back with 'Well, it would be much better if I could come and talk to you personally, then I could explain it a lot better.' Be suspicious of anyone who can't put together a written proposal, they are not likely to be professional or very organized about making the sponsorship work either. That is a general rule, however, and there may be exceptions. I recently came across an amateur racing driver who acquired a large sponsorship on the strength of a short handwritten letter but then came up trumps and managed to have his car resprayed in the company house style and organize himself a complete racing outfit with the sponsor's logos on it all within less than a fortnight.

One way of short-circuiting a long conversation is to say to all callers that you would like to send them your sponsorship application form which perhaps they would fill in and send in with any proposal document that they may have. Say that once your sponsorship 'committee' or 'policy group' has considered their application, you will write back and let them know the outcome. (You might also be unable to resist the temptation to add the immortal words 'Don't call us, we'll call you'!) I suggest using a plural word such as 'committee' to avoid getting yourself into long discussions about personal opinions. Mysterious 'other people' are much more difficult to argue with.

The sponsorship application form is a good idea because it can insist on all the answers to the vital questions which many proposal documents tend to leave out. It also makes people precis their proposal into a manageable space rather than writing an auto-biography. If you feel you are likely to receive large numbers of sponsorship proposals, do try it. The sort of questions you might ask on one or two sides of an A4 sheet of paper include:

- Title of sponsorship
- Contact
- Address
- Telephone number
- Brief sponsorship proposal
- What are the benefits to the sponsor?
- Why is sponsorship necessary?
- When will the sponsorship start and for how long will it run?
- What fee is required?
- What does this cover?
- What area/region/countries does the sponsorship cover?
- Any further details

It enables you in an instant to see whether the application is suitable or not. If you include on it a summary of your sponsorship criteria, it may save the sponsee the time and trouble of filling it in when he realizes that he does not, by any stretch of his imagination, fit the bill.

Write your refusal letters as soon as possible after receiving the applications in order to circumvent follow-up phone calls and to give the sponsorship seeker plenty of time to pursue other avenues. The more determined ones will be on the phone the next day to ask if you have made a decision yet and, if they are very pushy, they will badger you unmercifully with 'But this is to raise money for the underprivileged children of Madagascar. Don't you care that thousands are starving!' Saying 'no' can be very wearing, if you feel obliged to spend time justifying yourself.

But there is going to come a time when something will make you say 'yes'. The sponsorship proposal fits your criteria and most of the questions on your list can be answered positively. There is plenty of time to organize and publicize the sponsorship and the people you are dealing with seem professional and eager to please.

But before I go on to discuss negotiating with a sponsee, let's just pause a moment and look at the idea of finding the right sponsorship from another angle.

Making an approach

If you wait for people to approach you, you are taking a rather passive stance. This has the advantage that people have to sell to you so you are in the driving seat but, on the other hand, it also means that you may just miss a golden opportunity to link up with a unique sponsorship that may otherwise pass you by.

Armed with your sponsorship policy document, you should be able to go out and identify areas, organizations or events which perfectly match the bill.

Your prospects will need to be thoroughly researched before you make an approach because you will need to know, before you start talking to them, whether they really do match your sponsorship criteria or not, in order not to waste everyone's time. Equally, you should consider whether an organization will wish to get into bed with you. Environmental organizations, such as Friends of the Earth in particular, are now becoming very cautious about which companies they become involved with and drinks and tobacco manufacturers are not always welcomed with open arms by sponsor seekers.

You may wish to conduct your researches openly with the organizations concerned, explaining to them what you are looking for and asking them to put a proposal to you, if they are interested. This saves time and gets to the point immediately but is also likely to provoke dreams of tinkling cash registers in the eyes of your prospects and you may be better to make the approach indirectly and have some undercover research done first.

This is probably the right place to use an independent consultancy who can find out information on your behalf without actually revealing your identity.

Your advertising agency or public relations consultancy will know exactly how to find out the information you require but, if they start 'making enquiries on behalf of a client' it does not take a great deal of initiative for a prospect to get hold of a client list and put two and two together and then your cover is blown. Market research consultancies are experts at getting information incognito, so that is another possibility, but the most obvious option is to use a specialist sponsorship consultancy.

Whichever way you do it, you should give the organizations you are approaching enough information so that they don't send in ludicrous proposals that waste your time and theirs, but conversely do not make it such a tight brief that no organization could fill it exactly. A general idea of the sort of product area you are in; your sponsorship objectives; your target audiences; the area you wish to cover; and perhaps the timescale, should be adequate. The fee is a slightly more ticklish problem since if you reveal that you have £50,000 to spend all proposals may come in at £50,000 regardless. On the other hand, if you are too vague, you are making life difficult for the potential sponsees. Better perhaps to say that the budget is limited to a certain sum at present but more may be available for a really outstanding sponsorship, and then wait to see what comes in.

If you are fairly flexible in your approach you should be able to judge, from the quality of the response, those organizations which are likely to be easy to deal with and professional in their approach. I say professional with a small 'p' because this is terribly important and really, on the whole, it comes down to the quality of the individuals you will be dealing with rather than the clubs, leagues, orchestras or whatever it is that they represent.

On an occasion when I went through the exercise of looking for a suitable sports sponsorship for a major company, the quality of the responses was quite astonishingly varied. It ranged from a private aerobatics pilot who had photographs and sample designs ready for me within two days of our first meeting, to a major amateur sports organization which I rang five times before I could extract a response. I was told by a very off-hand telephonist that I had to speak to the secretary, the secretary was away, and that nobody else knew anything about sponsorship but the secretary. When the secretary returned (by the sixth call), he said he had nothing much to send but would very graciously see what he could find. Nothing ever arrived. Somehow this inefficient organization managed eventually to get itself a big sponsorship via a consultancy but I gather that the sponsors are very unhappy with it. Surprise, Surprise!

One of the advantages of being pro-active rather than reactive is that you can create your own events or sponsorships. This is particularly useful where you simply cannot match any available sponsorship to your own target audience or target area. This brings us back to research. For example, if you are a men's outfitters particularly trying to reach customers who are between 18 and 24, you will need to know precisely what the demographic profile, interests, lifestyle, perceptions and aspirations of such a group are.

You might, for instance, have outlets in twenty-nine towns with another five due to open and all needing publicity. The chances of finding something suitable to cover those thirty-four towns alone are remote so you might, in conjunction with a sports organization for instance, create your own competition. To take an imaginary example, it might be a national pool competition to be known as the Smart Man Pool Trophy and played between teams only from towns where there are local Smart Man branches. It simply takes imagination, creativity and a ready and willing organization looking for a sponsor to set them on the road.

On a much larger scale, international sponsored events are often especially created simply to help a company raise its profile in a particular country or countries. Sport is an international language, so is music, and what better way to reach a local population than through a major pop concert tour or a sporting circuit.

If you are trying to open up new markets in China or America or Tahiti, you will surely already be doing a considerable amount of groundwork in the country concerned and using local knowledge and expertise. But, as far as sponsorship is concerned, you should certainly in this instance use the experience of an international sponsorship consultancy who will be able to smooth the passage of what could otherwise be an extremely bumpy ride. The rewards however can be considerable.

We digressed slightly there, but it was a necessary diversion to help you decide whether to work on your own or to use a consultancy. Either way, your next step will be to take a closer look at your potential sponsorship. If the proposal sounds interesting on paper, then you should now look at the sponsorship and the people who are promoting it.

It is possible that you may have been approached by a sports marketing agency or sponsorship consultancy but don't just be content with meeting them. You really do need to go and see the decision-making organization. In the sports world it is quite common for sports organizations to use a consultancy to market their sponsorships and although the consultancy staff may be extremely professional and willing to promise that this, that and the other will happen, the ultimate decision will probably lie with the committee members of the sports body concerned. If they are all octogenarians with very firm ideas about amateurism in sport, you may find that they consider sponsorship only as a necessary evil to be kept very firmly in its place.

So, make a point of going to see your potential sponsorship in action. It is not a bad idea to go incognito in the first instance so that you see the organization as the spectators see it and not as a cushioned VIP guest.

If it's a sport you're interested in, pay at the turnstiles and stand on the terraces or the sidelines. Look at the publicity material, the programme, the way you're dealt with by the staff, the atmosphere at the stadium. Is this what you want to be associated with?

If it's the arts, go to a similar exhibition at the Royal Academy, get a ticket for the Malvern Festival or the Mozart Centenary Series Concerts.

And if it's an expedition, tourist attraction, book, or whatever, just take a look at it as Mr Average and see if you'd be aware of a sponsor's name.

When you make the direct approach, you will (or you certainly should) receive red carpet treatment. But don't be lulled into a false sense of bonhomie at too early a stage.

First, look at the people you will be dealing with – not just the directors, committee members and senior management. But ask also to meet all the people you will be working with on a day-to-day basis. If the general ambience of the organization is professional, helpful, happy and keen to please you, then you are off to a good start.

If you are looking for name awareness, then you should ask for facts and figures and firm evidence of TV coverage, press coverage and attendances over a period.

You should also ask (or check in advance) what restrictions there are on hoardings, banners and other vehicles where the sponsor's name may be displayed. The restrictions on this vary from sport to sport, and organization to organization so you need to know this before getting too enthusiastic about putting up a fifty-foot hoarding where no fifty-foot hoarding will be allowed. Once you know the rules, you can then investigate further for potential advertising sites.

Look at all the printed material and see where your company name or advertisements might appear.

If you require entertainment facilities, check exactly what you will be able to have in the way of seats, private facilities, meals and refreshments, car parking and so on. Ask if you will be able to meet the players, artistes or personalities involved on a regular basis.

You can check all the aspects of sponsorship that you should be investigating in this preliminary visit against the lists of possible sponsorship benefits outlined in Chapter 2 and detailed in Chapter 6.

Your potential sponsee should already have given you a proposal listing the benefits that they are prepared to offer and you can see this in practice on your visit and modify it as you think appropriate.

Negotiating the benefits

Once you are determined to go ahead with your sponsorship, you and the organization you are sponsoring will almost certainly be bursting to get on with it, not least because time may be short and you will need to get on with arranging the practicalities. You will almost certainly have already been presented with a package by the organization you are dealing with but that will probably be flexible both on benefits and on price.

The list of sponsorship benefits you will be given will probably be a very general one suitable for any sponsor from a bank to a brewery and it would be surprising if, after some investigation, you were not able to change or improve upon that to suit your own company image or product.

Sometimes in their anxiety to attract a sponsor organizations promise benefits they cannot actually deliver, so if you have any doubts about benefits being offered, check. For instance, a company I know was recently three-quarters of the way down the road to sponsoring a well-known sports club, totally sold on the idea that the club was going to be able to include their company name in its title. But the trouble was that the club's sponsorship negotiator had used it as a strong selling point without thoroughly checking that it would be allowed by the official sports body. It was not!

What are the benefits worth?

Inexperienced organizations inevitably make the mistake of equating the finance that they need with the sponsorship fee that they ask. But needing £150,000 to maintain an orchestra and offering to print the sponsor's name on the programme cover add up to a rather poor deal.

Putting a precise figure on the value of a sponsorship is almost impossible. You can really only compare it with the sort of sums you are spending in other areas of marketing and communications and see if it equates reasonably well. Some benefits are intangible and immeasurable but you could try putting a figure on each of the benefits listed in your package and see if the total is somewhere near what is being asked.

For instance, if you are being offered a free page in a programme, that is easy to value simply because you can find out what the normal programme advertising rates are.

On the other hand, how do you put a value on your best customer being able to meet the England captain? You can't. It might be worth nothing or it might be worth a million pound contract. It's really a question of your own instinct about what value these hidden benefits have for you.

You may also like to do some research into what the market rate is for similar sponsorships and, if your preferred organization is in the same price band, then you know you are paying a fair sum.

If you are particularly keen on a sponsorship but feel that the price being asked is too high and you are unable to get a reduction on the asking figure, the simplest way round it is to ask for more benefits than were included in the original package. This is a neat way of saving face since both sides give and take without appearing to do so.

One point you should be clear about in the letter or contract is what your fee covers in terms of the expenses of putting the sponsorship into action. If, for instance, it is agreed that your company name will appear on all the organization's headed paper, who is going to pay for the reprinting of that paper? If a car has to be repainted in a new livery, who pays for the painting? If a press conference is planned to launch the sponsorship, who will pay for the venue and the catering? More often than not, it is the sponsor who pays, but make sure that you know exactly what you are in for in advance.

The timescale

There is no hard-and-fast rule on the length of a sponsorship. Some have been running for as long as twenty years, some are one-year wonders. It ultimately depends upon the objective of your sponsorship. If name awareness is the dominating factor, then a long-term sponsorship will be much more successful in achieving public notice than a short-term one. If, on the other hand, the main purpose of your sponsorship is client entertainment, then going to see *The Nutcracker Suite* for ten seasons in a row is going to become rather tedious.

In practice, with the exception of one-off events such as festivals, exhibitions, expeditions or record attempts which are going to get a considerable amount of short-term publicity, a year is a very short time in sponsorship.

Three to five years seems to be the average length of time for a sports or arts sponsorship. If you have doubts, then a compromise is a two-year contract with a rolling option to renew every following year.

Tax considerations

Richard Baldwin, a partner in the firm of City accountants Touche Ross, has made a speciality of tax and sponsorship and has written various papers and an excellent booklet on the subject for the World Wide Fund for Nature. It is called *Business Support of Conservation – a Tax Guide*. It's intended for those interested in conservation sponsorship but the principles apply to any sponsorship.

He says 'Sponsorship is a tax allowable expense providing its benefits can justifiably be described as revenue expenditure such as advertising, promotion and publicity.

'But there are a few traps. Sponsorship of capital expenditure such as land or buildings may not be allowed. Neither, as you will be aware, can business entertaining be claimed against tax. So, if the sponsorship contains a very large element of client entertainment, such as at concerts or horse racing, then you may be closely quizzed by the tax inspector. However, provided that the advertising and promotional aspects of a sponsorship are emphasized and entertainment aspects are minimal, there is usually not a problem in practice.

'He may also look very closely at situations where company directors or higher-paid employees are thought to be receiving hospitality benefits such as a day out at Goodwood or Gatcombe where they receive free tickets and meals. It is not unknown for some tax inspectors to try and claim that this is a company perk on which the employee should be taxed.

'What definitely will not be allowed is a company chairman who tries to get his own hobby sponsored by his company. Many a budding racing driver has seen this as a way of funding his highly expensive motor car and has been very disappointed!

'My advice is that you ask your accountant to investigate any areas of doubt very thoroughly. If he is unsure of his ground, then he should in turn seek advice from one of the City accountancy practices which has a specialist in this area.'

The fee you will be quoted will almost certainly be excluding VAT which will be added at the current rate, assuming that the organization or individual you are sponsoring is liable to register for VAT, which will be the case for most major sponsorships.

The VAT may be reclaimed as input tax although, because some or all of their supplies are exempt from VAT, the recoverability of VAT paid is restricted for certain financial organizations such as banks, insurance companies and building societies.

And here's a trap for the unwary. If by any chance you are not paying cash but paying in kind (such as photocopiers, airline tickets, television sets) and you receive promotional benefits in return, your sponsee may be asked by Customs and Excise to send you a bill for the VAT on the retail value of those goods or services. In other words, they might have invoiced you £1,000 as a fee plus 15 per cent VAT for sponsorship services rendered but, if instead you gave them £1,000 of camera equipment, then Customs and Excise would consider that they should have billed you £150 VAT on top of that. This often causes considerable embarrassment to both parties, so is worth checking in advance. This scenario does not apply if the goods are a straight donation with no benefits in return.

Donations are not directly tax allowable so the tax inspectors may look closely at your sponsorship if the fee you are paying seems disproportionate to the benefits you are receiving. In other words, if your chairman wants to sponsor his 10-year-old son's cub football team to the tune of £10,000 in exchange for the team wearing the company name on their shirts, the Inland Revenue can quite justifiably claim that this is a donation and not a promotional expense and the whole sum may be disallowed.

Incidentally, although this is a book about commercial sponsorship and not about company giving, I should make it clear that, while it is correct to say that you cannot make a donation and claim it as a tax allowable business expense, it is quite possible to make very tax-effective donations to charities, if it *is* purely a donation that you wish to make.

Richard Baldwin explains, 'Let's say a company decides to donate £100,000 to a particular charity. It pays the charity £75,000 and pays the basic rate of tax, say £25,000, to the Inland Revenue. The charity can then claim this £25,000 back from the Inland Revenue (making the donation worth £100,000) and the company can claim relief from corporation tax, currently at 35 per cent. This means that a £100,000 donation has effectively cost the company only £65,000. This does not apply to close companies by the way, in other words those where less than five shareholders control the company. However, it is also possible to pay an annual donation for four years under deed of covenant which will provide corporation tax relief for such companies.

'Many of the big corporations have set up their own trust funds to make charitable donations. They simply make one huge annual donation to their trust fund which saves a considerable amount of paperwork and then make donations through a board of trustees to whichever charities or organizations they wish.'

Michael Norton's book *The Corporate Donor's Handbook* published by the Directory of Social Change explains all this in some detail.

Sometimes there is an overlap where a company funds an event, but the fee it pays is well over the value of benefits accorded by the sponsee because it wishes part of the money to be a straight donation. Then it begins to get complicated and you do need an accountant and don't discount asking advice from your tax office either.

The contract

If your sponsorship is a fairly simple one then a letter of agreement should be adequate, but if it is complex and involves substantial sums of money you would be well-advised to have a proper contract drawn up by a solicitor. But you should have something in writing, however small or straightforward the sponsorship agreement appears to be, which make the benefits, the timescale, the fee and the VAT position clear.

Lawyers seem to be able to turn perfectly plain English into incomprehensible gobbledygook which is understood only by other lawyers but the purpose of the exercise really is to iron out any ambiguities or loopholes.

The problem is that there are very few lawyers who have a great deal of experience in sponsorship and consequently yours may not necessarily be able to spot loopholes. I often wonder how the organization which sponsored a football club which reached an FA Cup Final felt when they saw the team walk out onto the Wembley pitch with another company's name on the team's tracksuits. Their name was on the players' shirts but there was obviously nothing in the contract which said another company could not have its name on other clothing.

Problems you may wish to avoid by putting suitable clauses into the contract are:

- *Competitive advertising* You may wish to insist that no competitor in your business is allowed to advertise within your sponsee's publications or venues or indeed on their clothing.
- *Sales exclusivity* If you have an agreement that the organization you are sponsoring sells your products within its boundaries, then you may wish to insist that no competitive products are sold.
- *Logos* Part of your agreement may be that the organization which you are sponsoring allows you to use its official symbol on your merchandise for the period of the sponsorship. Your sponsee will undoubtedly wish to retain some control over how and where this is used. Equally, if they are organizing the inclusion of your logo in promotional and advertising materials, then you should have the right to vet it for style and quality.

- *Joint logos* Alternatively, you may have a joint logo designed for a particular new competition or event. The copyright of this design is vested in the author (providing that they were commissioned and not employed) so be sure that the copyright is specifically assigned over to you.
- *Merchandising* Is joint merchandise to be produced? If this is on a major scale, then you will certainly need a lawyer experienced in this field to tie up the details on trademarks, royalties, design copyright and so on.
- *First options* Think ahead. If there is a chance, however remote, that your sponsee may achieve something out of the ordinary, like reaching a championship final or touring South America, then make sure that you have the first option to buy any further sponsorships going before they are casually offered to your biggest competitor.
- *Successes and failures* Most companies like to have a fixed fee for their sponsorship regardless of success or failure. This makes budgeting easier but, conversely, is it right that the same fee should be paid for a champion as for the man in last place? Undoubtedly, winners get more publicity than losers (Eddie Edwards excepted) which means more publicity also for the sponsor.

The contract should state when the sponsorship starts and finishes and whether there is an option to renew for a further period. If so, the sponsee should insist that he has fair notice of your intention to renew or withdraw in order to give himself time to look for a new sponsor. Six months is reasonable but this can be longer or shorter depending upon the type of sponsorship. Note the difference between an 'option to renew' and 'first refusal'. With an option to renew, the advantage lies with you, the sponsor, in that the onus is on you to choose whether or not to continue the sponsorship – provided that you have fulfilled your part of the previous sponsorship agreement and provided that the terms for the renewal have been set. In the case of first refusal, the sponsee offers a further period of the sponsorship under his own terms and can go elsewhere as soon as you say 'no'.

The contract should also state what fee is to be paid and when. Your sponsee will want your cheque as soon as possible but you will probably want to tie it in with your financial year, so you should reach a compromise on how the fee will be paid. Annually in advance on the date of signing the contract is common practice.

All the benefits to be received should be clearly listed and specified in detail where necessary. If you are to be given a sign at the entrance to the museum you are sponsoring it makes sense to specify that the sign will be 'at least 30 square feet in area' otherwise you may end up with a window sticker.

If it is very important to you that your guests meet the actors in a production you are sponsoring, you should make it clear that the actors will be expected to attend the first night sponsor's reception. Ambiguous sentences such as 'The producers will invite the actors to the sponsor's party' give no indication that attendance is mandatory and therefore the lazy and the unsociable can slink off with a clear conscience.

The same applies in any instance where the sponsorship depends not so much on the sponsee keeping his part of the bargain but on some third party, so beware of any clauses which guarantee delivery by a third party such as the governing body of a sport. You will need to understand the structure and regulations of that governing body as it relates to your sponsorship.

Television is an important part of many sponsorship deals but, again, the TV company is a third party and unless (as in the case of a sponsored broadcast) you have signed a deal with them direct, nothing is guaranteed. They may have signed a contract for the rights to televise an event but that is not a guarantee that they will do so. In practice, the chances of a major event such as the Derby or the Cup Final not being televised are remote but a technicians' strike or a hurricane is always a tiny possibility and you may wish to consider such a possibility when drawing up your contract.

However, the benefits you receive from your sponsorship will very much depend upon your relationship with your sponsee. If you are demanding and unreasonable and want every i dotted and every t crossed, then your relationship is likely to be formal and managed strictly to the book. If, on the other hand, warm friendships develop – as they usually do – then much more will be given on both sides than has been asked for or expected.

Nevertheless, I would advise anyone about to undertake a complicated sponsorship (or their lawyers) to read Stephen Townley and Edward Grayson's book *Sponsorship of Sports, Arts and Leisure: Law, Tax and Business Relationships*. It's not an easy read and it was published in 1984 so some aspects may be slightly out of date, but as a reference manual it is invaluable since it covers every legal and tax angle of sponsorship from breach of contract to the registration of trademarks.

Another useful and more recent reference book which goes into some detail on the legal aspects of sponsorship is *Sponsorship Endorsement and Merchandising* written by lawyer Richard Bagehot and published by Waterlow in 1990.

6 Making it work

The plan

By now this book will have seemed like an awful lot of planning and researching and structuring. I'm recommending that you do a great deal of groundwork first because I know exactly what will happen if you don't. Three or four exciting sponsorships will all come on stream at once and you'll be trying to juggle twenty-four balls in the air at a time when even the *Guinness Book of Records* reveals that the maximum possible is a mere ten!

Once you have signed the deal, then a lot of work is going to have to go into getting the lumbering machine into motion.

Maybe you are lucky or wise and have a sponsorship consultancy to do it all for you but, even so, it is as well that you, too, are aware of all the arrangements that need to be made so that you are running the show rather than the show running you.

I would suggest that first of all you get together with your contact at the organization you are sponsoring and make a list of deadlines under various headings such as – advertising, sales promotion, press publicity, client entertainment and so on. For example:

Barsetshire Cricket Club – advertising

- Programme – artwork by 18 March
- Ticket backs – artwork by 5 March
- Posters – artwork by 27 March
- Pitch hoardings – to be in place by 17 April
- Marquee banner – marquee up on 16 April
- Local papers – artwork by 5 April
- Clothing – team photograph on 4 April, first match 18 April
- Headed paper and printed material – as soon as possible

The same type of list will apply to all the other headings.

I hesitate to suggest that you make up a timetable or a flowchart but it's astonishing how easily things get forgotten when they are not written down. It's also amazing how long things take when they have to be designed, agreed by both parties, put into action and the goods delivered. If you know, for instance, that your deadline to get a hoarding sign onto a cricket clubhouse is 14 April, then you may be looking at a schedule like this:

- Inspection of ground for hoarding site – 1 March
- Agreement on site and design from club committee – 8 March
- Briefing of hoarding manufacturers – 9 March
- Site measurement by manufacturers – 14 March
- Quotes in from manufacturers – 19 March
- Agreement from department head on price – 24 March
- Go ahead given to manufacturer – 25 March
- Hoarding erected – 13 April

Yes, it could be done within a few days at a push but, if you have tedious company approvals and accountancy procedures to go through, and the boss is on holiday for a week, and the club committee doesn't meet for a month, or the groundsman is only there in the mornings, you will find that the wheels of organization can move exceedingly slowly.

Once you have a sort of working timetable or schedule, you should then be able to get on with delegating parts of it to in-house staff and briefing agencies and consultancies where necessary.

You would be wise to have regular team meetings so that everyone knows what everyone else is doing but do give authority for decisions to be made without waiting for the team meeting or you will never get anything done. Do involve secretaries in team meetings so that they know what is happening when you are out and can save much wasted time.

Those are the practicalities of organization. But let's go back a step and consider in detail some of the other aspects of sponsorship about which I have already written.

Image

Hopefully you will have matched the image of your chosen sponsorship with the one that you want to portray.

It can take years to change an image and while you may be able to do something about your own company's image, it is highly unlikely that you will be able to do much about changing the image of your sponsored organization, so it is important that you make the right choice in the first place.

Your first area of consideration will be how you are able to emphasize that image and this will vary considerably according to the organization you are sponsoring. Televised sport offers very different opportunities from wildlife conservation, for instance. In the former, the emphasis will be very much on placing the corporate identity in the right places to be picked up by TV cameras, in the latter it is more likely to be a question of keeping opinion-formers informed of your activities through press coverage.

Whichever way you do it, do make sure that the message is consistent. If the image is to be 'dynamic, pacy, modern' then diversions into 'Established in 1898' may confuse the onlooker.

Corporate identity

In terms of image, your immediate thoughts, once you have signed a sponsorship contract, will be to get your company name or product onto anything that moves within your sponsored organization. But pause a little and enlist the services of a top designer to see exactly how this should be done. It's absolutely no good slapping your company logo all over the place if it is going to look like an afterthought.

There is a lot to be said for sponsoring an organization which has a matching corporate image, or the same corporate colours, but one is very rarely that lucky and you may find that your tasteful pale blue and grey logo sits very uncomfortably with their red and orange one. Red Star, the British Rail express parcels delivery service, chose to sponsor Harlequin (rugby) Football Club. Harlequins' shirts are claret, chocolate, grey, pale blue, green and black. Red Star's colours are red, white and yellow so they had nine different colours to contend with, but the result was memorable to say the least!

If you do find yourself in a mismatch situation, then one or both sides may have to come to a reasonable compromise. You should not expect a hockey team which has been wearing emerald, yellow and red hoops for 100 years to blossom into sky blue and claret but it would be perfectly reasonable to expect vehicles, boats and individuals to be dressed in your corporate colours.

Given that a team or orchestra or group cannot change, you may yourself have to compromise in order to achieve maximum legibility.

One of the best examples of corporate branding is that of the Stella Artois Tennis Tournament, the major pre-Wimbledon men's grass court championships. The red and white of the Stella Artois branding is in evidence everywhere from the court-side perimeter hoardings to the ball girls' uniforms. However, it is done with class and consistency which adds considerable style to the event, rather than cheapening it.

Advertising

This section is almost an expansion of the last one. But I've segregated it to make the distinction between the visual way of creating a corporate identity and putting the message over via the public relations and client entertainment route.

There are many ways of getting the advertising message across (even if it's only your company or product name) and these include advertising hoardings; perimeter boards and poster sites; printed material; clothing; vehicles and equipment.

Advertising sites

These have three possible audiences — the audience at the event (including your guests), those who pass the venue or site and TV and other media. For most sponsors TV and media will be the most important audience, so do check with your liaison executive at your sponsored organization exactly what the rules are in terms of the number of sites you are allowed to have and the sizes and, if necessary, check with the TV companies themselves on sizes, siting, wording and so on and indeed the length and type of coverage they intend to give the event.

If you intend to site hoardings or banners specifically in order that they may be picked up by TV you must, absolutely must, look at that site through the eyes of a camera. If the TV cameras are sited up in the roof of an athletics stadium, you would be extremely foolish to judge the site from track level. The angle of the board must be right — it may have to lean backwards or be set at an angle, for instance. And check the site at the same time of day that the board will be seen. What looks fine at 9.00 a.m. in the morning may be struck by the sun at just the wrong angle in the afternoon and suddenly become a mirror rather than an advertisement.

Don't try to include too much wording on a hoarding. Experienced buyers of perimeter boards know that one word is far more effective than forty and, alongside hoardings stating 'Midland Bank', 'Electricity', 'Bic' and so on, you often will see an unreadable jumble, which at one metre reads: 'Fred Bloggins & Sons, Plumbers Merchants,

345–353 Corporation Road, Barchester, Telephone: 345678. 'We can obtain anything!' Maybe they can, but at 100 metres, they are throwing their money away.

Are there any obstructions in the way such as posts, or stewards, or steps which you may need to consider? If you look at your board in an empty arena, you may be thrilled, only to be horrified later on when you see that your perfect TV site is right behind a bank where 2000 people stand and they blot it out completely.

Not only should your message be brief but the style of the lettering should be simple. You may need to have letters thickened or separated slightly to make them readable at a distance. It may be against all your company's corporate identity regulations but the public probably won't spot the difference. Colours, too, are important. Strong colours and contrasts are best – white on red, dark blue on yellow, pink on black, or something similar.

Your sponsorship consultancy or hoarding advertising sales agent should advise on all this, but sometimes the customer thinks he knows best!

While TV coverage is of major importance, don't neglect the paying customers. They will undoubtedly pick up on many of the TV hoardings but you should also consider placing hoardings, posters and banners in other sites – particularly in view of those areas where your guests will be sitting. There's nothing more frustrating than to be entertaining the chief executive from one of your best client companies, and spending a fortune on carefully placed hoardings for TV, only to find that he can't see them, and have him say 'Thought you'd have your name about a bit more, Old Boy.' So look to getting the identification around where it can be seen by all the audiences important to you.

That may also include sites which cannot be seen from within a stadium, arena or concert hall. Sometimes a venue is situated as a perfect advertising site in itself. Stadiums on the flight path to Heathrow have made the most of this for instance by using their huge roofs as billboards. Twickenham simply uses theirs to advertise itself but the Brentford Football Club stand roof advises 'Next Time Fly KLM'. Bradford's Valley Parade, the stadium where there was the appalling fire in 1985, is set on the side of a hill. National & Provincial Building Society sponsored the new stand and their name on the roof overhang can now be read from the other side of the valley, half a mile away. It doesn't have to be a stadium either, it can be a museum, a recycling plant, a woodland, a theatre – any building or area may be suitable but make sure it's tasteful. Presumably you would not want to sponsor the purchase of a beautified piece of coastline and then have you company name cut into the chalk, would you? Heinz sponsored the purchase of Cape Cornwall and their name is simply inscribed on a small plinth at the site.

Performers and staff

Sport is the main area where the participants are likely to wear your company name or logo, and the maximum size of logo allowed varies from sport to sport so, again, you would be well advised to confirm the rules and regulations in relation to your chosen sport before embarking on an impossible path. Association Football allows a company name or logo of up to 75 square centimetres, rugby football allows a mere 9 cm × 9 cm and tennis allows 13 square centimetres. Sports where one competitor is pitted against another, such as tennis or golf and where the camera lingers longer on individual players, are usually more limited than fast-moving sports with many competitors. These figures are usually based upon a limitation of what television will allow, but tempered with what the governing body will stand as blatant commercialism. Soccer, you will observe, is much more commercial than rugby union!

So check first and then experiment. What looks good from three metres away may be unreadable from thirty, so exactly the same principles apply as with hoardings. Even football shirts allowing a massive 75 square centimetres produce some awful failures. I remember watching a televised match involving Chelsea a few years back and after a while beginning to wonder why it was that all the players seemed to have a light shadowy smudge on the fronts of their shirts in exactly the same place. I later discovered that this had been a sponsor's name!

So, where names on clothing are concerned, you should take the following points into consideration:

First, as with perimeter boards, use contrasting weights of colours. White on pale blue is unreadable, black on yellow stands out very well.

If clothing is striped or patterned, look at the options very carefully. You could add a plain, separate background, site your logo in between the stripes or even take it at an angle across the stripes as Virgin have done on the shirts of Crystal Palace Football Club.

Use your company symbol on its own only where you are obliged to use it very small, or when it is instantly recognizable (i.e. Shell, British Rail, Rank, MacDonalds). What may be a familiar and friendly company symbol to you is probably just a mysterious squiggle to a million TV viewers.

Long company names make for very small writing in a limited space. Where there is a size restriction, the name Guardian Royal

Exchange Assurance is, for example, one tenth as legible as the name JVC. So shorten where you can.

Stylish logos which may look good in print may not necessarily look good on clothing. The names which stand out best are those in chunky simple typefaces. Thin, elegant Roman lettering, letters too close together and interwoven letters are all unreadable from a distance. Again, you may need to thicken, separate and adapt your logo in this instance.

Watch where you place the logo. Caps and collars are ideal because they frame the face which must appear in any picture. Second choice should be the upper chest. And it gets worse as you go down. You may not always have the option, of course. Sportsmen who perform in various states of undress such as boxers, swimmers and Sumo wrestlers offer somewhat limited opportunities for labelling! Look at the name and logo on a real person not on a flat item of clothing. A logo placed beautifully on the right breast of a flat jersey can end up under an arm or in a rumpled midriff on a three-dimensional human being.

Incidentally, although I want to try to avoid an overemphasis on sport, that is obviously where most performers wear a uniform kit. However, there are other organizations which wear a standard dress style such as musicians. But you are unlikely to be able to persuade a symphony orchestra or a choral society to wear your logo on their dinner jackets or evening gowns as part of the deal.

But that is not necessarily going to be the case where lighter music is concerned. There is no reason why a marching band, for instance, should not wear your colours and your company name on their tunics, shoulder flashes, drums, flags or anywhere else for that matter and, unless they are performing on television, the size of such logos is really a matter of whatever is mutually acceptable.

Nor need we concentrate on performers. There are support staff who could very easily be dressed in corporate colours and wear your company name. Some of these may briefly appear on television, others may not. But consider team managers and coaches, physiotherapists, ball boys, mechanics, course builders, judges, stewards, timekeepers, referees, marshals, attendants, grooms, bar and catering staff, guides, information staff, administration staff, stagehands, collectors, distributors, conservation workers – there is even the audience. Need I go on?

An investigation into the type of outfits worn by those involved in your sponsorship will enable you to come up with a surprisingly long list of clothing which can be used to promote your company name and image.

Printed material

You are more likely to be offered advertising space or identification on printed material by a sponsorship seeker than on anything else. Virtually all sponsorships will produce some form of printed material whether it be headed paper or programmes, tickets or reports. A number of different possibilities are listed below but whatever you are offered, you must ensure that you have some final say-so on design. If your company name is cheaply printed in the wrong typeface onto existing notepaper, it may reflect very badly on you.

So you may find yourself involved in the expense of hiring designers and getting reprints of paper done in order to maintain a desired level of quality. If it has not been agreed in the beginning who will foot the bill for the change of corporate house style for the sponsee, this may come as an unwelcome surprise.

Don't impose your identity too heavily in the wrong places or the impression you give may be a negative one. As with advertising hoardings and clothing, you may have to compromise a little to achieve a pleasing result.

Advertising checklist

Here are a few suggestions for places you may like to consider as possible vehicles to carry your corporate identity or advertising:

Sport and record attempts

- *Sports kit* – (may also be subject to an agreement with a kit manufacturer to display their logo) shirts, jerseys, shorts, socks, footwear, caps, hats, trousers, skirts, athletic vests, tracksuits, training kit, rain jackets, drivers' overalls, jackets, breeches, wet suits, swimwear, helmets.
- *Official wear* – tracksuits, suits, blazers, ties, scarves, sweaters, dresses, handbags, hats.
- *Leisure wear* – sweatshirts, T-shirts, leisure suits.
- *Back-up staff* – tracksuits, blazers, shirts, ties, skirts, trousers, suits, rain-jackets, stewards' waistcoats, programme sellers' coats, anoraks, fireproof overalls, mechanics' overalls.
- *Equipment* – (already highly likely to be the subject of a separate agreement with a manufacturer) rackets, bats, balls, skis, bows, rods, bowls, saddlecloths.
- *Hoardings or advertising sites at venues* – pitch or track perimeter, stand walls, roofs, roof overhangs, inside walls, windows, ceilings,

walkways, steps, seats, entrances, track, pitch, rink, green, flags, floating balloons, marquees, information signs.
- *Vehicles and transport* — cars, trucks, vans, vehicle and horse transporters and trailers, coaches, bonnets, doors, boots, spoilers, petrol tanks, van sides, windows, wings, frames, mudguards, sails, hulls, decks, balloon fabric, balloon baskets, parachute canopies, official coaches, cars and transport.

Arts

- *Performers* — stage outfits, band uniforms.
- *Official wear* — suits, blazers, shirts, ties, dresses, hats, handbags.
- *Back-up staff* — blazers, ties, shirts, skirts, sweatshirts, T-shirts.
- *Hoardings at venue* — walls, roof, entrance portico, entrance interior, ceilings, marquees, arenas, concert halls, bars, lobbies.
- *Printed material* — information leaflets, programmes, tickets, posters, events lists, maps, headed paper, promotional literature.

Conservation, environmental and community projects, tourist attractions, exhibitions and shows

- *Paid and volunteer staff* — overalls, anoraks, rainwear, gumboots, sweatshirts, T-shirts, shirts, blazers, ties.
- *Hoarding sites* — building exterior walls and roofs, entrances and doorways, windows, information boards, information kiosks, directional signs, counters, display areas.
- *Equipment* — bottle banks, skips, tools.
- *Vehicles* — on-site transport.
- *Printed materials* — visitor guides, maps, instruction leaflets, programmes, catalogues, reports, letter headings and compliments slips, press release paper, envelopes.

Media relations

On the whole, the media are interested in four basic things to fill their pages or their programmes — news, human interest stories, odd and unusual features and information useful to their readers or viewers. They are not interested in promoting a company's name just for the sake of it. So bear this in mind in terms of sponsorship.

Major news is usually something that is of major national importance and interest — politics, war, crime, disaster.

Human interest means the Royal Family, politicians, the peerage, personalities, sportsmen, film stars, TV personalities, children and (almost human) animals.

Odd and unusual stories are much loved by the press when they can get them – the biggest, smallest, funniest, bravest, rarest, oldest and youngest are all typical stories of this nature.

Information comes in many forms. Each different type of media informs in one way or another but some inform on a personal level so that the reader or viewer can make use of what is offered – sport, arts, travel, TV, films, music, motoring, beauty, fashion, finance, property, gardening, cooking – and so on.

So, for your sponsorship to get major media coverage, it must fulfil one of the above criteria.

The sponsorship announcement and major events

These days, I'm afraid, it is unlikely that the announcement of a sponsorship is going to attract more than a paragraph in the national press unless it fulfils one of the first three criteria. As I said earlier, sponsorship in itself is no longer front page news as it was when Liverpool secured the sponsorship of Hitachi back in 1978 – the first football club in Britain to do so.

You might make a bigger splash if the sponsorship is in some way unique – the biggest of its kind, the first in its field, the youngest or oldest participant, the most successful (Alain Prost) or the biggest failure (Eddie Edwards), an unusual clause in the contract, anything to make good copy.

Is there a personality involved who is newsworthy in his own right? Would Barbour have sponsored Captain Mark Phillips' three-day event at Gatcombe had it not been for the royal connection? They actually pulled out after a perfectly reasonable period of three years but, of course, the press immediately speculated that it was because of the royal divorce. An ex-husband of Princess Anne is presumably regarded as less news-worthy than a current husband. Would Ian Botham have attracted so much publicity for his long-distance walks and consequently raised so much money for Leukaemia Research if he had been but a modest and unassuming county cricketer?

The most attractive personalities to the press are those who are already in the news for one reason or another, although this can sometimes backfire in that the press will certainly be more interested in an update on the scandal or the strife involved than they are in the launch of sponsorship. The Prince of Wales, for instance, could be regarded as a coup for any organization at a launch, but HRH has a tendency these days to use such events as an opportunity to make a point about something almost totally different so, when that hits the headlines, the original purpose of his attendance is forgotten. If you do find yourself involved with a 1960s pop star or an ancient athlete, try to find a peg for the press – 'Forty years to the day since he scored the winning goal for Blackley in the 1952 Cup Final' or 'Once a hell-raiser in the sixties, now plays polo with the gentry.'

Human interest plus the odd and unusual makes a story out of something that is not genuine news. Add a really good photo opportunity and you have an even better chance of getting your sponsorship launch covered.

I was recently in just such a situation with the sponsorship of an amateur sports club where a good photograph could have made the difference between a quarter page of coverage and a quarter of a centimetre. Pleas to provide famous players, not-so-famous players or players' children fell upon deaf ears and we ended up taking a picture of chairman shaking hands with chairman. The chairmen were quite delighted with their picture but naturally the press simply ignored it.

It takes imagination and often hard work on the part of the sponsor or his consultancy to create a scenario that photographers will relish. It also takes cooperation on the part of the sponsored organization. For example, someone obviously saw a couple of good stories and photographs in a recent Boat Race. For a start, it was the first time that there were two female coxes. It was also a nice contrast to have the heaviest-ever oarsman at 6'6" alongside his diminutive 5'2" cox. And naturally both were wearing Beefeater Gin sweatshirts.

But be cautious about plastering people, things and places with your corporate identity. However good the photograph, most picture editors simply will not use a shot that is blatant advertising. You can usually get away with clothing featuring logos or slogans but hoardings placed carefully in the background will be equally carefully cut out by either photographer or picture editor.

Timing is vital, too. Modern technology may have brought news-paper production kicking and screaming into the twentieth century but in some cases it has also taken a step back. For instance, pages are now made up much earlier than they once were so, major news excepted, the earlier you can arrange for your manufactured news to be staged, the better chance it has of being covered. So breakfast press conferences and early photo-calls are more helpful to the press than lunchtime or afternoon events.

Similarly, which day you choose is also important. It's probably too obvious to point out, if you are launching a sports sponsorship, that Cup Final Eve or Derby Day is not a good choice but think ahead about the sporting calendar for the date you have in mind and the sort of coverage that it is likely to get on the next day. Genuine news is always going to get preference over PR puffery but, on a thin day, editors may be glad of that brilliant photocall you organized. Good days to get into the sports pages are usually Thursdays or Mondays but for other types of sponsorship, seriously consider a Sunday. No one wants to 'work' on a Sunday of course, which is why newspapers in particular often have a problem of filling the Monday papers and your story will have a better chance of being chosen.

So, when you plan the launch of your sponsorship, look at it from the journalist's or photographer's point of view. Is it a story or is it a picture or, better still, is it both?

There are six categories of media which are likely to be interested in the sponsorship launch:

1 *National media (TV, radio, national press)*: News editors, specialist editors or correspondents (i.e. sport, arts, environment, education) and picture editors. Specialist editors will almost certainly cover the story as a matter of course. News reporters and photographers will only be despatched to attend if there is the smell of a good story.

2 *Local media*: News editors or specialist editors of the local newspapers and radio stations in the area of the sponsoring company and/or sponsored organization. These can be relied upon to attend and will be looking for a local angle on the story and how the sponsorship will benefit their readers.

3 *Specialist press*: Magazines and periodicals of a specialist interest in the area of the sponsorship (i.e. sport, education, tourism, environment, theatre, arts, music, etc.). Given a good angle, they may use the opportunity to expand the story into a longer feature.

4 *Trade press*: The sponsor's own trade press (i.e. *The Grocer, Accountancy Age, Construction News, Computer Weekly* etc.) will be interested in the reasons for the sponsorship from a trade point of view and in the reasons for the choice and the expectation of results.

5 *Communications press*: Any announcement of a major marketing initiative will be of interest to this specialist area of the press (including probably *Marketing, Marketing Week, PR Week, Direct Marketing, Precision Marketing, Campaign and Sponsorship News*). Like the trade press, they will be interested in the thought behind the choice, the benefits and the fee.

6 *Company publications*: Most major companies will have their own company newspapers or magazines and usually other pub-

lications, such as company brochures and annual reports. The house journal is an ideal vehicle to explain to the workforce the reasons for the sponsorship and the benefits it will bring to the company. The company brochure or annual report does the same thing to a different audience, such as shareholders.

The one-off opportunity

More often than not, once the initial launch is over, it is very difficult to create more stories about the sponsorship as such. What more is there to say unless the sponsorship is renegotiated or there are problems over the contract, in which case the publicity is going to be good for neither sponsor nor sponsee. This very situation happened when *Today* newspaper sponsored the Football League. After a year they managed to pull out, the principal problem being a certain reluctance on the part of their fellow newspapers to mention a rival publication.

Sometimes a problem can attract major publicity. As, for instance, in 1987 when Tottenham Hotspur played Coventry City in the FA Cup Final. Somehow half the Spurs players were given shirts with no sponsor's names on them and the next day Holsten were reported to be absolutely livid, the contract was said to be in jeopardy and the club secretary was forced to resign. It made all the national media from TV to newspaper cartoons, and a rival brewery was inspired to use an advertisement featuring one of the Spurs players with a blank shirt and the caption 'Bet he drinks Carling Black Label!' How players who had been pulling on white shirts with large blue logos on the front for several seasons could manage not to notice that the logos were missing on Cup Final day remains a mystery to me, but nevertheless it was wonderful publicity.

A similar situation happened with Daley Thompson at the 1986 Commonwealth Games. Daley apparently took sudden exception to the fact that he, a teetotaller, was obliged to wear a number bearing the sponsor's name (Guinness) and so scribbled out the offending word. Result: lots of close-up shots of Daley's chest and massive publicity for Guinness.

It takes a good publicist to spot an opportunity for media coverage whether it is accidental or manufactured. I suggest that you and your public relations staff or consultancy think in advance about what could happen and plan how to react to different situations. Unless you do this, you can be sure that Parkinson's Law will swing into action and when a major publicity opportunity does present itself, it will be on a Sunday afternoon and no one can either be contacted or be bothered to make the most of it. This scenario could cause a major problem if the story is negative rather than positive, so it isn't just a question of making a PR scoop when an opportunity comes your way but also of heading off impending disaster. For instance, let me throw in a few possible publicity opportunities and problems:

- Your sponsored pop star, wearing a T-shirt with your name all over it, is photographed sticking two fingers up at the camera.
- A streaker does a cartwheel on a cricket pitch right in front of your perimeter board.
- A member of a sports team is overheard by a journalist to say that he thinks your lager comes straight from the Thames.
- Striking employees start grumbling to the press that your company has managed to find £2 million to sponsor a major sports event but won't give them a 4 per cent rise.
- Three people are badly injured in an accident on a big dipper you have sponsored.
- There is a TV technicians' strike and all the TV coverage you had expected will not happen.
- A world record attempt you are sponsoring ends in tragedy when the driver is killed.
- A Hollywood star agrees to act in a play you are sponsoring.

Situations such as these could be managed into huge publicity successes or, handled badly, could mean disaster. Be prepared.

Corporate logos

One of the purposes of the corporate logo in certain types of sponsorship is for it to be seen on television or in newspaper photographs. See the section on advertising regarding the style of such logos but, apart from the coverage of the event, there are other opportunities to get the logo onto television or into the media via the moving or the static image.

First, do make sure that all official shots of your sponsored team, sportsman, musician or personality are taken so that they show your logo to its full advantage. Photographers do not tend to make this a priority unless forewarned. You do not want your hefty rugby league team standing with their arms folded, if those beefy arms neatly cover your name on their shirts. If necessary, arrange your own photographer and have a representative present to make sure that the name shows up well.

Portrait photographs of individuals can present the same problems. Mind you, it is quite easy for picture editors to crop pictures right down to cut out a sponsor's name on a shirt, although on some occasions the pictures have to be cropped so tightly that they almost end up as a pair of eyes staring out of the page.

When space permits, action photographs are usually preferred by picture editors and, in this case it is more difficult to crop out the sponsor's name.

All major newspapers keep photo libraries of major sports stars and other personalities. If you want to avoid a situation where they use last year's photograph featuring last year's sponsor, then it could be a good investment to send a pack of suitably captioned photographs to all the major newspapers to keep on file.

If a picture editor needs a shot in a hurry and his own or a commercial picture library cannot supply it, then the chances are that he'll approach the organization, sports club or individual concerned. It is, therefore, worth checking with your sponsored organization exactly what sort of picture library they have, if any.

You will almost certainly find that it is not very good and the professionalism of such a small element of publicity does not necessarily relate to the grandeur of the organization either. I once threw mighty Liverpool Football Club into utter consternation and irritation because I made the perfectly commonplace press request for a head-and-shoulders shot of one of their players for the following week's programme at Watford. After about half an hour of being transferred from one person ('it's not my job, you know') to another, I got as far as the suggestion that the club shop might sell me one or I could ask the player himself. I gave up in exasperation in the end and the sponsor missed a small plug.

If the organization itself isn't geared up to keeping a photo library, then you should consider helping it along a little by arranging some photo sessions to start up a good library which the press can draw on and, when I say press, I mean any publisher whether it be the opposing team's programme editor or the local advertising agency. Team or group shots, head and shoulders portraits and action shots will all be useful as will shots of the stadium – with your signboards somewhere in the background of course. Keep both black and white 8 in × 6 in on file and 35 mm colour transparencies. TV programmes use a lot of colour shots of individuals so will welcome good photographs for their libraries. These should be 35 mm landscape only.

The same theory applies not only to sport but to arts, personalities, events or whatever you may be sponsoring.

In the case of unusual sponsorship, where photographs do not already exist, your chances of having a picture reproduced are quite good. For instance, if you were to sponsor a package of young athletes, one of whom might suddenly smash a major record, then an action shot of that athlete (wearing your kit) would be quite a desirable commodity. Similarly, shots of community activities — people picking up litter, recycling paper, planting trees, painting houses — aren't always easy to find in picture libraries and a little forethought and investment in a good photographer may pay dividends later on.

Before you commission a photographer, consider for what purpose you will be using his photographs. Once upon a time, whoever commissioned the photography owned the copyright but the Copyright Act 1988 has turned that on its head and the copyright now rests with the photographer. Effectively, this means that you can pay a photographer to do a day's work for you for a particular purpose but he can still go out and sell the photographs elsewhere unless you have agreed to the contrary. This can be a considerable problem if you intend putting the photographs to several uses. I suggest that you identify as exactly as you can the type of use the photographs will be put to and ask your photographer to quote a price accordingly. Naturally, the fee for a shot of a conductor in action for a concert programme will be rather less than the fee for the same shot which may be used for programmes, posters, press handouts, and so on.

If you intend using the pictures for purposes which you have yet to identify, then you can pay a fee that will include the copyright but you must make this clear in writing when you commission the photographer. If you commission a great deal of photography, then a copy of the Copyright Act 1988 is worth the investment but a series of articles called 'The Right to Copy' appeared in *The Photographer* in 1989. These can be obtained from The British Institute of Professional Photography, 2 Amwell End, Ware, Herts SG12 9HN for £1.50.

From the photographer's point of view, the Act is a big step forward. From the client's point of view, I think it could present many, many problems.

Press office

What the media require above all else is information. They want it supplied accurately, knowledgeably and swiftly. So if you, the sponsor, want to establish good relations with the press and want to encourage them to mention your company as often as possible, then you will create a more receptive climate if you help them to get what they want. Efficiency is rated much more highly than an over-abundance of good food and wine.

The type of press office you set up will depend upon your sponsorship. What is necessary for the sponsorship of a major car rally or arts festival lasting two weeks is not going to be appropriate for the sponsorship of a programme to save the red squirrel or to publish a series of books on learning foreign languages.

In the case of most sponsorships, the organization you are sponsoring will probably have either a press officer or someone designated to look after publicity. They will normally have a million other things to do so and, with the best will in the world, will not always remember to mention the sponsor's name at the appropriate moment.

If the sponsorship is a very major one, let us say well into six figures, and you feel that media publicity is a vital part of your sponsorship package, then do look very closely at your sponsee's press set-up. If you feel that it needs boosting, then you might consider doing just that as part of your sponsorship deal. This could mean detailing your sponsorship or PR consultancy to spend part of their time concentrating on press publicity; it could mean seconding one of your own press office staff to the sponsored organization; or it could even mean funding a press officer for it.

The success of any press office depends upon the people running it. One way to help a press office without being obtrusive is to supply photographs, as I've already mentioned, but also to gather and publish information which they can make available to the press.

You should aim to have your company name or logo on your sponsee's press release paper, if nothing else. This will reinforce the message that you are the sponsor and, certainly if your company name is within the title of the event, that your name should be included rather than deliberately excluded.

You may also like to take a look at the sort of information that your sponsee normally supplies to the press and see if this can be enhanced in any way. Do they supply biographies of the actors, musicians, players and personalities taking part? Can they provide technical or historical information? Are they keeping records of progress or updating statistics?

If you're running a short-term event such as a festival, tournament, rally, concert series, tour or record attempt, then an efficient press office can not only bring you better publicity but also foster good press relations for the future.

Set up separate facilities for the press — a room, a marquee, a Portakabin, a bus or whatever the venue will allow.

This should primarily be a centre for gathering information but, if you have room, include other path-smoothing facilities. These will vary widely from event to event but include a writing area; telephones — free phones, pay-phones, card-phones, or special lines paid for by the newspapers who require them (many journalists don't dictate these days but simply type into a portable computer and send the story down the line direct); fax machines; quiet rooms for radio interviews; bar and refreshments; toilets; a main conference room with seats and a top table on a dais for post-event interviews.

The press centre should be permanently manned by staff who are on-the-ball and know what's happening; in the case of an ever-changing situation such as a car rally or golf tournament, press releases giving out the latest details and facts and figures will be extremely useful as will photographs of the major competitors.

After the event, the press will appreciate a conference or briefing to meet the players or performers, a few facts and figures of the day's performance and then an opportunity to ask questions. Even so, inevitably there will be a rush afterwards to get an 'exclusive' few words with the stars.

Good publicity may appear to happen by accident but it very rarely does. Organizations which receive a lot of coverage tend to be those that have prepared for any eventuality well in advance, give the press what they want, when they want it, and are generally readily available and instantly responsive.

Television coverage

Television is, of course, simply one element of the media so, strictly speaking, it should come under the previous heading. However, since it is arguably the media leader in terms of the coverage it is able to offer and the size of the audience it attracts, it merits a separate section on its own.

Sometimes sponsors place too much emphasis on the actual televising of an event considering the size of the audience the programme will attract. The sight of the runners in the 1.30 at Market Raisen flashing past the company name for one second on television is no doubt a big thrill for the chairman, but entertaining twelve important customers at the same race is probably a much more effective sales technique.

Some types of sponsorship are more likely to receive TV coverage than others. You may make the news once with an environmental or expedition sponsorship, or with a museum opening, or a record attempt. But sport is currently the only sponsored activity which has the benefit of regular TV coverage, since it provides entertainment and news at the same time.

In terms of announcements of sponsorships, events and photo stories, the press and publicity executives of the organizations which you are sponsoring should inform the news rooms of the TV networks in exactly the same way as they inform radio, newspapers and magazines. Depending upon the efficiency of the organization you are sponsoring, you would normally expect them to handle the press but there is no reason why your own public relations department or PR consultancy should not add their own expertise for the common good.

While attracting news or feature coverage will depend very much on the story or picture value of your sponsorship, coverage of sport on a regular basis is more likely to be determined by the sort of television audience the event will attract.

First, the sport will probably have an exclusive agreement with one of the TV authorities or networks which will have been negotiated between the head of sport and the management committee of the particular sport's official body. Once upon a time, it was a two-horse race between BBC and ITV but now there are more options with BBC national and regional TV, the ITV networks and Channel 4, British Sky Broadcasting and the Cable channels, all with hours to fill. But, of course, while the chances of getting on television are now greater, unless we are all destined to watch TV twenty-four hours a days, the size of the audience will remain the same but will be dissipated among more channels. Hence precise targeting of your audience, matched with the audience of your particular sponsored sport or event, becomes even more important.

Most spectator sports are shown on television at one time or another. The popular ones are self-evident — snooker, cricket, soccer, horse-racing, rugby, athletics etc. and all make good television. Some sports such as Formula 1 motor racing or darts, in my opinion, don't make for particularly thrilling TV but receive huge coverage nevertheless because there is such a great interest in them as sports. Other activities such as angling and rifle shooting are never likely to make for successful television because, from a spectator's point of view, they are pretty dull fare.

If you are sponsoring a major sport, then the official negotiating body or their agents will almost certainly have included TV coverage in the contract, in which case you should check whether this is guaranteed or whether it is simply that they are hoping for TV coverage on the chance of a strong current and a following wind.

'The ITV networks are really only interested in major sports these days' says Bryan Tremble, an editor with Thames Television. 'It means that the quality of competition will be high, and public interest will be high and that means good viewing figures for us which is very important since we rely entirely on income from advertising. And where an important sport is concerned, we're obviously bidding against the BBC so the fee we pay goes up, too.'

'We're also not so interested in the same major sports at a lower level and neither are the public really. The problem is that local competitions are in poor venues, the organization is much slower and doesn't make entertaining television and the quality of competition is much lower. So the net result is that we have to spend considerable time in actually helping to stage the event to make it interesting for the viewer.'

'However, with the arrival of the satellite television companies which have channels designated solely for sport, there are a huge number of hours to fill. So I see no reason why competition at lower level and coverage of lesser sports shouldn't go to these channels with the finals or the major events being shown on the public channels as well.'

The message would appear to be that if TV coverage is very important go for a major sport and sponsor the League, the Cup, or a major competition. If your budget is small, then come into a major sport at a lower level or sponsor one of the minor sports but remember that the type of TV coverage you will receive is likely to be inconsequential.

Before signing anything, check carefully what you will be allowed to have in the way of branding at any particular event. This will vary considerably from sport to sport. Tobacco and hard spirits sponsors will find it more difficult than others to get an event heavily branded (if they are allowed to sponsor an event at all).

You also need to know where and when the event will be shown. Will it just be in one region, for instance, or will it be nationwide? Will it be sold into Europe or even to countries worldwide? What time will it be shown? Six o'clock in the morning on BSkyB Television isn't going to achieve the same viewing figures as 8.00 p.m. on BBC1.

If you're sponsoring a team or an individual, then the likelihood of television coverage will depend very much on the success of that team or individual. The 'Big Five' football clubs appear regularly on television because they are successful, even if half the audience is screaming at the television 'Not them again!'

'We have to answer to advertisers,' says John Taylor, another Thames Sport editor. 'ITV can pull in an audience of eight million for Manchester United versus Arsenal but I'm afraid Norwich versus Coventry will rate an audience of perhaps three or four million.'

This is a Catch 22 situation of course. People want to watch sports with which they are familiar, they want to see famous teams and star performers, and these tend to be the ones which are shown on television. But then the unknowns never get shown and never get famous. John Taylor agrees, but says, 'In a sense that isn't our problem. We have to show the events which will get the biggest audiences because they will attract the highest advertising rates, which will enable us to pay the high fees the sports organizations

140

expect. If the organization then demands that we cover lesser events as part of the deal, then the fee we would offer would go down accordingly and they don't want that! The BBC don't have advertisers but they still have to justify the high fees they are paying by keeping their viewing audiences up.'

However, Channel 4 and satellite television do offer opportunities for the minor sports, and for sponsors too. American Football would still be firmly restricted to the USA if it had not been for Channel 4, but the interest generated was huge and Budweiser Beer reaped the benefit.

Predictably, arts programmes are allocated less time on TV than sport and sponsors also get a pretty raw deal in comparison – no perimeter boards round the concert hall if you're an arts sponsor and considered lucky if you receive a mention in the titles or the continuity announcement. This is a continual source of annoyance to sponsors. If the 'Whizbang Toys Child Musician of the Year' is constantly referred to as the 'Child Musician of the Year' and Whizbang Toys are not allowed to have any banners or hoardings in the auditorium, then Whizbang are wasting their money. If the sponsor pulls out and the arts organization can't fund an event, then there is nothing for television to cover and everyone loses.

Television is rather more generous to charities because the Broadcasting Acts allow it to be so. Indeed, several major TV programmes, such as *Children in Need* and *Telethon* are now devoted to fund-raising and millions of people not only watch but take part in sponsored events. Worthy activities such as tap dance marathons and bathing in baked beans make good stories, even if the viewer has to put up with large cheques featuring the Cleckheaton and Grimethorpe Building Society being thrust in front of the camera at regular intervals. Companies creating sponsored events in this way are also taking a gamble in that there is no guarantee that their event will be covered and, even if it is, that coverage is likely to be very brief.

But there is no doubt that often even a brief appearance on television is a very powerful way of creating awareness and heightening the emotions. One tiny animal charity I know was so overwhelmed with funds following a TV news story that it now has more money than it can ever spend on saving donkeys in a far corner of the world.

Liaise closely with the organization you are sponsoring and the programme makers and, advises Bryan Tremble, 'It's often a good idea to work through one of the big sponsorship consultancies who understand the problems from both points of view.'

Client entertainment

Sports and arts sponsorships in particular score heavily in terms of client entertainment but some of the other types of sponsorship such as record attempts, exhibitions and tourist attractions offer possibilities as well.

As I've indicated before, the philosophy of entertaining clients is really quite simple. It gives the sponsor an opportunity to meet his customers in an enjoyable setting where they can get to know each other on an informal basis and thus cement business relationships into friendship as well.

What clients want out of a day out are the things that they cannot arrange for themselves. They like luxury with excellent food and abundant drink, they like their paths to be smoothed − car parking on the doorstep, reserved best seats, someone to look after them. They like to see behind the scenes where the general public can't go. They like entertainment and excitement. They like to meet the famous, they like to be made to feel important, and, above all, they like to be able to go away and brag about it to their friends and relatives afterwards.

Client entertainment is big business these days. There are numerous firms which specialize in it and there is even a magazine, *Corporate Entertainment and Hospitality*, devoted to the subject. If your sole objective is to treat your clients to a day out, then it is very easy to buy an entertainment package from a company which will get you to Wimbledon, or Henley, or Glyndebourne, or the FA Cup Final, or the Derby, or virtually any major event you care to name. Tickets will be organized, guests invited, meals laid on, car parking arranged, paths smoothed, palms crossed and, in fact, the hospitality company will do everything for you apart from make out the guest list − and they would probably even do that, if you asked.

Hospitality packages range from around £100 a head upwards but for prestige events you can expect to pay considerably more − well over £1,000 a head for a finals day at Wimbledon.

So why sponsor? The difference in the eyes of the guest can be quite a major one. It is rather like the difference between being Oxford or Cambridge in the Boat Race. All the oarsmen have the pleasure of participating, they all have the hard work and excitement of the build-up and they all get a rowing Blue. But, at the end of the day, one boat will be the winner and one the loser and there may only be a few feet in it.

When you buy a corporate hospitality package your guests will have a lovely day out, watch the event in comfort and be wined and dined well. But they may also notice that your marquee is one of several dozen crammed in along the banks at Henley and that yours is nearer the start than the finish; they may have been invited to the same event last year by another company anxious for their business and been wined and dined better and further up the bank; they may expect to meet some of the stars of the event and be disappointed; they may be even more disappointed to find that your hospitality is at a local hotel and that they have to be bussed to the event itself.

The major sponsor, on the other hand, should have none of these problems. His marquee or seats should be in the prime position nearest the action, arrangements should be the most efficient, his food the best and his little extra touches the most memorable because he is not buying a package and can control exactly what he gets.

His branding should be obvious around the event where appropriate, not just for the benefit of the TV cameras but where the guests can see it as well. It should be on banners, hoardings, programmes, tickets and other publicity material so that the guest is always aware that the sponsor has a prestigious connection with the sponsored event.

And the sponsor should be able to arrange for his guests to meet some of the participants in the event. What greater delight and prestige can there be for a guest to go home and say they have met Graham Gooch or Malcolm Pyrah in person?

On the subject of meeting the famous, don't necessarily expect sparkling cocktail party conversation from pop stars or an interest in anything but horses from jockeys. Some guests can be struck totally dumb when confronted by a famous name and reduced to simply asking for an autograph. It's even more difficult for the performer or sportsman to make conversation out of nothing.

Many sports people in particular regard meeting the sponsor's guests as hard work and will avoid it if they can. Many's the time I've been left gabbling inanely in the middle of a group of dumb-struck guests and uncomfortable sportsmen who didn't know what to say to each other. It's hard work!

Making small talk is not a qualification for being an athlete or an artiste so you can make life easier for such individuals by liaising with the sponsored organization in advance and gathering information about the players, or the artistes, to pass on to the guests and, likewise, supplying information about who the guests are and where they come from to the sportsmen or women or performers who will be meeting them. It doesn't have to be a biography, even a list of names will help.

Professional sports teams, musicians and others who earn their living from their talent usually do what they are told, when they are told. So, if it's a question of spending the day in Birmingham on the sponsor's stand at the Motor Show then that's what they do. They don't always find it easy or even enjoyable and sometimes they become mysteriously invisible when required to 'come up and chat to the sponsors'. Knowing footballers, I was once quite astonished to hear that one of the big clubs' sponsors had players positively queuing up to meet their guests. 'How on earth do you do it?' I asked. 'Easy,' came the reply from the company's sponsorship consultant, 'I just slip a £50 note in each back pocket.' Knowing the club, I wasn't then quite so astonished. I hope you don't find yourself reduced to such tactics.

On the other hand, amateurs who are not quite so used to being regarded as glamorous are often very happy to meet sponsors. A few free beers in the bar after the game and a chat about their favourite sport is reward enough for being sociable. But the problem with amateurs is that they have to earn their real living in other ways and are, therefore, usually neither willing nor available to take time off during working hours to be present at the sponsor's sales conference or annual dinner dance.

Sometimes the organization you are sponsoring is genuinely unable to fulfil a request because it simply does not have the power to force amateur athletes to break training schedules. In 1988, one of the sponsors of the British Olympic team had arranged many fund-raising events for Seoul. The British Olympic Association genuinely fulfilled the request that, where possible, Olympic athletes should be present at these events. The trouble was that Olympic athletes to most people meant Daley Thompson and Steve Cram and the people who did turn up were the wrestlers and cyclists and archers of whom the public had never heard. So don't make assumptions that the famous will make themselves available. Get it clear from the start.

Think carefully about which guests you are going to invite to your event. You obviously want the decision maker. But the decision maker is not always the buyer or the seller of your product.

I remember when I was in the tourism business that companies were always very insistent upon getting the managing directors of travel agencies along to events, but in fact it was not the MDs who were selling on to the public, it was the lowly counter clerks who hardly ever got invited to anything.

So an invitation to the right person is essential. It is a tricky situation. You must not offend the assistant buyer by inviting the managing director, equally you should not irritate the managing director by inviting only the assistant buyer. If it means more than one invitation, or organizing more than one event, then the investment may be necessary.

Your second dilemma is whether to invite the customer on his or her own or whether to include their spouse and – one step further – their children.

If you have chosen your sponsorship wisely, you will have matched the sponsorship to the customer profile anyway, and this to a certain extent will determine the audience. A midweek day at a golf or cricket championship isn't likely to appeal to wives and children and it may be that your prospects are the type who don't mix family and business anyway. But, on the other hand, there are many businesses where families are heavily involved, particularly retail businesses.

Mike Smith, a master baker from Burnham in Buckinghamshire, is a typical example of this. He works a six-day week running his bakery and only has Sundays off. He is entertained once a year by Allied Mills who sponsor a 'Harvester' Historic Racing car and invite clients to Brands Hatch. He and his wife and two sons thoroughly enjoy their day out. 'It certainly makes a difference to me that the whole family is invited,' he says, 'because in my business we don't have time for many days out together and the boys love it. They meet the driver, they sit in the car and have their photographs taken. They think it's wonderful.'

Many companies look hard at bills when it comes to inviting children, but not Allied Mills apparently. 'I noticed that many of their guests were teenagers,' says Mike Smith. 'In small businesses such as ours, they could be the owners or managers of tomorrow so, from Allied Mills' point of view, entertaining those teenagers is a good investment for the future.

'There's no doubt that I am influenced by the day out. Not only does it make you see the company in a warm light, but it's also an opportunity to meet people in the organization that may otherwise only be a voice on the other end of the telephone.'

Whom ever you decide to invite to an event, you would be wise to make a checklist of all the things that need to be remembered:

- Who exactly is to be invited – are names and title correct?
- Are wives, husbands or, more tactfully, 'a guest' to be invited?
- If there is any restriction on guests (i.e. if it's a stag boxing dinner, then women are excluded or perhaps it is not a suitable event for young children) you should tactfully make this clear in the invitation to avoid embarrassment.
- When are they to be invited? If you send out invitations too early, people will forget about it. If you leave it too late, they'll be busy elsewhere. Four or five weeks in advance is about right for most occasions.

You can make life easy for your invitees by enclosing a reply card or a reply form and addressed envelope. You would be amazed at the inertia that overtakes some people when it comes to picking up a telephone or writing a letter. It will also make things easier for you, too, since the replies will come in that much quicker. If no replies are forthcoming from some invitees, phone round to check. Give yourself enough time to invite replacements where the answer is 'no'. Inevitably, there will be last-minute cancellations and people who simply don't turn up, so have some last-minute stand-ins you could invite – this is often a nice perk for staff.

If you can, send out final information about a week to ten days in advance. Don't leave it until the last minute or you'll be inundated with anxious phone calls about Royal Mail reliability.

Don't send valuable tickets through the post unless you have to. It's better to arrange a meeting point where these can be collected. If you have to post tickets, send them by recorded delivery and make a note of the serial numbers, too, so that you know who has had what.

When you mail out your final information pack, it should contain:

- A map and description of how to get to the meeting point. If guests are driving, send a car park pass or, at the very least, a description of the nearest parking place.
- Tickets or passes as necessary.
- A plan of the venue if necessary.
- Final details of the venue; the date; the time the guests should arrive; a timetable of what is happening in case they are delayed; and the approximate time they should expect to leave.
- The name of their host for the day.
- Details about what sort of catering they can expect so that they don't have a five-course lunch on the assumption that you are just going to give them a sandwich when you've prepared a banquet. Ask any vegetarians to phone you in advance so that they can be catered for.
- Advice about what to wear. It's so much nicer to be warned in advance that it's going to be freezing or that everyone will be in dinner jackets. Women in particular hate being in the wrong clothes. It's utterly miserable being stuck in a March blizzard in an open stand at the Grand National in a frock and a picture hat when you should have been wearing wellingtons and a sheepskin coat.
- Any information that will build up the anticipation. A brief biography of the star conductor they are going to meet, the success story of the showjumper named after your company, or a picture of the yacht that it is hoped will break the world record.

146

Do think of all the things that could go wrong. Have a list of emergency numbers that guests can ring in case of disaster — your office number for daytime calls, an overnight number and a number where you can be contacted at the venue. If you are not the only contact make sure that they have the name of the person who is.

At the venue

Do check out the venue beforehand. Never take anyone's word for anything and confirm every detail in writing.

Check the venue itself. Is the room, the marquee or the hospitality bus the right size? Does it have all the facilities you require? Will it be warm enough? Are there enough toilets? Will everyone be able to see? Is there enough lighting? Is there a microphone? Do you need special flooring? Can it be decorated in your corporate colours?

Check the catering and be pernickety in advance. If the menu states cold meats and salad, you should know exactly what those cold meats and salad are going to be. It could mean spam and lettuce!

Make sure everyone knows what time you will be arriving and what time you require coffee to be available, the bar to be open and the lunch served. Find out the name of the person who will be in charge on the day and make sure that they know where to find you or whoever will be representing you.

Check which table linen, cutlery and crockery will be used. You may have bone china and silver cutlery in mind, they may be thinking you want paper plates and plastic knives and forks. What colour will the table linen be? Could it be set out in your corporate colours?

If you're in a marquee or a rather bleak room, consider how it might be decorated to make it more welcoming. Should you have flower displays, artificial plants or festoons of balloons? Should you have banners and flags displaying your company logo? Should you put up an exhibition stand of some sort?

Take care of the tiniest details of both the venue and the catering. Customers will remember that the heating failed or the smoked salmon ran out long after they have forgotten that they saw the Bolshoi Ballet.

Looking after people

If you've invited people for 11.00 a.m. you can be sure that one at least will be sitting unashamedly on your doorstep at 9.30 expecting to be entertained while you're in a mad panic to get everything organized. So be prepared in advance and arrange for amusing diversions for early arrivals. Detail someone to look after them,

147

arrange coffee or drinks, provide daily newspapers, programmes or anything to while away the time. There will also be those who arrive at 3.00 p.m. with no apology expecting you to have held up lunch for them. So make sure that the late arrivals can also be coped with in some way.

Have enough staff available to ensure that there is always someone to entertain the guests but not so many that it appears like a company jolly.

British people are incredibly reserved so help people get to know each other. Badges are often good ice breakers because they can be an easy way of starting a conversation: 'Oh! I see you're from Buggins' Biscuits, my son-in-law works there.'

But, if you don't want to emblazon people with badges, perhaps because the guest list is too small, then effect introductions as far as you can and get conversations going. Particularly look out for people on their own. What's worse than spending a day at Ascot and never speaking to a soul?

Sit-down meals are better than buffets for starting conversations and place names ensure that you don't end up with all the guests on one table and the staff on another. Don't leave gaps on tables where there are non-arrivals. Keep an eye on the guest list and shuffle names at the last minute so that all the tables except one are absolutely full.

Make sure that drinks are generously available but don't force alcohol on people. You will get a few who pour whiskies down as if there's no tomorrow but most people these days drink surprisingly little because they are driving, so be sure to have plentiful supplies of soft drinks and mineral water.

A few words of welcome will set the tone of the day and you can take the opportunity to explain what the format of the event will be as well. If people are coming to watch a new sport or a complicated modern opera, then you can make it more enjoyable for them by telling them a little about it first. Better still, you may be able to persuade a famous star to do it for you. Alternatively, give guests an information sheet when they arrive. Not everyone knows how to place a bet, for instance; not everyone knows how points are scored in boxing, tries in rugby, or is fluent enough in Italian to understand the plot of Don Giovanni or La Traviata. It's safer to assume that, like Manuel from *Fawlty Towers*, people 'know nothing' and inform them rather than leaving them to their own devices so that they only half enjoy a day because they don't want to admit their ignorance and ask.

Keep people entertained without making them feel pressured by rushing them from place to place. If they want to sit at the bar all day, let them. It's much better to announce, 'We're going down to the thirteenth hole now because Faldo's due there in ten minutes. If you'd like to come, please follow me,' than to force people into a Cook's Tour group.

Guests love to be shown 'behind the scenes' so, if you can arrange a visit to the stables, on to the stage, into the dressing rooms, into the pits, into the green room, into the press box, into the weighing room, on to the scoreboard platform, or into the wings; or if they can sit in the car, on the bike, in the boat, try on the helmet, feel the bow, stand on the pitch, walk the course, kick the ball, enter the Royal Box, then you will have made them very happy.

If your event is an outdoor one, be prepared for it to be postponed or cancelled at the last minute because of weather and have a contingency plan ready to swing into action. If you let people sit about miserably waiting for the rain to clear, your day will be a failure but, if you've thought about it in advance, you might all have a better time than you could ever expect.

One easy-to-organize time filler is a quiz. Have it prepared ready in advance. Divide your party into tables which must each compete as a team. This creates a convivial atmosphere straight away.

Your quiz can last ten minutes or two hours as necessary if you divide it into rounds. Give each table a sheet for each round to fill in their answers and collect each one at the end of each round and keep a running total. This way you'll be able to end at any time. Rounds can be on any theme from general knowledge to very specialist subjects. If you're at an open-air Shakespeare play, then you can perhaps have a Shakespearean round, a famous actors and actresses round, and so on. You could even have a charades round to get people participating, laughing and enjoying themselves. Award prizes at the end appropriate to the day — miniature racing cars for motor sport, records for concerts, signed bats for cricket, and so on.

If a quiz is not appropriate, then the alternatives are videos, films, slide shows, talks by famous stars of the past, a look behind the scenes, or even a coach ready to whisk people off to the local stately home or museum for the day. Be a good scout — 'Be prepared'.

Quizzes and competitions don't have to be restricted to wet weather. A small quiz or competition is a good ice breaker and adds interest to the day. The reason why people enjoy horse racing is the excitement of betting. But there is no reason why you shouldn't organize a sweep or competition for any event — Who will get a clear round? What's the attendance today? What will the score be?

If possible, make sure that the winners are presented with their prizes by one of the stars of the event — a musician, an actor or a player. And make the prizes worth having, too. This doesn't mean that they have to cost a great deal. Some people would much rather have a signed programme than a cheque for £100.

You may have arranged for the players or participants to come up and meet your guests. Bear in mind what I said earlier about the possibility of this being something of a conversational struggle and help it along where you can. Don't leave eighteen-year-old tennis players to walk majestically into a room on their own and make brilliant and witty conversation as they skim charmingly from group to group. You must look after them, make introductions, find mutual points of interest and get brief conversations going. It's hard work, but if you make it easy for everyone your guests will love it and your 'star' will be happy to perform again next time.

If you have a whole team to cope with, get someone who can act as a spokesman. It usually works quite well if the manager or the captain can stand up and introduce their team members one by one and say a little about each of them. Done with humour, this can raise a lot laughs – Elton John used to introduce himself by saying, 'When I became chairman of Watford in 1976 (his days of platform shoes and outrageous outfits) I was 6 ft tall and had pink hair. Now I'm 5 ft 8 and I've got no hair!' It never failed.

Do arrange a photographer for the day so that people can be pictured enjoying themselves and make sure that they get a copy soon afterwards. A photograph with someone famous will be treasured for ever.

Finally, having had a good day's entertainment, met a few famous people, seen behind the scenes, eaten and drunk well, the final seal will be set on your guests' day when they receive a parting gift.

Try to be original. Plastic ballpoint pens and keyrings are cheap but pretty forgettable. There are any number of souvenirs on the market but mostly it's the same old stuff – ashtrays, notepads, pens, plastic wallets. It isn't always easy to be economical and unique!

The most popular items are those which arouse slight envy in others (especially potential customers). Try to create something which is a memory of the day such as a miniature version of the car they have just seen racing, or a signed tennis ball, a cassette of the concert they have just heard, a copy of the book written by the actor they have just watched and so on. T-shirts and sweatshirts usually go down well, too, but have a variety of sizes available. Better still, replica team shirts are a huge success but a very expensive gift. Some people are grateful for anything. Others are irritatingly greedy. 'Can I take another five for my children?' you will hear quite frequently. Give in gracefully, if you must, or try the innocent line, 'Well, I think we only have enough to give one to each guest but if you'd like to wait another three and a half hours until everyone's gone, we'd be happy to let you have the odd spare.' (But, on the other hand, if he's your best customer, perhaps you might make the odd exception!)

By the way, it isn't always necessary to take people to a public event to make them feel special. Some people who have considerable purchasing power can become quite blasé about invitations to Covent Garden or Ascot. But if you can arrange with your sponsee for guests to see the practice sessions for the European Figure Skating Championships or the dress rehearsal of *The Taming of the Shrew* they may, surprisingly, feel rather more privileged.

Staff incentives

Most companies see sponsorship as a way of reaching customers but your own staff can be just as important. This is particularly true in the case of a service industry where the person behind the counter is perhaps the only contact the customer has with his bank or building society, supermarket or garage.

I could fill another book on the subject of staff and customer relations but, if your staff are the make or break of your business, then you should already be investing considerable time and effort into training and motivating them.

Britain is not a country renowned for the quality of its service. We have all been into shops where the assistants are more interested in discussing last night's date than they are in wasting their valuable time in serving you. Things are changing slowly but sometimes the sentiments don't always match the words. Every hotel these days seems to have a receptionist who answers the phone in a monotone gabble ... '*GoodmorningGoldStarGodivaHotelsofCoventryTraceyspeakinghowmayIhelp you?*' They've been trained to say the right words but obviously don't feel motivated enough to really mean them!

Motivation is not about earning more money. A survey amongst salesmen once surprisingly revealed that money came fairly low on a list of motives. Number one was, in fact, their relationship with their boss. And the same principle surely applies throughout any industry whether it's the managing director in a power struggle with his chairman or the food packer being bawled out by her supervisor. People want to feel appreciated and appreciation does not necessarily mean money.

Staff can be motivated in many ways, not least by encouragement, praise, involvement and interest in their work. What staff hate is to be taken for granted, to be treated like work processors, and having their working lives rearranged without being consulted.

Sponsorship can in fact be another very positive way of motivating staff. However, before you launch gaily into a new sponsorship programme, you may be wise to inform your staff what it's all about. They are not necessarily going to criticize your direct mail, advertising campaign or PR activities in terms of value for money, but sponsorship fees are usually well publicized and, given what I have said earlier about misconceptions about sponsorship and donations, you could come in for some damaging internal criticism if the benefits are not clearly explained.

Every organization has its own method of communicating information, whether it is a regular staff meeting or a company newspaper, but whichever method you use, get the correct version of the story in before the popular misconceptions are allowed to occur. That may mean inviting your staff to the launch party, or it may mean arranging a separate briefing for them, but do it sooner rather than later.

Another internal PR exercise that is usually well received is to take the star performers in your chosen sponsorship on a tour round your premises. Not only will the staff enjoy the experience of meeting famous people, but it will help them to understand the pleasure similar meetings must give your customers and the sales benefits that will bring to the company. It will also help the stars of your sponsored organization to understand you, their sponsor, better. If you are going to expect ballet dancers to discuss widgets authoritatively at post-performance parties, then it may help if they actually see a few widgets in production and then the conversation may flow more freely!

There are several other ways you can involve staff in the sponsorship. First, from a simple entertainment point of view, if it is a sponsorship where the purchase of tickets is involved, negotiate a special rate with the sponsee for your staff. This may mean free tickets or discounted tickets for which you may be expected to pay but, if staff feel that they, too, have some perks out of the sponsorship it should make them feel positively towards it.

If you are sponsoring a tourist attraction or a local cricket club, the cost in terms of staff tickets may not have to be very great but, if it is a rather more prestigious sponsorship such as an opera at Covent Garden, then tickets for everyone are going to be an expensive investment.

You could try a ballot or a competition for a pair of tickets or you could organize a special staff day. Many arts venues, theatres in particular, are happy to put on performances solely for the sponsor's guests and there is no reason why the same should not be done for the sponsor's staff, if perhaps on a slightly less lavish scale. If you invest annually in a staff outing, sports day or party, you could simply combine the treat and the sponsorship at very little extra cost.

Staff are more often going to be involved in a sponsorship as the workers rather than the guests because you will need to have company representatives around to entertain customers, make conversation and to make sure everything runs smoothly. More often than not these will be PR, marketing and sales staff. Many sponsoring companies give their area sales managers a number of places at an event which they have to fill and they are then responsible for their own guests. This works very well since the representative has a good opportunity to get to know his customers better.

But don't neglect those lower down the scale. If your secretary has been working until 7.00 p.m. every night to get invitations out for you, don't send her off without a second glance on Friday evening, and then regale her on the following Monday with happy tales of what a good time was had by all at Silverstone over the weekend. She might have been an asset at the event as well.

But do make sure that staff who are going to work at the event do precisely that — work. The event should be enjoyable but the reception desk should not be deserted at 2.15 because that's the time of the first race and Sophie wants to see it. Nor should guests be left to their own devices for hours at a stretch because Trevor finds the bar much more interesting than they are.

Linked promotions and competitions

Not enough sponsors take this aspect of marketing into consideration and yet the right sponsorship can form a totally suitable and attractive theme for any sales promotion campaign.

Once advertising has awoken interest in a product, the purpose of sales promotion is to persuade the potential customer to make a purchase. Where the hand is hesitating between picking up Persil and Brand X, the sales promotion incentive may just tip the balance.

We are all familiar with the sort of schemes that are used by manufacturers of fast moving consumer goods — money-off vouchers, two for the price of one, free draws, competitions, free gifts, on-pack offers and so on. So unless your sponsorship is designed strictly to enhance your corporate image, you should certainly consider sales promotion opportunities offered by a sponsorship. Here are a few examples:

Samples and give-aways

If you're in the fast moving consumer goods market and trying to increase sales or indeed launching a new product, then one of the problems will be persuading people to try it let alone buy it. However, if the sponsorship is at a suitable venue, you have a ready-made sampling audience who will be eager to accept your free 'gift'. Suitable products are fairly obvious but include snacks, sweets, drinks, cigarettes, newspapers and magazines, shampoos, perfumes etc.

Thing about whether you will be able to use the venue staff to give out the sample or whether you should hire promotional staff to do it for you and where they will be sited. The best time to give out gifts is when people arrive and have time to kill, not when they are leaving and anxious to be off. But is the wrapping paper going to cause a massive litter problem?

Consider how you will follow up this sampling test. I can remember going to a big athletics meeting sponsored by a biscuit manufacturer. I was given a sample of an extraordinarily delicious new biscuit as I entered the ground and, craving for more, asked were I could buy a packet. 'Oh, we haven't got any for sale!' I was told.

So, should you have the product on sale at the venue? Should you encourage an increase in stocks in the venue's catchment area in anticipation of increased sales? And should you record and quantify those sales for a period after the event? If it works, it's worth doing elsewhere, if it doesn't, then you need not waste your money.

Sales outlets

As a major sponsor of an event, you will expect to have a very high profile on the occasion with advertising hoardings well in evidence. But you should also consider having a more practical presence, if it is appropriate.

It makes sense for equestrian sponsors such as Barbour, for instance, to have a stand at a three-day event. With the name Barbour on everyone's lips, the urge to purchase a waxed coat may come upon some people and the sales opportunity should not be wasted. The same common sense applies to any product which has an obvious link with the event that is being sponsored. It would not be appropriate for salesmen to go round trying to flog life insurance to opera-goers at Covent Garden but car owners may welcome the sight of an AA caravan at a county show.

If you are, as part of your sponsorship, going to take a sales site at the stadium or venue, you should certainly demand that you have exclusivity as part of the contract and that, as part of the deal, no other raincoat manufacturer, bank or building society ends up in the next stand.

Taking this a stage further, some companies as part of their deal have negotiated a permanent sales outlet on site with total exclusivity to their product. Kodak is such a company who have arrangements with various tourist attractions including Alton Towers where they have sponsored the cable cars as part of their trade agreement for exclusive photographic sales rights to Alton's two and a half million visitors a year.

Displays and literature distribution

Naturally you will not be giving away free samples of video cameras or motor cars but there is still plenty of opportunity for promoting these items. Where the venue is suitable, you may wish to organize a display stand, test drives or demonstrations to inform and encourage potential purchasers. People hanging around waiting for the rugby match to start or the concert to begin are usually eager for some time-consuming amusement.

At some events you may find you stand besieged by children picking up armfuls of literature, wanting to sit in the driver's seat and fiddle with the gears. The temptation is to chase them away as time-wasting but don't be too hasty. Children can sometimes have an extraordinary influence on their parents' purchases, so if you are nasty to little Johnny, Johnny's daddy may just cross out that cheque he was about to write you. Second, Johnny will one day grow up and become a customer and he will remember. How many stories of the rich and famous begin with, 'I knew I wanted a Rolls Royce from the age of seven!' Ambitions for the future sometimes begin at a remarkably young age!

Have something active for people to do or watch on the show stand, like a game of skill, a competition, a draw, a video or other entertainment. Do not follow the example of a stand I saw recently. It was set up by the local community police and consisted of two small piles of unidentifiable literature guarded by two burly uniformed policemen who stood solidly in front of them all day. I think the stand had about two visitors!

Free entry qualifiers

One highly effective way of sponsoring an event is to have an on-pack promotion offering free entry to an event.

Obviously this is only suitable for certain types of event where the venue has the space to cope with large numbers. It would hardly be appropriate for a theatre or indoor concert but would be an excellent way of attracting people to a race meeting, a festival, an outdoor tourist attraction, or an exhibition.

You must first come to some agreement with the event which you are sponsoring about how this free entry will be funded. Will free entry for an estimated 50,000 people be included in the up-front sponsorship fee? Or will you pay them either a full or discounted price for each entry qualifier?

This is the type of promotion which requires considerable advance planning so it is not suitable for a sponsorship arranged at short notice. Advertising and sales promotion agencies will obviously have to be briefed, campaigns designed, media space booked, special wrappers printed, the product distributed, and so on.

You will also need to think about the practicalities at the event. For instance, it may be necessary to reserve one gate or turnstile solely for these special entry tokens to avoid any possibility of dishonesty either by ticket sales staff or by the public. In fact you would be wise to ensure that the qualifiers are invalidated as the visitors hand them over so that they do not mysteriously reappear later in the day! It is important that a promotion which catches the public's imagination isn't ruined by casual management at the final hurdle, so every possible problem needs thinking through.

Given that the promotion is properly advertised, promoted and managed, sales of your video cassettes, gin, car wax, chocolates or stockings should go up measurably. This, coupled with all the other sponsorship elements such as branding at the event, could be an extremely effective way of raising a product's profile.

Competitions

Most types of sponsorship link in very well with competitions. What the sponsorship will give you is a theme with a genuine link with your company or product and the opportunity to offer prizes that come away from the old favourites of cash, cars and holidays.

Sports sponsorships are ideal for this. Prizes such as tickets to major events or competitions, particularly if they are overseas, are likely to draw big entries especially if there is the added spice of meeting some of the 'star' names.

But, if you want to be more original, then think in terms of a prize that cannot be purchased by a member of the public — a ride in a record-breaking car or in the driver's cab of a restored steam engine, a flight in an aerobatics aeroplane or sponsored balloon, a chance to sing with a famous pop group or train with a top rugby team, a private viewing at a new museum or the chance to be the starter at a world record attempt – all these things cost little but will remain in the memory of the winners for ever. They also have a much better chance of attracting media coverage with consequent publicity for the sponsor.

Direct marketing

Many leisure organizations still have not woken up to the fact that direct marketing is an invaluable tool for their own promotion and publicity, let alone for the purposes of providing a unique benefit to potential sponsors. Letters requesting further information are simply answered and discarded, payments by credit card are filed away in the accounts department and mailing lists of members kept in out-of-date ledgers so all these potential customers interested in theatre going or gardening or clog dancing are simply lost souls doomed to enquire yet again if they require further information. Meanwhile, the organization spends its money on media or poster advertising to a mass audience when it might have been far more cost effective to direct mail those who had expressed a firm interest.

But things are improving. Some sports bodies, clubs and entertainment venues are able to offer sponsoring companies an extremely highly targeted audience and, for an appropriate product, direct access to potential purchasers is an extremely valuable benefit.

Some organizations will already have, for instance, a mailing list of members. It may be nothing more sophisticated than that – a list of names and addresses – but it will at least be a list of people who are clearly identified as being interested in golf or opera or motor racing or antiques and the profile of golf players may be exactly the profile of your potential customers.

If you have researched your sponsorship properly, you should have already identified which sponsorship vehicle it is that matches the profile of your customers. Volvo, for instance, identified that golf was the ideal match for their customers.

But you may identify a particular sport or art as a wonderful match and then discover that the method of reaching its audience is not as easy as you might think. Some sports are very well organized and it is easy to reach their participants. Take orienteering, for example. To go orienteering more than once or twice you must be registered as a member of a local club which is affiliated to the British Orienteering Federation. Therefore, the BOF has, on its computer, a membership list of 7000 individuals and families, including information on their sex and age, which could be an invaluable tool to a potential sponsor such as a footwear or sportswear manufacturer, for instance.

157

But orienteering is a comparatively minor sport with very little spectator interest. At the other end of the scale is Britain's national sport, football, watched by some half a million people every week. What a wonderful way to reach an 85 per cent male CD audience, you might conclude. But getting through to them is a marathon of organization. You can't simply say to the Football League, 'I want an advertisement in every football programme' and then deal with one person. You have to liaise with ninety-two clubs at varying levels of efficiency and with varying sizes and styles of publication. The ill-fated football supporters' membership scheme was always going to be a nightmare of administration but it could have provided a huge mailing list of up to one and a half million names and addresses.

So, if you have assessed a particular sport or arts organization (or any other sponsorship vehicle for that matter) as perfect for direct marketing, be very sure that the organization can deliver the goods you want before signing the contract.

First, do they have a membership or mailing list that can form part of the sponsorship package and second, do they actually own it. Hopeful phrases like, 'I'm sure all our affiliated clubs will let you have their membership list if we ask them' are likely to produce a third of those clubs responding with a flat 'no', a third never getting themselves organized and a third sending in lists on everything from computer print-outs to school exercise books. Never rely on lists to be provided by third parties who haven't signed the contract!

If, however, a membership or mailing list is available, then you should check:

- How up-to-date it is. Widows are not amused to receive letters addressed to their husbands.
- Whether several members of the same household are each on the list. Identical letters to husband, wife and three children can cause much irritation and mutterings about 'Waste of money'.
- The recipient's age if this is important to you. Information about high performance sports cars and pop record collections sent to retired people may cause a smile of amusement. Information on football pools and wine clubs sent to children will definitely do you more harm than good. So make absolutely sure that unsuitable recipients can be filtered out.
- If you need any other information from the list. Can the sexes be divided? Can it be divided regionally or into postcode areas if required? Does it register anything else such as the number of bookings made, method of transport used. In fact anything that will help you, the sponsor.
- How the list is kept? These days the chances are that it will be

on computer and you should be able to get a print-out or labels or the information transferred on to a disk that matches your own set-up. But do not assume that this is the case and find yourself presented with a handwritten ledger or a jumbled box of file cards.

Some organizations may be unwilling to let you have a copy of their mailing list (perhaps because of the Data Protection Act) but will mail your material for you. This is much easier in one way although you have less control in others. For instance, if it is very important that your mailing is received before 1 April, you must be very sure that your sponsee has not delayed his own mailing until 2 April because he's decided to wait for another enclosure to be printed to save postage.

You should also be clear whether this service is included in your sponsorship fee or whether you are expected to pay for postage, print-outs, envelopes and handling.

If no mailing list exists, is there some vehicle that will enable you to create your own? For instance, is there a magazine, handbook or programme in which you could advertise or put an insertion to solicit a response? Are there entry points to the stadium or the venue where you might station staff to give out competition entry or survey forms. At smaller venues such as squash clubs, is there a noticeboard or registration point where you could place posters or literature. This method will naturally not guarantee the 100 per cent coverage of a mailing list but on the other hand it will pick up those many people who are just casual visitors to a venue and not card-carrying members, season-ticket holders or on a mailing list.

Research

'Many companies have recognized an important role for sponsorship and have made adequate provisions in terms of finance and staffing to resource it efficiently,' says Ken Parker, Director of Research Services Ltd. But he then qualifies it with the ominous words, 'Yet there are still a number of organizations undertaking expensive sponsorship without having clearly defined pre-determined objectives.' The net result of this laxity is that if there are no clearly stated objectives then it is difficult, even impossible, to measure the effectiveness of that sponsorship.

'Most major sponsorships undertaken today are by companies who wish to communicate to wide audiences. I believe that the objectives should, therefore, fit within four main headings: to establish or increase brand or company awareness; to create or strengthen brand image; to communicate a message to specified targets; to provide corporate hospitality facilities.

'In order to measure the effectiveness of sponsorship against the first three objectives, two basic approaches could be used.

'Dipstick research which is conducted at specific points in time, for example just before the sponsorship and immediately after it. The subtraction of the first stage findings from the second gives the result. This method, while being a useful indicator, does not, however, give the long-term effects as, for example, tracking study research which is continual monitoring of performance over time. For instance, RSL's Sponsorship Tracking Study monitors all the leading sports and arts sponsorships and sponsors. This allows a sponsor not only to evaluate his own performance but to compare it with the performance of others in the same field.'

- Spontaneous awareness of sponsorships
- Brand prompted awareness of sponsorships
- Event prompted awareness of sponsorships
- And most importantly the effect of sponsorship on brand or company image'

A tracking study is only going to be of use in a major sponsorship. Ken Parker himself suggests £250,000 million as a guideline. So a company spending £50,000 or even £150,000 on a sponsorship has to look for other methods of measurement. For instance, Fez Labady, marketing services manager for the Birmingham Midshires Building Society says, 'I am simply interested in local media coverage. We do a number of small sponsorships in the West Midlands area and in return for our money we expect the organization we are sponsoring to make sure that the event and our name get into the media.'

Ken Parker believes it is important to maximize the number of mentions in the media but not to use it as a proxy for effectiveness. He quotes the example of the 1990 World Cup – 'There were ten sponsors each paying the same for the sponsorship but not getting the same level of exposure from perimeter board advertising. In the UK only two – Coca-Cola and Mars – achieved respective levels of sponsorship awareness and attained positive effects on their image. The remainder did not support the sponsorship effectively and achievements in the UK were low.'

That seems a perfectly reasonable and achievable result which can be measured in terms of space or name mentions. Other sponsors may have other criteria or even a number of criteria.

But whether you are spending £2,000 or £2 million, the message is the same. Set reasonable objectives and make sure that you can somehow measure them.

Your company is almost certainly conducting some form of research already, in which case you may need to look no further than your current market reasssurance consultancy for advice and expertise. The problem is that there are many different kinds of research and just as sponsorship consultants often specialize in a particular area so do researchers.

If in doubt about where to start, try the Market Research Society. They publish an excellent free booklet called *Organisations and Individuals Providing Market Research Services*. Not only does it explain the different types of research but it also explains how to brief a researcher and lists over 400 consultancies and the services they offer in some detail. It is available from MRS, 15 Northburgh Street, London EC1V 0AM (Telephone 071 490 4911).

Put all the information in a smart folder and it will arrive as an exciting package waiting to be opened.

7 Finding a sponsor

What can you offer?

This book is principally intended for sponsors and potential sponsors but essentially sponsorship is a buyers' market, so there are many more people seeking sponsorship than there are companies anxiously looking for someone or something to sponsor.

Every large company managing a package of sponsorships will tell you that each day brings a mailbag of hopefuls asking for money to finance some venture or other. Most of these have a very short life indeed, in fact about as long as it takes to travel from desk to wastepaper basket. Many are badly worded, badly presented, are inappropriate or offer little in the way of benefits to the sponsor and, in fact, are a complete waste of time for all concerned. By now you will have read the preceding chapters which detail exactly what a sponsor should aim to achieve from his sponsorship. From this you will have realized that it is not simply a question of a company handing over a large cheque in order to achieve a warm feeling of benevolence. The decision is made, or should be made, for very hard-nosed business reasons to achieve proper objectives.

Time and time again, I have heard sponsorship seekers when asked what fee they have in mind saying, 'Well, we need £120,000 to cover our expedition expenses' or 'I really need £50,000 a year to enter all the top competitions.' The firm message to all those looking for a sponsor is – *it's not what you want, it's what you can offer.*

To give you an analogy, it would be like a newspaper offering advertising on the basis that they need to fund the news-gathering of their reporters, or a restaurant pricing its meals on the total cost of all the food purchased for the day. So, in this case, it is generally a question of purchasing a number of benefits for an all-inclusive sponsorship fee.

Many people confuse 'sponsorship' with 'donations' simply

because sponsorship is an oft-misunderstood word used to disguise a request for a money.

For instance, it is common practice for people to run marathons, swim multiple lengths of swimming baths, slim drastically and otherwise set themselves targets to raise money for charity. You'll have been asked many times yourself 'Will you sponsor me to run in the local fun run on Saturday?' and you'll have filled in a form committing yourself to ten pence a mile knowing perfectly well that you are actually handing over a donation. A donation is money or goods handed over with no expectation of benefits. Sponsorship is the payment of fee with *every* expectation of benefits, even if they merely involve the creation of corporate goodwill! The trouble is that once the word sponsorship becomes misused in this way, companies have every justification in viewing all requests for money with deep suspicion.

So your first task as a sponsorship seeker must be to ask yourself what benefits you or your organization can offer and to equate these benefits with value for money. Incidentally, benefits don't necessarily have to be tangible. If a company is seeking to improve its image, then the benefit could very well be that the sponsorship will project them as contributing something to the community without apparent reward.

On the following pages you will find checklists of possible sponsorship benefits which you may be able to offer. These are simply starters to set you thinking because hopefully you will be able to add further benefits of your own.

Answer honestly; just because *you* are so involved in your sport or expedition or film, do not assume that everyone else is going to be obsessed by it too. That is highly unlikely – the decision will almost certainly be made on your ability to reach a target audience suitable to your potential sponsor.

Before you start ticking off sections of the lists, it may help you to go back to Chapter 2 which details some of the advantages of sponsorship. Although they are all unlikely to be appropriate to the 'product' that you are offering, they will at least give you some clues.

Before you begin, let's also have a look at some of the reasons why companies say 'No' without appearing to give you a chance to put your case:

- The sponsorship will not, in any way, help them achieve their objectives.
- The sponsorships they are being offered simply do not match either the target audience they are trying to reach, or the message that they are trying to communicate.

- They have a firm sponsorship policy and your sponsorship does not fit their criteria. For example, they only sponsor projects involving the environment and the disabled; they do not sponsor individuals; they only sponsor amateur and not professional sport; etc.
- They confuse sponsorship with donation, assuming that they are being asked for money with very little return for their investment.
- They receive hundreds of sponsorship proposals every year – most of them total non-starters because they are so unprofessional in the way that they are presented and worded and principally because they offer so little in the way of benefits.
- They are concerned that if they are seen to sponsor one sport, event or project they will be an immediate target for other sponsorship-seekers. It seems easier to have a 'No sponsorship' policy.
- They see 'sponsorship' as somehow frivolous and are concerned that staff will react badly if the company is having to draw its belt in in other ways such as through redundancies.
- They are genuinely unaware of all the benefits that sponsorship can bring and how it can slot into the company's marketing and corporate communications policies.
- If they *are* aware of all the ways in which sponsorship can be used, then they will also know that it will mean the involvement of a large number of executives from chairman down to brand manager and that someone will be required to spend considerable time coordinating everything.
- The executive who has to make the sponsorship decision may simply feel that he does not have the time to mastermind putting all these options into practice, even if he does not have to manage everything himself.
- Some sponsorships require a considerable amount of executive time to be spent entertaining clients and often this entertaining has to be done during evenings or weekends. An afternoon out at a football match can sound fun but it may become very wearing if you are required to be there every Saturday. (But, conversely, to a soccer fan it could be sheer bliss.)
- The executive who makes the final decision may be personally prejudiced against the proposed sponsorship simply because he isn't interested in pop music or yachting or rare butterflies. And, although personal prejudice or favour shouldn't enter into a sponsorship decision, there is no doubt that it often does!

Sponsorship seeker's checklist

Audiences reached

This is going to be a vital element of your sponsorship proposal, so it is extremely important that you think carefully before filling in the answers. If necessary, do some research and gather any information you can from your national organization.

Sports and arts

1 Where are the participants or spectators in your sport or art form? (Be specific about areas or countries.)
    Locally
    Nationwide
    In Europe
    Worldwide

2 How many people participate in your sport or art form?
    Locally
    Nationwide
    In Europe
    Worldwide

3 How many people watch your sport or art form live?
    Locally
    Nationwide
    In Europe
    Worldwide

4 How many people watch your sport or art form on TV?
    Regionally
    Nationwide
    In Europe
    Worldwide

5 What type of TV is this? (Name networks and channels, if possible.)
    Regional
    Networked ITV
    BBC Regional
    BBC National
    Satellite
    Cable
    European
    Worldwide

6 How many people follow your sport or art form through results, media reports and reviews even if they neither participate nor spectate?

  Locally
  Nationwide
  In Europe
  Worldwide

Give annual figures broken down into population totals, then percentages of males, females and, if possible, the age ranges. If you are looking for a sponsorship for a club, team, competition, event or individual, then give the total figures plus additional figures for the more specific requirement. (For example, 400,000 per annum watch Rugby League Football live every week during the season and Wiggington average gate is 9437.)

7 What equipment are the participants in this sport or art form likely to buy (e.g. rackets, boots, skis, clothing)?

8 Is there any product that the participants in this sport or art form are highly likely to buy (e.g. drinks, chocolate, glucose tablets)?

9 Are there any products that the spectators or audience of this sport or art form are particularly likely to buy (e.g. drinks, tobacco, foods, clothing, vehicles)?

10 What demographic profile are the participants, spectators and viewers?

 You may not be able to give entirely accurate answers to these questions yourself (the sponsoring company will know exactly where its market lies) but it will at least help you to focus your mind on the type of company to approach. For instance, if the Pony Club Camps are principally attended by girls aged between ten and fourteen it is a waste of time approaching Johnnie Walker or Benson & Hedges.

Books

1 How many people will buy/read your book?
  Locally
  Nationwide
  In Europe
  Worldwide

2 Is it aimed at any particular target markets (e.g. do-it-yourself enthusiasts, gardeners, antique collectors)?

3 Is it timed to coincide with any particular event or anniversary (e.g. the launching of a liner, the end of a war, the death of a famous personality)?

Expedition and record attempts

1 How many people will be following your expedition or record attempt?

Within your specialist area
Nationwide
In Europe
Worldwide
2   Will the venture be using special equipment (e.g. clothing, food, boats, survival gear, insurance)?
3   Do the followers of such a venture buy similar equipment?

Museums and tourist attractions

1   How many people will visit your attraction each year? (Break down into groups if possible, e.g. adults, children, foreign visitors.)
2   Are these groups likely to be the purchasers of any particular products at your attraction (e.g. food, drink, films, souvenirs)?
3   Are they likely to be purchasers of any specific products in general (e.g. fast foods, sweets, soft drinks)?

Conservation, environmental, community and charity projects

1   How many people are directly involved in the project (e.g. setting up bottle banks, creating cycle paths or running rescue services)?
2   How many are indirectly involved (e.g. using bottle banks, likely to use cycle paths, collecting or giving funds to the charity)?.

Image

What sort of image does your sport, art form or sponsorship project convey (e.g. young, old, upper class, aggressive, fast, gentle, caring, green, community-conscious, dare-devil, refined, safe, family)?

This is an extremely important point for a potential sponsor since, not only does your audience have to match the target audience he is trying to reach, but the sponsorship you are offering must also match the image he wishes to create. For example, if Dior wish to present themselves as high class and sophisticated, they are certainly not going to consider banger racing as a possible sponsorship.

Advertising and promotional opportunities

In what ways could the name of your sponsor be promoted?
1   In the title of the event or attraction (e.g. The Cornhill Test, The Rumbelow's Cup, The Guinness World of Records, *The Shell Guide to the Countryside*).
2   On the clothing of the participants (e.g. sports shirts, expedition gear, museum attendants' uniforms)?

3   On advertising hoardings within or outside the venue (e.g. round the perimeter of the track or pitch, above the main entrance, on the roof, on the walls)?
4   Incorporated within advertising for the event or attraction (e.g. newspapers, magazines, posters, leaflets, direct mail).
5   Incorporated in publications linked with the event or attraction (e.g. programmes, fixture cards, information leaflets, guides, maps, follow-up books)?
6   Incorporated in other information material linked to the event or attraction (e.g. videos, slides, photographs, postcards, films)?
7   Incorporated in clothing and souvenirs linked with the sport, team, arts group etc. (e.g. replica sports clothing, souvenirs, badges)?

Direct marketing opportunities

1   Does your sponsorship project have names and addresses on a database or mailing list (e.g. club members, requests for information)? If so, what information does it contain?
2   If you sell tickets or supply information, do you keep a record of such requests in any other way, such as a card index or letters file?
3   Does that audience buy a regular magazine or programme for information on your sport, club, event, etc?
4   Have you any other method of reaching people (e.g. door-to-door leaflet delivery, distribution of literature at entrance to a venue)?

Sales promotion opportunities

1   Will there be opportunities to promote to the spectators/audience at your events?
2   Will there be purchase opportunities for the sponsor's product at stalls, exhibition stands, shops?
3   Will there be opportunities to hand out samples or literature to the audience or crowd?
4   Will there be on-pack ticket offers for your event?
5   Will there be competitions linked with the event?
6   Will you or members of your team be willing to be involved in the sponsor's own events (e.g. sales conferences, exhibitions, factory visits)?

Star status and prestige

Individuals

1 Are you a household name without having to be identified as, for instance, cricketer, painter, mountaineer (e.g. Ian Botham, David Hockney, Chris Bonnington)?
2 Are you well known by those interested in your field (e.g. First Division footballer, county cricketer, successful artist, author or playwright)?
3 Are you fairly well known by those interested in your field?
4 Are you relatively unknown?

Teams/orchestras/groups

1 Is your team/orchestra/group well known:
   Locally
   Nationwide
   In Europe
   Worldwide
2 Is it performing in an area of major interest (e.g. football, Grand Prix motor racing, international concert halls)?
3 Is it performing in an area of specialist interest (e.g. contemporary dance, real tennis, medical research)?

Endorsements

1 Will you as an individual, or your team, be willing to endorse the sponsor's product?
2 Is there likely to be any conflict of interest with other sponsors or advertisers?

Merchandising

Will there be any opportunity for the sponsor to take part in a joint merchandising scheme for clothing or souvenirs or other related products?

Client entertainment

1 Will your event be a suitable occasion for your sponsor to entertain clients?
2 What facilities will you be able to offer?
   Best seats

Private boxes
Private suites
Marquees
Bar facilities
Buffet facilities
Full dining facilities on the premises or nearby

3   Will your sponsor and his guests be able to get 'behind the scenes'?
4   Will they be able to meet some of the star performers?
5   Will your sponsor be able to receive an extra allocation of tickets for major events for customers and staff?

Miscellaneous benefits

1   Will your sponsor have exclusive rights to you or your event or will he be competing with numerous other co-sponsors and advertisers?
2   Will he be able to have a 'no competitive advertising' clause in the contract?

Media coverage

Will your sport, art form, event, expedition, attraction etc. be covered by the media? (Note whether this is likely to be regularly, occasionally or rarely.)

● National TV
● Regional TV
● National newspapers
● Regional newspapers
● Local newspapers
● National magazines
● Specialist press/magazines
● In-house newspapers/members mailing lists

If you start making notes as you follow the above lists, I think you'll be pleasantly surprised at all the benefits that you could offer a potential sponsor and you will no doubt be able to think of benefits other than those listed.

The more facts and figures you produce and the more creative suggestions you make, the more likely an organization is to be impressed with your professionalism. But don't bombard them immediately with all this, just have it to hand if necessary. If you don't have the information at your fingertips, then do some research and find out − even if it means investing money to do so. If, for instance, you want to run a National Pub Games Championship, then a potential sponsor will need to know how many people play pub games, how many pubs offer what variety, the profile of the participants and so on.

What you should end up with then, is some notes which may look something like this:

National Pub Games Championship

Let us assume that you represent the National Publicans Association and your members would like to do something to encourage more people to use pubs on Mondays and Tuesdays, and to encourage them to come in earlier in the evenings.

You envisage a National Pub Games Championship. Teams from competing pubs would play on a home and away knock-out basis, locally, then regionally culminating in a national final comprising the sixteen top teams. You have already spoken to the TV companies and they are interested in the possibility of televising the finals.

Each pub enters a team of four in any of the games to find the national darts, shove-ha'penny, pool, bar billiards, skittles and petanque champions. Additionally the sixteen finalists will also be required to compete in a multidiscipline competition to find the Pub Games Champions of the Year.

You don't have the money to finance this as an organization although naturally you have access to all your members so encouraging entry will not be a problem.

You therefore have to look for a sponsor. Obviously a brewery will not be a suitable sponsor because there will be a competitive advertising situation. A competition sponsored by Watneys won't stand much chance in Courage pubs. A spirits or soft drinks company with a broad-based distribution pattern is a strong possibility; a snack supplier or a tobacco manufacturer are other likely candidates. So what you need to do is to put together a package to suit any of those options and then refine it as you go along. Your sponsorship notes will probably look something like this:

Audiences

(Note: The figures are fictitious.)
- 23,000,000 people over eighteen visit a pub at least once a year.
- 12,000,000 visit once a week or more.
- 8,000,000 visit virtually every day.
- 6,000,000 play pub games occasionally.

- 4,000,000 play pub games regularly.
- 90,000 are members of pub games' teams.
- There are 50,000 pubs in the UK.
- Over 30,000 of them have facilities for one or more games:

Darts	23,000
Pool	17,000
Bar billiards	1,000
Skittles	400
Petanque	200
Shove ha'penny	1,800

- 53 per cent of a pub's clientele drink beer (52 per cent beer, 41 per cent lager, 11 per cent stout).
- 37 per cent drink spirits (43 per cent gin, 28 per cent whisky, 12 per cent vodka, 10 per cent Bacardi, 9 per cent others).
- 23 per cent drink wine (45 per cent wine, 55 per cent fortified wines).
- 85 per cent buy snacks regularly.
- 42 per cent smoke.

Image

- Adult
- Alcohol
- Social
- Fun
- Competitive
- Participatory
- Entertaining
- Make friends
- Travel
- British tradition

Advertising opportunities

- The name of the event e.g. 'The Dry Ice National Pub Games Championship'.
- Promotional posters for the event at each pub.
- Fixture cards for the event.
- Finals day programme.
- Sponsor's name on finalists' shirts or kit.
- National and regional advertising of the event.

Sales promotion opportunities

- Special promotional evenings on the nights of the local and regional competitions to include extra displays, samplings and simple competitions and draws.
- Linked merchandising sales such as T-shirts, baseball caps, badges etc.
- Celebrity visits to regional finals to throw the first dart or shove the first ha'penny.

Client entertainment

Opportunities for client entertainment at the finals e.g. best seats at the venue, lunch, meet the teams, meet the stars.

Media coverage

- Extensive coverage in local papers of local rounds, regional papers of regional rounds and national papers of the final.
- Regional TV and radio coverage of the regional finals.
- National TV and radio coverage of the finals.
- Feature coverage in general and specialist magazines and programmes.

That was purely an imaginary example but you, too, could now have the beginnings of a package to offer your potential sponsor. The next step is to turn it into a proposal.

The proposal document

Your proposal document should reflect the sponsorship you are presenting. It would, for instance, be ridiculous to circulate a full-colour brochure, if you are simply seeking £10,000 to fund a local point-to-point meeting. Equally, it would be totally unprofessional to send out a photocopied letter if you were offering a £5,000,000 Grand National sponsorship.

What the reader of your document will want is something which explains exactly what you are offering logically, informatively and, above all, briefly. In other words: This is the 'product' (the sport, event, book, museum), this is the sponsorship we can offer you alongside the product, these are the sponsorship benefits and this is how much it will cost.

It sounds so logical and simple but very few documents actually run to that pattern. I have seen numerous beautifully-produced sponsorship brochures mailed out by organizations which tell you all about the wonderful work they are doing and talk vaguely about 'sponsorship opportunities' and then don't tell you what sort of benefits a sponsor will get or how much the organization expects to receive for those benefits. The onus is then on the potential sponsor to think up his own benefits and guess how much to offer. But who would be bothered? Alan Preece, formerly Public Relations Controller for Asda, confirms this: 'One of the biggest faults I find in proposals is that people won't tell you what they want. They wax lyrical about their organization without coming to any conclusion and telling you what they need. Somehow you're supposed to work it out!'

At the other end of the scale, I regularly receive handwritten or photocopied proposal documents from individuals such as the Barsetshire County Champion Windsurfer who need £5,000 to compete in the UK National Championships and in return will 'be very pleased to help the sponsor in any way including making personal appearances.' And who wouldn't give their right arm to meet the Barsetshire County Champion Windsurfer?

As mass mailings of sponsorship proposals tend to look exactly what they are – mass mailings – they have a very low success rate. If you are asking for a large sum of money, then it is only courteous to write personally with a well-presented document.

It is not necessary to have this printed – it is much better to get it typed on a word processor, then it can be individually altered and tailored to whoever you are approaching. Use plain A4 paper, typed on one side only and with generous margins in which the sponsor can make notes. If you then fit the sheets neatly into a thin card presentation cover, you have a perfectly adequate and suitable document.

Start with the background to the event or whatever it is you are offering for sponsorship and make it short and to the point. Who? Why? What? Where? When? are the good old journalist's maxims you should apply. A page is ideal, two is more than enough. James Poole, Head of Corporate Affairs for Barclays Bank receives 500 sponsorship proposals a month and says, 'What I want is the facts: the need for the money, the benefits, the timescale and the cost – preferably on one sheet of paper!'

Follow on with the sponsorship opportunity: who the participants are, who the audience will be – how many; what demographic profile they are; what image your 'product' conjures up.

Then list the benefits: reaching the target audience; creating an image; the advertising and sales promotion opportunities; the suitability for client entertainment; the media coverage and so on. But say also that you are prepared to be flexible in order to accommodate any particular requirements a sponsor may have.

Finally state the terms of the contract — the timescale and the fee. You may feel uncertain about how much to ask for and how long the sponsorship should be for. Briefly, in terms of time, a year is too short, ten years is probably too long and something around three years is usually ideal and acceptable to a sponsor.

In terms of a fee, you have to equate what you are offering with what it's worth to your client, so try to put a figure on that. One way of doing it is to try to put a figure on every benefit you are giving and total it up at the end so that you can judge a sensible fee to quote. But sometimes it is simply a question of gut feeling and knowing what else is happening in the market. The tangible benefits may not appear to add up to very much but, particularly in the case of environmental or charity sponsorships, the sponsor is likely to see an element of corporate responsibility in his fee so it becomes partly a donation and he is, therefore, less likely to be sticky about the price. On the other, he is far more likely to ask for a budget of where his sponsorship fee is to be spent.

Some companies accept sponsorship fees quoted without a murmur, others can be very difficult.

I've seen it both ways. One managing director I know spends £3,000,000 a year on advertising and £500,000 on PR without a query but insisted that he got a penny by penny breakdown of the value of the benefits of a £20,000 sponsorship in terms of advertising, sales promotion and public relations.

On the other hand, I've seen a company sign away £250,000 without comment for what appeared to be some very minor benefits.

Once you have written your proposal, your next major task will be to compile a list of potential sponsors. But there is one short cut which is worth trying before you spend too much time on this and that is to create a situation where sponsors come to you. This means publicity and you can either pay for it through advertising or try to persuade suitable press to make a story out of it.

In this instance, advertising probably means the specialist marketing press, or the trade press of likely industries. It also means a financial outlay which you may not be able to afford. The best options are *PR Week* or *Sponsorship Insights* which both have sponsorship seeker classified advertising sections.

The marketing and communications press may also publish editorial details of your sponsorship if it is interesting enough, but this tends to be the exception rather than the rule. You are more likely to be successful with your local paper or with the trade press of the industries you feel are likely targets, again providing there is an interesting story to be told. From a local news point of view, an angle such as 'Town's famous athletics club to close unless sponsor can be found' may jog a nearby company into becoming your saviour and thus attracting considerable local goodwill. From a trade point of view 'New pop museum seeks music industry partner' may attract a sponsor ever on the lookout for publicity.

Sometimes – rarely – you may be lucky enough to make the national media. Eddie 'The Eagle' Edwards managed to get several stories in the national sports pages both about himself and his subsistence-level existence for the sake of his sport. But Britain's first ski-jumper, and the world's worst at that, is a grand story anyway so don't count on such luck if you are looking for sponsorship as fifth-placed driver in the South Derbyshire Motor Club rally. Sponsors are looking for big successes – Eddie Edwards excepted!

If media publicity fails, or if you don't wish to use that method for some reason, start approaching companies on an individual basis. First, jot down the likely areas of attack. For instance, if you want to publish a book on slimming, don't list doughnut makers; think in terms of slimming magazines, slimming clubs, low-calorie drinks manufacturers, low calorie food manufacturers, leisure wear manufacturers and so on.

A few obvious names will come to mind but you will need to do some research to come up with a reasonable list. There are many directories, publications and organizations which list this very information. But your most helpful source of information could be your family, friends or colleagues. Check what contacts they have in your chosen fields or if they know anyone in the advertising or public relations business who may be able to find out for you. Milk your contacts for all they are worth – as the saying goes 'It's who you know.' If all else fails, throw yourself upon the mercy of the specialist magazine which covers the particular industry you want to approach and ask for some leads – some names of companies producing slimming products, some leisure wear manufacturers. The chances are that you'll get a few names at least and maybe even some publicity.

As an alternative to approaching a company direct, an often more effective route is to go through their agencies or consultancies. Look at *Hobson's Sponsorship Yearbook* and *Hollis Press and Public Relations Annual* which will give you an idea of which consultancies are handling which clients and, if any are appropriate, try going down this route. As far as the bigger sponsorship consultancies are concerned, it may be worth sending them a brief sponsorship proposal to keep on file. It may never see the light of day but, on the other hand, it's entirely possible that a client will suddenly make a decision to go in for a particular type of sponsorship and the consultancy will be required to come up with suitable ideas at very short notice. So your file could be a life-saver for them as well as for you. But check first what the consultancy requires from you, who it should be sent to and – important – whether they charge a commission or not.

Some consultancies act only on behalf of their clients and will therefore not charge you a commission, but equally they will not actively go out looking for sponsors for you. Your proposal is simply likely to remain on file for possible future reference. Some consultancies will charge you a commission which can range from 10 to 30 per cent of the sponsorship fee, but even so your proposal may remain on file for ever. And the less you require in terms of a fee the less effort the agency is going to put into finding you a sponsor. Thirty per cent of £1 million is worth having, 10 per cent of £1,000 is not even worth opening the file drawer for!

There is a further alternative, which is that if you represent a prestigious enough organization or are a personality in your own right – national sports organization, regional theatre, major charity, well-known artist – the consultancy may suggest that it takes you on as a client in your own right and actively seeks sponsorship for you on a fee basis. This is expensive and you may not be prepared to take the financial risk but it does guarantee time and expertise spent on your behalf in looking for sponsors. See Chapter 4 if you are interested in pursuing this route. You may not have to pay a straight fee – a combination of fee and commission may be acceptable instead.

If you want to pursue the do-it-yourself method of finding a sponsor, then little points can make a big difference between success and failure. For instance, whether you are approaching a company direct or through a consultancy, it is important that your proposal should be addressed to the right person. 'The Managing Director' isn't good enough. Nameless individuals tend not to feel so obliged to reply as those who are addressed personally. In the case of a smallish company, your best bet is to phone and ask for the managing director's secretary, who will know better than anyone who does what in the company, and ask her for the name and title of the person responsible for sponsorship. If she says that the company has no sponsorships, ask for the name of the person responsible for marketing or public relations. Make sure that you get the spelling right. You may have a wonderful sponsorship to offer but addressing someone as Smith instead of Smythe will put you at the back of the field straight away. In the case of a very big company, I'd suggest you phone the public relations department for the same information. A few companies, such as Mars, will refuse to give you the names of individuals so you may have to use back-door methods of obtaining this information or be reduced to addressing letters to the marketing department.

But in most cases this will not be a problem. So you then need to put your proposal to Mr Smythe and opinions here differ on the best method of approach. Should you call, should you phone, should you write?

Personal callers who 'drop in' without appointments are likely to get short shrift ninety-nine times out of a 100 and, although it can sometimes work, it is something of a time-wasting gamble.

You may like to both write and phone but which comes first is really up to your personal preference and self-confidence. If you can put yourself over as likeable, warm and confident, then it certainly does no harm to phone first and then your follow-up letter will be expected and read.

The difficulty is likely to be getting through to your prospect. Some executives prefer to answer their own telephones in which case you will have no problem speaking to the person concerned. Others like a secretary to field their calls and particularly to ward off sales people. So, Mr Smythe's secretary will first ask your name and what company you are from. If she recognizes neither, you may get, 'Can you tell me what it's about?' Long explanations about sponsorship of windsurfers will almost certainly result in, 'I'm afraid Mr Smythe is out and may not be back for some time – a very long time! Please could you write in.'

If you do get through to the decision maker, think first about structuring the call without sounding as though you're selling double-glazing. Many executives can be charming and helpful, others (even those in public relations) seem to take a singularly nasty enjoyment in putting people down and that can be a disheartening experience.

The chairman of one of the major insurance companies recommends that you should 'Find out a company's policy before wasting their time and yours by sending off a proposal. For instance, we're in the business of insurance and, in terms of life insurance, obviously we like people to live longer. Therefore while we might, for example, be interested in sponsoring research into heart disease, we wouldn't contemplate motor racing.'

That's sound advice. If you can't speak to your prospect himself, then you may well be able to speak to a public relations officer or a marketing assistant who will have a good idea of the company's corporate communications or marketing policy and of the sort of sponsorship areas it may be interested in. They will certainly be able to send you a company brochure, house journal and annual report which will again provide you with useful information.

Armed with this knowledge, you can now send off your proposal, tailored to your chosen company's policy and requirements.

Don't just go for one potential sponsor and wait expectantly for their enthusiastic reply — you'll be disappointed. Write to batches at a time; follow up with a phone call if you don't hear within two or three weeks so that you can cross them off your list. Many companies are very good at responding but you won't always get the courtesy of a reply. Sales people (for that's what you are to a potential sponsor) are expected to chase if they are really keen.

You may have to go through this tedious procedure dozens of times before you get a break or you may strike lucky first time. But your chances of a lucky strike will be that much greater if your proposal document is professionally presented and you appear to have at least some knowledge about the company you are contacting.

Don't be too disheartened by negative responses. You'll learn as you go along and may have to adjust your proposal and your fee accordingly. Many companies, long experienced in fielding sponsorship proposals, simply send out an obviously word-processed letter which covers everything from mountaineering to mud-wrestling: 'Thank you for you letter ... blah ... unable to assist you ... blah ... sorry to disappoint you ... blah ... wish you every success with this venture.' Others have the infuriating habit of glancing at your proposal, seeing the dread word 'sponsorship' and passing it straight on to their charitable trust. You can spend hours working out a commercial proposition, emphasize all the opportunities for advertising, sales promotion and client entertainment, address it personally to the marketing director, and then get a letter back from someone called 'donations coordinator' stating 'I'm sorry we don't undertake any form of commercial sponsorship.' It's like going to buy a pair of shoes and being told by the shop that they don't sell apples!

Some PR-orientated companies, however, are more helpful and give clues on why they are saying 'no' and, if a pattern emerges, you may need to rethink. For instance, a sponsorship proposal for a commercial tourist publication sent, amongst others to a petrol company and a fast food chain, received one absurd and one quite helpful response. The petrol company stated that they had 'discussed your letter with our Appeals and Donations Committee but regret we are unable to respond positively to you in this instance.' The fast food chain was more blunt but gave a helpful clue: 'We do not feel that the uptake will be from our core target market of 18–34, C1/C2 people.'

From time to time, you may find that the boot is on the other foot and someone, usually from a PR consultancy, is phoning you and asking what you have available in the way of sponsorship. This is because there is an increasing, and welcome, trend for clients to brief their consultancies to take a more pro-active look at sponsorship as a communications option.

What usually happens is that the consultancy phones a dozen suitable charities, sports or arts organizations for proposals and ideas. The PR executives always exude charm and enthusiasm and invariably need something 'by tomorrow' because, as ever, they have left everything to the last minute. Full of excitement, you drop everything to work slavishly to produce suitable proposals, send off irreplaceable slides and other material by special delivery and then wait anxiously for the result.

Ninety-nine times out of 100 the result is a resounding silence, for the majority of PR consultancies never bother to extend the courtesy of telling you that your proposal has been turned down, or even to return your precious material. And, if you phone up to find out what's happened, you'll find that the executive who was once so friendly is suddenly always 'in a meeting' and never returns your calls.

Frankly, this doesn't say much for those consultancies who don't practise what they preach — good public relations — so they're the ones to avoid when your organization is itself looking for a consultancy! But, irritating though it may be, it is worth trying to provide what is required for that one in a hundred times when you do hit the jackpot. A PR or sponsorship consultancy or advertising agency has usually built up a good relationship with their client so that what they recommend has added weight. And that in turn should make for a much more rewarding relationship between you and the sponsor.

On the happy day that a consultancy or a company shows interest, this is the point where you must arrange a meeting and probably on your territory since your potential sponsor will need to see what it is you are offering and where and how you operate.

Don't be casual about it. If he's coming to look at your rugby club, make sure that he sees it on a match day where there is plenty of excitement and atmosphere; if he's going to sponsor your orchestra, take him to a concert which is going to be sold out; if you want him to sponsor your museum, then take him on a day when the place is bursting with visitors. If your project is entirely new, then produce visuals, plans, maps, slides, people — anything to bring it to life. Prime all the people your potential sponsor will meet beforehand so that they know exactly what is going on and won't make terrible gaffes like 'If we don't get some money pretty quickly, I'll be out of a job!' or 'Huh! I suppose you'll be wanting us to have 'sponsored by Doggy-Dins' on our dinner jackets then?'

Your sponsor will not only be interested in the material benefits of what is on offer, he will also want to get an impression of the people who will make it work. If that impression is a negative one, then it's goodbye!

However, if your potential sponsor seems positive and asks plenty of questions about sites for hoardings, availability of tickets for clients and so on, then he is obviously very interested and will want to arrange a further meeting to discuss the details.

Advertising agency and public relations staff may be despatched to sort out the details and, between you, you should be able to come up with a list of benefits which must then be turned into a contract.

Unless you're a one-man band asking for a very low sponsorship fee, it is advisable to involve a lawyer to turn your list into a legal document. It is unlikely that your solicitor will have had much experience of sponsorship contracts but he should be able to spot any pitfalls or anomalies that you may miss. If you have friendly relations with any organizations which already have sponsors, you should also ask their advice on ambiguous situations which may arise because they may already have been through it, in which case their experience will be invaluable. Similarly, governing bodies and parent organizations should be able to offer expertise.

One final point, once the contract is signed and the first cheque handed over, please don't heave a sigh of relief and forget all about it. Your organization is being paid a large sum of money to make that sponsorship work. Your sponsor will have delegated people to do just that from his end but he will expect, quite rightly, to receive a considerable input from you and your staff.

If you want to know what I mean, go back and read Chapter 6 again which details numerous ways of maximizing a sponsorship. The more you can generate ideas and publicity for your sponsor, the more likely he is to sign for a further period – which is precisely what you want.

8 Working in sponsorship

If you've read this book right from the beginning, you'll by now have realized that there are many aspects to sponsorship and that the sort of knowledge you require is quite wide-ranging.

Most of the people I've met who are hoping to 'work in sponsorship' are young people, usually in their early twenties, who are dying to get a job in sport. And why not? It's much more fun working with something that you enjoy and can relate to than with widget production.

Let's first look at the types of jobs that are available in sponsorship.

Sponsorship consultancies

These are companies which have an expertise in all aspects of sponsorship, so can advise clients on obtaining the best value from their sponsorship, maximizing all the benefits and managing it for them. Some act as brokers for sponsees looking for sponsors and these are usually known as sports marketing agencies rather than consultancies. Some act as both agencies and consultancies.

You are likely to find the following people working in sponsorship consultancies.

Managing director

The managing director will have had many years of experience in the business in all areas. He will have an enormous range of contacts in sport, arts, in companies and organizations and will be the main provider of new business.

He will almost certainly have started the business himself, having gained wide experience from working in other organizations, and is likely to be in his forties or fifties.

Board director

The managing director of a small consultancy may well run his business with a secretary and a couple of assistants, but in a large consultancy of twenty or more people, he will have a board of directors who help to manage the consultancy. These directors will also have had many years of experience and have come up through the ranks, and will probably have particular areas of expertise such as motor sport, arts, design or finance. One director will also often be designated as new business director and it will be his job to keep in contact with people, make cold calls, arrange meetings and generally try and win new accounts for his consultancy. Board directors will usually oversee a team of people working on a range of accounts and will usually be in their late thirties and forties.

Account director or manager

An account director does not have a seat on the board so the title can be rather confusing to the uninitiated. Account directors look after either one very big client or a small range of clients, often in a specialized area. This usually relates to the type of sponsorship rather than to the type of client, e.g. it may be athletics, tennis, yachting, orchestras, the environment and so on. The account director is responsible for day-to-day management of the account and liaison with the client and will usually have two or three people working for him. He is likely to be in his late twenties or early thirties.

Account executive

Account executives are mostly in their twenties and will have had anything between one and five years' experience in the business. They are the worker ants of the sponsorship business and it is their job to do all the day-to-day work involved in sponsorship – the booking, the arranging, the writing, the checking, the liaison. They will assist the account director and attend meetings and events with him, gaining experience and learning as they go.

Junior or assistant account executive or graduate trainee

Not many consultancies take on staff at this level. Most people want staff with experience. They don't want to have to spend valuable time training juniors. However, some of the bigger consultancies are prepared to take on talented graduates with an eye to the future. Others are prepared to take on people of 18 or 21 straight out of college to do the donkey work. To begin with this is usually the routine and mundane jobs that no one else either wants or has time to do. It might be as boring as stuffing invitations in envelopes or photocopying documents, but it is a fine opportunity for observing and learning.

Secretary

Secretaries are often the unsung heroines behind the boss and know as much about the business and the clients as the executives for whom they work. Secretaries, of course, do all the typing for their managers but are often involved in the sort of work that junior account executives are given. Some secretaries are happy with nine-to-five jobs and have no ambition to further their careers. Others see it as a stepping stone into account work.

Sponsoring companies

This is slightly more difficult to define since many companies do not actually use the title 'sponsorship manager' for the executive responsible for sponsorship. But as a rough guide these are the people likely to be involved in sponsorship.

Chairman/managing director/chief executive

Often the decision to invest in sponsorship will be made by the chairman – particularly in smaller companies. He may have a personal interest in a particular sport or art form and therefore will take a considerable interest in the management of his sponsorship.

Below managing director, sponsorship invariably falls between two stools and may either be managed by the corporate affairs/public relations department or by the marketing department. This very much depends on whether the objectives of the sponsorship are to boost the company's image or to sell more products. In some cases, different departments manage different types of sponsorship, and in others the two departments may work together. There are no hard and fast rules.

Corporate affairs

The corporate affairs department (also known as public relations) is responsible for the creation of the company's public image. It is a very political department whose role in life is to ensure that the organization is seen in the best possible light by its publics. This may involve dealing with the press, with shareholders, with employees and customers. If sponsorship is run by corporate affairs, then the objective of the sponsorship is likely to be for reasons of company image, to be seen as a caring organization, for instance, or to create goodwill in the community.

Companies are likely to have a corporate affairs director, a corporate affairs manager, a public relations officer, a company newspaper editor, a public relations assistant and a couple of secretaries.

Marketing

This is the department which is responsible for the development and sale of the product. It will be responsible for consumer research, advertising, direct marketing, sales promotion and product public relations. Sponsorship will certainly come within this department if the objective is to promote the product rather than to heighten a corporate image.

There will usually be a marketing director, a marketing manager and a marketing assistant. Sometimes, also, a marketing services manager, an advertising manager, a sales promotion manager, a print buyer or a publications manager, a product publicity officer and secretaries. Particular brands within a company (e.g. different chocolate bars or breakfast cereals) will also almost certainly have their own brand or product managers who have total responsibility for the entire marketing of their own particular brand and this includes sponsorship. Some companies even have both corporate marketing departments and product marketing departments.

Sales

Some organizations separate sales from marketing, particularly where there is a huge sales force to be maintained in which case there may be a sales director as well as a marketing director who will run a sales force with a national sales manager, regional sales managers and a team of sales representatives. But some companies don't separate sales from marketing and the sales force may well come under the sales and marketing director.

There are certainly more permutations than that and every company is different.

Very few organizations use the title 'sponsorship director' preferring rather to put the executive or executives responsible into corporate affairs or marketing as seems most appropriate. He may be given the title 'sponsorship manager' and have one or two assistants and a secretary. If no such title exists in the organization, then it is likely to be the public relations manager, marketing manager or brand manager who is responsible.

Organizations seeking sponsorship

Every organization looking for sponsorship, be it the national organizing body for a particular sport, an orchestra, a theatre, an environmental organization, a TV company, a publisher, or whatever, will have someone responsible for finding and managing sponsorship.

Some organizations, realizing that they do not have any expertise in this field, use a sponsorship consultancy as their marketing agent, others prefer to do it themselves and this will often fall to the director, company secretary, marketing manager, sales manager or public relations officer. This person not only needs to have the necessary expertise to devise a sponsorship package but the personality and the contacts to sell it as well. Usually this a one-man or one-woman job situation. They may have a secretary and possibly an assistant.

Have you the right experience?

It is unlikely that you are reading this chapter as a 55-year-old dentist thinking that you would like a change of career. More likely you are a student or a young executive attracted by the idea of sponsorship. Or maybe you're a keen rugby or tennis player desperate to work in the sport you love.

Ask yourself the following questions:

● Are you a good communicator?
● Can you write well?
● Can you think logically and match actions with objectives?
● Do you have a tidy mind and enjoy attention to detail?

- Are you confident in dealing with people?
- Are you likeable and easy to talk to?
- Are you a good organizer? Do you cover all eventualities or are things left to the last minute or forgotten?
- Do you feel that some jobs are beneath you, like photocopying or making coffee?
- Do you mind working evenings and weekends?
- Do you have any relevant qualifications?
- Do you have any relevant experience?

If you're already halfway through a career, then the questions get tougher:

- Have you worked in a consultancy in a marketing-orientated field?
- Have you any experience of marketing, sales promotion, advertising or PR?
- Do you have any useful contacts or experience to offer a prospective employer – preferably ones which are unique?
- Do you have any other unique selling points which might interest a prospective employer?

Let's begin with the school leaver and start with qualifications. If you are about to make a decision on which college course or university degree to take, the most relevant course is likely to be in marketing, media studies, advertising, public relations or anything involving communications. There is no course in sponsorship, I'm afraid; it has to be learnt by experience. Your school careers officer will have all the relevant directories of the college courses on offer.

You'll leave college all bright-eyed and bushy-tailed, start applying for jobs and find yourself being rejected, often without even getting an interview, simply because you 'have no experience'. It's a Catch 22 situation we all have to go through. And you can avoid it by trying to get some useful experience while at college. But more of that shortly.

Your curriculum vitae (your CV)

Unless you 'know someone', the chances are that all you are going to be able to sell yourself on is your letter of application and your CV. And the two important elements here are presentation and content.

It amazes me that some people ever get jobs at all because their applications are so dreadful. If you are an employer advertising a junior executive's job and you receive 100 applications, the task of wading through them all is extremely tedious so you start to look for ways to reject people.

My own method is to give all of them a quick scan and then weed them out into 'Yes', 'No' and 'Possibly'.

First to go are the 'Nos'. These are the applications written on bits of paper torn out of notebooks, photocopied letters addressed to 'Whom it may concern', letters apparently written by seven-year-olds who have only just learnt to do joined-up writing, letters which begin 'I saw you're advertisement in the *Sunday Times,* and would like to aply for the job of marketing assistant.' (You think I exaggerate?)

The 'Possibly' pile consists of those applications which are well-presented but a little dull or those which sound interesting but aren't so well presented.

The 'Yes' pile consists of applications which are beautifully presented and interesting to read and reveal that the applicant has a personality as well as useful experience.

So, before you even think about content, think about presentation. What is your handwriting like? Your prospective employer may not be a graphologist but he'll instinctively guess something about you from your writing. Is it an illegible scrawl, a rounded immature hand, or are you quite proud of it? Take advice from other people. If your writing is poor, type your letter of application and develop a decent signature at least. If people are always commenting on 'what nice writing you have', do your letter of application by hand.

Don't write on lined paper, notepaper with flowers in the corner, pink paper or purple paper. Use black or blue ink on white, beige or grey paper and use a fountain pen not a ball-point or felt-tip. And don't address prospective employers chummily by their first name. This may all seem very trivial but first impressions count for a lot, and tiny, tiny things can mean the difference between rejection and interview.

Personally, I find bad spelling and punctuation an immediate source of irritation. Some people are not so fussy but, if you are going to work for an organization which is in the communications business, then it's better not to take the risk and to get someone else to check your application before sending it. Amazingly, I don't think I have ever received an application which hasn't had at least one small error in it. The odd typing mistake is acceptable but misplaced apostrophes, and obvious spelling mistakes really are not. . . . ' Its always been my ambition to work in sponsorship. . . . '

Your CV should always be typed and a couple of pages is enough. It should contain basic information such as your name, date of birth, address, daytime telephone, sex and marital status. Then list your educational qualifications, your job experience and your interests outside work.

Your qualifications will give your prospective employer an idea of your level of intelligence. GCSEs in woodwork and Bible studies aren't going to impress him. A first class degree in English probably will but it doesn't actually prove that you can do the job. It just gives you a few more bonus points towards the 'Yes' pile.

The sections that will really interest him will be your previous job experience and, if that is a bit thin, then your interests outside work.

Short-term work experience

When I was a student, I spent five years closeted in college learning about art and photography but gaining no real experience of the working environment whatsoever. Fortunately, colleges are more enlightened these days and most students are sent out on work experience. This may be a week, a fortnight, a month or a year but it will be an absolutely invaluable insight into companies or consultancies.

Your college will almost certainly have good contacts with organizations where they regularly place students, but try to ensure that you go to one offering experience relevant to the job you eventually want to get. If necessary, make the contact yourself by writing or phoning and asking if you can come and work for them for a couple of weeks.

Your immediate reaction would probably be to write to the personnel department, but personnel departments of large organizations tend to get so many applications from students that there is a standard formula for reply, and you may simply end up in a filing cabinet. I would suggest that you start by phoning the managing director's secretary, making friends with her and explaining your situation. She will know everybody within the consultancy or company and will put you in touch with the right executive to contact. It will then be a question of either you personally, or your college lecturer, selling yourself to him.

You will tell him about the course you are doing, what your ambitions are and how a couple of weeks' work experience in an organization such as his will be invaluable in your future career. You will say that you don't mind sticking stamps on envelopes, running errands, or making coffee and that you won't expect to be paid. But don't be too astonished if you get a negative response.

You might think that any organization would welcome the opportunity to have someone working for them for no pay. But *they* are doing *you* the favour and not the other way round. They have to invest time in you. Even if it's simply the time to explain how the photocopier works, it's still time that might profitably be used elsewhere. It's also quite difficult to find jobs for someone who is only transitory so, unless you are very lucky, they necessarily tend to be rather mundane tasks.

But while you're tidying the stationery cupboard or stuffing press releases into envelopes you will be observing the life of an organization and absorbing a lot of useful information.

Don't be afraid to ask questions and to be interested in what is going on. Obviously you would not interrupt people in the middle of a crisis, but most executives are generally quite flattered to be asked to explain what is going on. If your questions are intelligent, you will be noticed and, when a job does come up for a junior executive, you may well be approached. So let them know if you change your address or start work somewhere else. Believe me, consultancies would much rather offer a job to a student they know and like than go through the time-consuming process of advertising and interviewing. Also, try and make friends with someone at the organization and keep in casual contact so that, if a job does become vacant, you'll be the first to know.

A block of work experience of at least a fortnight is the first positive step you can take towards getting something positive on your CV. The second is to take a part-time or summer job that will be relevant to your future.

Part-time work experience

It may be that you need to supplement your grant by earning extra money anyway. Most students find it fairly easy to get work in shops, bars or restaurants, but if there's any chance that you can get work in an organization that will help you in the future so much the better — even if it's only working in the bar of your local rugby club or being a programme seller in your local theatre. Once you've made contacts and your face is familiar, you may be in a position to apply for the more interesting jobs.

You'll need to have a rough idea of what sort of sponsorship you want to go into and the chances are that it will be sport or possibly the arts. You will almost certainly have an interest in a particular sport or hobby yourself. For instance, you may be an avid football fan or enjoy amateur dramatics, in which case follow up this interest.

If it's sport, then there are numerous options. Most professional sports clubs employ an army of casual staff on match days or race days so it's simply a question of applying to the stadium manager to see what's available. You'll probably be welcomed with open arms but be prepared to accept one of the less prestigious jobs initially such as car park attendant or turnstile operator, and then keep your eyes open for something that may be more relevant to your future ambitions. You might, for instance, get a job in the commentary box, in the press office or in the entertainment suites. There is one snag, however. If you love watching your particular sport, you may be better getting a job in a sport you aren't quite so keen on. Car park attendants are paid to attend the car parks and not to watch the races!

The same theory applies to arts venues and here, of course, you have a better chance of employment in London or one of the bigger provincial cities. Theatres and concert halls need programme sellers, usherettes and catering staff and once in-situ, you'll be able to keep your eyes open for more exciting opportunities.

You will get paid for all this casual work, maybe not a great deal but it will all help to boost the grant. In the unlikely event that money isn't your prime consideration, then there are a great many more options open to you which will give you excellent experience and where the offer of your services will be received with great delight.

If you are an impoverished student you may not be able to afford to work without being paid, but if you are already in full-time work and simply looking for a change of career, then I'd strongly advise it – anything to add weight to your CV.

All amateur sports and arts associations, and indeed many professional ones, rely on a proportion of volunteers to keep them going. If you can be earning money as a turnstile operator for your local rugby league club, it doesn't appear to make sense to volunteer to be an unpaid ticket seller for your local rugby union club. But that rugby club may very well welcome your services in a publicity capacity. You could act as volunteer press officer, writing stories and giving information to your local paper; as the publicity officer organizing the printing of posters and fixture lists; you could be the programme editor, writing and managing the production of the programme; the fund-raising manager running raffles, lotteries and special events; or the sponsorship manager devising sponsorship packages and trying to sell them to local companies. Any of these things will bring you extremely useful experience and will certainly help you in your search for a job in sponsorship.

This is also the sort of thing that looks good on a CV of anyone who hasn't previously had a full-time job. It shows someone with enterprise and initiative – the key elements that a prospective employer will be looking for.

Look, too, to make the most of the 'Other interests' section of your CV. If you have any unusual interests – pot-holing, parachuting, morris dancing or collecting signed cricket bats, put them in. They will attract the prospective employer's interest and may just make the difference between the 'Yes' pile and the 'No' pile. Don't put in things like 'reading, knitting and going out with friends'; fascinating pastimes though they may be, they don't exactly awaken the imagination of the reader.

The secretary route

I shall just digress a moment here to talk about secretarial skills. Do learn to type and, better still, to use a word processor. Technology is moving so fast these days that anyone not able to operate a word processor or simple computer is going to be at a severe disadvantage, particularly at the lower end of the job scale.

Young women have a distinct advantage over their male counterparts in the job market. Makes a change, doesn't it! Secretaries, particularly in London, are always in demand and therefore it is quite easy to get yourself into the desired organization as a secretary or typist. Simply phone up and ask for whoever deals with personnel and say you'd like to be considered for a job when they next have a vacancy. Keep phoning and eventually you'll get an interview and a typing test. In London I doubt you'll wait long, although it may be more difficult in the provinces.

Once in an organization, you have to prove that you're keen, can do a little more than type, are a good organizer, aren't a clock watcher, can show initiative, can make useful suggestions and, when the first junior vacancy arises, you'll be the first to apply for it and quite likely to get it.

Young men are not quite so fortunate. It's a rare male school leaver who would admit to an ambition to be a secretary. Social pressure to do something more masculine would simply be too overwhelming. I suppose it is because, traditionally, women's jobs have tended to be servicing jobs which most men would consider to be beneath their dignity. This is a pity because any man with secretarial qualifications would have absolutely no difficulty in getting a job and, simply because he's male, be first in line for promotion when a vacancy arises. But, if you're male and you feel that this back-door method of getting the job of your dreams is not the route for you, do at least learn to type!

Where to look for vacancies

You have now got some useful experience, you know how to put together a good CV and letter of application but where do you look for a job? There are three possibilities – advertisements, recruitment consultancies and the direct approach.

Advertisements

I'm afraid that the newspapers aren't bursting with advertisements for junior sponsorship executives. Big companies tend to promote from within and consultancies are so overwhelmed by unsolicited applications that they simply don't need to advertise. However, that doesn't mean that it can't happen, so it is definitely worth keeping your eyes open.

Likely sources for advertisements are the trade magazines although, on the whole, these tend to advertise the more senior vacancies. That's fine if you're a public relations officer looking to become a sponsorship manager, but not so helpful if you're a graduate. However, they include *Marketing Week*, *Marketing*, *Campaign* and *PR Week*. In addition, *Sponsorship News* is published monthly although this rarely contains appointments advertisements. It's a good idea to read these publications anyway just so that, at an interview, you can talk intelligently about what is going on in the marketplace.

As far as national newspapers are concerned, you should certainly look at *The Guardian* which contains a media section on Mondays and at *The Sunday Times* appointments section. All the other serious papers are worth reading, too, but don't go to the expense of buying them all, go to your local library.

Any job that is advertised nationally will receive a huge number of applications, so bear in mind what I said earlier about getting your CV right.

Recruitment consultancies

Your second option is to go to a recruitment consultancy. The problem here is that, with the exception of specialist graduate recruitment consultancies such as Graduate Appointments (which are certainly worth contacting), most recruitment consultancies are looking for people with some kind of work experience because that's what their clients want. And many sponsorship consultancies do prefer to use a recruitment agency simply because they know an advertisement will bring in an overwhelming number of replies.

However, don't let that put you off. Look through the trade

magazines and study the advertisements put in by the recruitment consultancies. You may see something you can apply for, but even if you don't it's worth phoning and asking if they accept graduates on their books and, if not, ask if they are able to recommend anyone who does.

Some recruitment consultancies are better than others. Many will just say 'Send in your CV' and you'll never hear from them again. Others will take the trouble to call you in for an interview, find out what you want to do and may come up with some leads.

If you have experience that is relevant such as public relations, marketing, sales promotion or advertising, then the recruitment consultancies will be much more interested in you. Many, however, have the absolutely infuriating tendency to put you in a slot according to your last job so that if you are an advertising manager trying to move into sponsorship, the chances are that they will keep trying to send you on interviews for advertising jobs. So be firm!

Direct approach

This calls for initiative. It can be hard work and time-consuming but, equally, it can pay dividends. Your three likely sources for jobs are again the sponsorship consultancies (including sports marketing consultancies, sponsorship agencies who sell sponsorships, advertising agencies, and public relations, sales promotion and marketing consultancies which may also involve themselves in sponsorship), companies who are already sponsors and organizations looking for sponsorship. Annual publications such as *Hobson's Sponsorship Yearbook* and *Hollis Press and Public Relations Annual* are very useful for leads, as is the monthly magazine *Sponsorship News*.

The number one targets for job-hunting hopefuls are the sponsorship consultancies. CVs come pouring in from all directions and invariably end up in a dusty file never to see the light of day. Sometimes you won't even get a reply, more usually it will be a polite letter of refusal saying that they have no suitable vacancies at present but will keep your letter on file in case anything suitable arises. Very occasionally, you will be given an interview.

Even more occasionally your letter saying that you are an expert in underwater polo will arrive just at the point where they have won an account to manage an underwater polo sponsorship for a client and are wondering what on earth it's all about. But I'm afraid that this scenario is highly unlikely.

Robin Ford, Managing Director of Option One Sponsorship, says, 'We get hundreds of applicants for jobs. All get a reply and we try to be helpful where possible; a few get interviewed and we take on one or two. At graduate level I'm looking for people who can demonstrate that they have initiative, are good administrators, can handle detail and are fast learners. For the more senior jobs I prefer to take people who are already in consultancies. There aren't enough people well-qualified in sponsorship to go round but, as a second choice, I'd take people from sales promotion, advertising and PR agencies in that order. I need people with marketing skills, but we get many letters from junior tennis champions and leisure centre managers who see themselves 'in sports marketing'. Really they don't have the experience I need. That's not to say that someone who has been successful in a particular sport couldn't get a job in sponsorship, but it would be more likely to be a sports marketing agency or an organization seeking sponsorship which could make good use of their contacts from a sales point of view.'

Those may not be very encouraging words if you're a PE teacher in Newcastle, but don't give up. Remember the saying 'If you really want something that badly, you'll get it.'

Somehow you need to get yourself into an organization to meet someone so that you can sell yourself for their future reference. People remember faces much better than they remember one more letter amongst so many. But no one has the time to interview every job-seeker and why should they? Their job is to earn money for their consultancy or promote their company, and interviewing for non-existent vacancies isn't productive.

However, there are various ploys you can use. Work experience is one of them. You don't necessarily have to be a college student either. If you can afford to volunteer your services as a dogsbody for nothing for a few weeks and are accepted, then that will get you some experience and get you known within the company.

Contacts are another. Speak to everyone you possibly can who may be able to give you some leads. Your college lecturers for a start, parents, friends of the family, friends of friends of the family — anyone who may know someone with some knowledge of sponsorship or communications.

Don't necessarily go asking for a job. It's often better to simply ask for advice. While your mentor will be answering your questions, he will also be assessing you and, if he receives a favourable impression, may just mention your name in the right ear when a vacancy occurs.

If you really have no contacts of your own, then try approaching people cold. You could try sponsorship consultancies, sports or arts or other appropriate governing bodies and companies who you know run sponsorships. Simply explain your problem to the switchboard and they will put you through to whoever they consider to be the most appropriate starting point. It's not their role to refuse to help you but they won't want you clogging up the line so they will endeavour to comply with your request as quickly as possible. You may end up in sponsorship, personnel, public relations or with some totally bemused executive who will be cursing the switchboard under his breath, but you'll have made contact and should take it from there.

I know a young accountant who at the age of 24 decided that he didn't like figures and wanted to work in sports sponsorship. He had no appropriate qualifications but used his initiative and telephoned thirty sponsorship consultancies to ask if there was anyone who could spare him half an hour just to give him some advice. He got fifteen interviews out of this and six months later was offered a job in a small consultancy. So it can be done and is a good method of making contacts – as long as everyone doesn't start using this ploy, of course!

The interview

Once you have got to the stage of an interview, you have then got to sell yourself in half an hour or so and, as with your CV, presentation and content are the two important elements.

First, presentation. If you want to work in sponsorship then you are going to have to be conventionally presentable because you will be dealing with clients and, although your employer may not be prejudiced against Mohican haircuts or purple lipstick, some of his clients may be, and he'll take that into consideration.

So, like it or not, it's a suit or smart jacket and tie for men, and a suit, jacket and skirt or dress for women. You need to look smart and classically fashionable and, unfairly, this is a lot more important for women than for men. Thigh-high skirts, six-inch fingernails, see-through blouses and very heavy make-up will all count against you.

Give a good firm handshake when you meet your interviewer, wait to be asked to sit down and be careful how you sit. Your interviewer will instinctively read your body language, so if you sit on the edge of your seat it will indicate nervousness and timidity; if you slouch back it will indicate casualness and superiority. Try to look alert and interested but, at the same time, appear relaxed. Don't smoke unless offered a cigarette.

Believe it or not, interviewing is much harder work for the interviewer than for the interviewee since he or she has to keep the ball rolling and therefore can't relax into silence and wait for the next question. So interviewees who answer 'yes' or 'no' and are not very forthcoming are hard work and unlikely to be offered a job.

You can impress an interviewer in various ways. First, if you are sensible you will have done some research on their organization and be able to display a knowledge that will indicate initiative and genuine interest in what they are doing. Asking as well as answering questions again displays an enquiring mind and someone who is going to think about what they're doing and not just mindlessly do what they are told and no more. When asked questions, display an enthusiasm for what you are talking about, show that you are pleasant and have a sense of humour. Don't give out any negative vibrations such as hesitating if asked if you mind working long hours, or looking pained if asked if you mind making the coffee. And don't ask searching questions about salary, holiday entitlement and whether you'll get to meet Boris Becker until you've been offered the job, or you'll give the impression that you're only concerned with the money and the glamour and not with the job itself.

I've been guilty of many of these things in the past. When I was 22 I was offered a job as a photographer on *The Times*. I was thrilled but must have looked a little disconcerted when told I'd have to work every other weekend. 'Think it over and ring me tomorrow' said the picture editor. But when tomorrow came and I phoned to say 'Yes' he replied that he didn't think I wanted the job and had offered it to someone else. He probably hadn't done so at all but my negative reaction made him change his mind. So if you get offered a job there and then, unless you absolutely don't want it, say 'Yes' with enthusiasm and ask for the terms and conditions to be put in writing which will give you more time to consider the pros and cons. Once the job has been offered you, then is the time to negotiate on salary, holidays, hours of work and so on. A company which has decided firmly that it wants you will be much more prepared to make concessions that one which is still hesitating.

Once you start to work in sponsorship, you will find it enormously demanding not only on your time but on your creative and organizing ability as well. There will be occasions when crisis will seem to follow crisis and when unexpected disaster will strike just as you thought everything was running so smoothly. But, on the other hand, you will find it exciting, challenging and rewarding and there aren't that many jobs which can offer those benefits!

Appendix The Independent Television Commission Code of Programme Sponsorship

Foreword

(a) The Broadcasting Act 1990 (the Act) imposes a statutory duty on the Independent Television Commission (the ITC), after appropriate consultation, to draw up, and from time to time review, a code which sets standards and practice in the sponsoring of programmes and identifies the methods of sponsorship to be prohibited or to be prohibited in particular circumstances. The ITC may make different provision in the code for different kinds of licensed services.

(b) This code applies to all television programme services licensed by the ITC under the Act: ITV (including TV-am), Channel 4, DBS, non-domestic satellite services and licensable programme services. It also gives effect in the UK to a number of requirements relating to television sponsorship in the EC Directive on Television Broadcasting (89/552/EEC) and the 1989 Council of Europe Convention on Transfrontier Television. **Compliance with the code is a condition of an ITC licence and licensees should ensure that relevant employees and programme makers, including those from whom they commission programmes, understand its contents and significance**.

(c) Whereas the ITC is prepared to give general guidance on interpretation of this code, it will not normally preview programmes or consider specific proposals before production. Independent producers or potential sponsors should seek guidance on specific proposals from the relevant licensee. The ITC may require sponsorship which does not comply with this code to be withdrawn.

(d) The Act reserves the right of the ITC to specify requirements which go beyond the rules set out in this code. The ITC may give directions to exclude methods of sponsorship not referred to in the code.

(e) If rules are breached the ITC may impose financial penalties or shorten or, in certain circumstances, revoke a company's ITC licence.

(f) This code applies with effect from 1 January 1991 to channels previously regulated by the IBA (ITV, Channel 4 and DBS). Other channels and cable operators, previously subject to Cable Authority guidelines, are not required to implement the code before 3 October 1991 when the EC Directive comes into force. Until then they may, as an alternative, continue to be subject to the Cable Authority Code of Practice on Programme Sponsorship (Second Edition, March 1990).

(g) There will be separate provisions applying to sponsorship on Oracle Teletext.

(h) To assist licensees and others reading this code, specific rules are printed in bold type.

(j) The detailed rules set out below are intended to be applied in the spirit as well as the letter.

Contents

Definition of programme sponsorship

Definition of programme sponsorship

A programme is deemed to be sponsored if any part of its costs of production or transmission is met by an organisation or person other than a broadcaster or television producer, with a view to promoting its own or another's name, trademark, image, activities, products, or other direct or indirect commercial interests.

NOTE:
This code does not apply to sponsorship by religious or charitable interests, which are dealt with in a separate code.

Part I: Principles

This part sets out the policy basis of the code. The <u>practical application</u> of these principles, with exceptions that may be justified and acceptable, is set out in Parts II and III.

1 **Any television programme may be sponsored, unless it falls into one of the excepted categories listed in Part II.**
2 **No sponsor is permitted any influence on either the content or the scheduling of a programme.**
3 **Any sponsorship must be clearly identified at the beginning and/or end of the programme.**
4 **No promotional reference to the sponsor, or to his product or service, is permitted within the programme he has sponsored.**
5 **No sponsored programme may contain within it any promotional reference to any other product or service.**
6 **No programme may, without the previous approval of the ITC, be sponsored by any person whose business consists, wholly or mainly, in the manufacture or supply of a product, or in the provision of a service, which is not acceptable for television advertising pursuant to the ITC Code of Advertising Standards and Practice.**
7 **Product placement is prohibited.**

NOTE:
'Within' a programme is defined as programme time exclusive of front, end, bumper credits and advertising breaks.

Part II: Specific requirements

8 Unsponsorable categories

The following programme types must not be sponsored:

(a) News

Programmes and news flashes comprising local, national or international news items must not be sponsored. However, some specialist reports presented outside the context of a general news programme may be sponsored: cultural reports, sports reports, traffic reports, weather reports or forecasts. **Business and financial reports where they contain interpretation and comment must not be sponsored.**

NOTE:
'Outside the context of a general news programme' means separated in some clearly apparent way eg by programme end credits or a commercial break. The use of the same presenter(s) as for the news programme would not be acceptable.

(b) Current Affairs

Not sponsorable are current affairs programmes containing explanation and analysis of current events. The definition includes programmes dealing with political and industrial policy, or with current public policy.

9 Sponsor influence

No person or organisation may sponsor a programme:

(a) **which contains within it material which, intentionally or otherwise, has the effect of promoting his product or service (but see the separate rules for game shows and events);**
(b) **which, had it not been sponsored, might reasonably have been expected to contain editorial content which might**

conflict with the sponsor's interests eg programmes offering consumer advice on the purchase or use of products and
services of the kind marketed by the sponsor.

10 Sponsor credits

(a) **Any sponsored programme must have either a front or
an end credit or both.** Credits may be aural or visual or
both.

(b) There may also be bumper credits (ie entering and/or leaving
any commercial break) which may be aural or visual or both.

(c) **Front sponsor credits must precede, and not be inte-
grated within, any element of the programme except its
title. End and bumper credits may overlap the programme for not more than five seconds.**

(d) **There must be no programme sponsorship credits within
programmes, with the exception of game shows only,
where there may be two factual aural references to the
sponsor's provision of the prize/prizes only. No undue
visual or aural prominence must be given to the sponsor's
name or branding on the prizes.**

NOTE:
*A game show is defined as a programme whose format is a
competition developed for television involving tests of knowledge,
intelligence or skill.*

(e) **A front credit (or, where there is none, the end credit)
must identify the sponsor and explain the sponsor's
connection with the programme** (eg 'sponsored by', 'in
association with', 'supported by' etc). **It must not suggest
the programme has been made by the sponsor: so
expressions like 'brought to you by' are not acceptable**
(but see rule 15).

(f) **Any credit may refer to but must not show the sponsor's
product or service and must not include slogans or
descriptions of any kind.**

(g) With the exception of credits under 14(b) below, any credit
may include the sponsor's name, trademark or logo without
restriction as to size, and employ animation or musical effects.
On-screen presenters are not acceptable.

(h) Trailers

The primary purpose of a trailer is to alert viewers to any forthcoming programme. The sponsor's presence should therefore remain secondary. **There may only be one reference to the programme's sponsors**, which can be aural and/or visual, **lasting not more than five seconds.** (See also rule 17.)

(j) Advertising campaigns

There must be no extracts from the sponsor's television advertising in any sponsor credit, or in any trailer or sponsored programme.

(k) ITV and Channel 4 only

A sponsor's name must not be used in a programme title except when the title is that of a sponsored event covered by the programme eg The Rumbelows Cup Final.

(l) ITV and Channel 4 only

(i) **A front credit must not exceed 15 seconds in length where one sponsor is involved; and 20 seconds where there is more than one.** There is no limit to the number of sponsors for any programme.

(ii) **End or bumper credits must not be more than 10 seconds in length** (even where multiple sponsorship is concerned).

11 Programme sponsor references

There must be no promotional reference within the programme itself to the sponsor or to any of his products or services.

NOTE:
'Promotional' means any reference, visual or aural, which is not clearly justified by the editorial needs of the programme itself. (See also the rules separately applying to game shows (rule 10(d)) and events (rule 16).)

12 Other product or service references

Visual or aural references to another advertiser's product or service which are not promotional are not prohibited.

13 Prohibited and restricted sponsors

(a) **The following are prohibited from programme sponsorship:**

(i) **any body whose objects are wholly or mainly of a political nature;**

(ii) **any person whose business consists wholly or mainly in the manufacture or supply of:**

(a) **tobacco products;**

(b) **pharmaceutical products available only on prescription;**

(c) **(without the previous approval of the Commission) any other product or service which may not be advertised under the ITC Code of Advertising Standards and Practice.**

NOTES:

(i) *Sponsorship is not acceptable from a manufacturer or supplier of tobacco products whose name is chiefly known to the public through his tobacco business, even though he may market other non-tobacco products or services.*

(ii) *Sponsorship references to non-pharmaceutical brands which do not include the name of a company otherwise disqualified by (ii) (b) are acceptable.*

(b) **Advertisers who are prohibited from advertising their goods or services during some types of programmes and/or during certain time periods are also prohibited from sponsoring those types of programmes and sponsoring programmes during those time periods.** This rule may be waived by the ITC if the sponsorship arrangements are able to avoid the difficulties (for example, the possibility of causing offence) that were the reason for the original advertising prohibition: prior ITC approval would be required. On the other hand the ITC reserves the right to impose restrictions on sponsorship associations between particular categories of advertiser and particular programmes going beyond those in this rule.

14 Product placement

(a) Product placement is defined as the inclusion of, or reference to, a product or service within the programme in return for payment or other valuable consideration to the programme maker or ITC licensee (or any representative of either). **This is prohibited.**

(b) When a product or service is an essential element within a programme, the programme maker may exceptionally acquire that product or service at no, or less than full, cost. This is not product placement. **It is acceptable providing no undue prominence is given to the product or service in question and rule 11 is applied if the programme is sponsored.**

NOTE:
A basic credit lasting not more than five seconds may be included within the end credits of the programme for the product or service, except where it has been provided by the programme sponsor. (See rule 10(g).)

Part III: Further guidance

15 Advertiser-supplied programmes

The constraints set out in the European Directive (see FOREWORD) upon editorial influence by an advertiser are especially difficult to reconcile with any programme made for, or wholly (or very substantially) funded by, an advertiser. An ITC licensee who wishes to transmit such a programme will need to take very particular care to ensure that it conforms with the provisions of this code. The licensee should note also that:

(a) **No programme wholly (or very substantially) funded by, or provided to a licensee by, an advertiser or his agent shall include within it any promotional reference to the advertiser or to his product or service.** (Exceptions to this rule may be made in the case of programmes of unusual cultural or historical value.)

(b) **An advertiser-supplied programme must be preceded by a front credit lasting not more than 10 seconds identifying the advertiser and his relationship to the programme and followed by a similar end credit; other credits and sponsor references are not permitted.**

16 Coverage of events

(a) Programme coverage of events and locations (eg the Fosters' Oval) which have been sponsored, or at which advertising or branding is present, may itself be sponsored. An event or location sponsor may also be the programme sponsor.

(b) **Visual or aural references to any advertising, signage or branding at an event must be limited to what can clearly be justified by the editorial needs of the programme itself.**

(c) Such advertising or branding is acceptable providing the event has a bona fide non-television status. Three conditions of that status must be satisfied:

    (i) **the event must be officially recognised by a sporting or cultural body, or other official body, whose existence is independent of advertising, promotional or television interests;**

    (ii) **television coverage must not be the principal purpose of the event;**

    (iii) **members of the public must be present irrespective of whether or not the event is televised.**

(d) On-site advertising and branding arrangements are otherwise a matter for agreement between the relevant official body and the television companies.

(e) Aural and visual references in the programme coverage to event sponsors should be sufficient to identify the events or elements (eg individually sponsored races or a sponsored prize ceremony) within it, and should provide appropriate recognition to the event sponsor. **They must, however, clearly be justified by the editorial needs of the programme itself.**

(f) Tobacco advertising, signage or branding

Coverage of tobacco-sponsored events, or events at which there is branding, signage or advertising for any tobacco company, must be consistent with the requirements of the Voluntary Agreement reached between the Minister of Sport and the Tobacco Advisory Council 19 January 1987. In particular, ITC licensees must ensure that:

    (i) **static signs for tobacco companies at sporting events are not located within camera sightlines for prolonged, uninterrupted periods: for example, they should not be placed in or at scoreboards, set playing positions, rest areas etc, that are likely to come** within the scope of the television cameras, or between a participant and the camera;

(ii) there is no display of tobacco house or brand names or symbols on participants and officials, their vehicles, equipment and/or animals likely to come within the scope of the television cameras. Auxiliary personnel, such as caddies, mechanics, grooms etc are to be regarded as participants;

(iii) the design or combination of colours used in the visual presentation of the set for small arena sports does not resemble or depict the product of the sponsoring tobacco company.

17 Sponsored support material

Off-air material made available to viewers as back-up to a programme may be trailed at the end of the programme and may be sponsored. **Any such sponsorship must be credited in that trail, which may be additional to any programme end credit. It must adhere to the relevant requirements for <u>front</u> credits.**

Support material may be separately trailed and the sponsor credited as set out in rule 10(h). Sponsored support material may include books, videos, tapes, information packs and other publications as well as off-air activities such as conferences, exhibitions, festivals and performances, and helplines. **The sponsorship must be clearly identified on any support material publication, and the rules generally set out within this code should, unless clearly inappropriate, apply.**

18 Product licensing and merchandising

Difficulties may arise under the code where a programme maker or broadcaster (or other programme rights holder) is paid a royalty or other fee for the right (ie licence) to market a product based upon one or more characters or other elements within a programme. This is not deemed to be sponsorship <u>providing</u>:

(a) **the programme, including all its elements and characters, has been developed independently of the product licensee OR the main characters had a prior literary existence independently of any merchandising;**

(b) **no <u>actual</u> product marketed is featured in the programme,** though name, general appearance and characteristic features may be the same;

(c) **neither the programme nor transmission of the programme is funded, wholly or in part, by the product licensee.**

Programmes which breach any of these conditions will not be accceptable for transmission.

19 Acquired programmes

The code applies also to acquired programmes, including those programmes acquired from outside the UK. Films made for the cinema and coverage of sporting and other events taking place outside the UK, however, may deviate from the code where this is unavoidable.

20 Informational services

A programme may include informational services (eg timing or other data electronically generated directly on screen) at reduced or no charge in return for a screen acknowledgement to the information provider, which may appear when the information is displayed. **The information provider must not additionally sponsor the programme (because that would conflict with the rules on sponsor credits set out in rule 10).** The provision of information on-site at any event is not covered or restricted by this paragraph.

Index